Las ɑ
Españas

Terror and Crisis in Contemporary Spain

The Cañada Blanch / Sussex Academic Studies on Contemporary Spain

General Editor: Professor Paul Preston, London School of Economics

A list of all published titles in the series is available on the Press website. More recently published works are presented below.

Kingdom: José María Aznar and Tony Blair's Personal Motivations and their Global Impact

Xavier Moreno Juliá, *The Blue Division: Spanish Blood in Russia, 1941–1945.*

David Lethbridge, *Norman Bethune in Spain: Commitment, Crisis, and Conspiracy.*

Antonio Miguez Macho, *The Genocidal Genealogy of Francoism: Violence, Memory and Impunity*

Carles Manera, *The Great Recession: A Subversive View.*

Nicholas Manganas, *Las dos Españas: Terror and Crisis in Contemporary Spain.*

Jorge Marco, *Guerrilleros and Neighbours in Arms: Identities and Cultures of Antifascist Resistance in Spain.*

Martin Minchom, *Spain's Martyred Cities: From the Battle of Madrid to Picasso's* Guernica.

Olivia Muñoz-Rojas, *Ashes and Granite: Destruction and Reconstruction in the Spanish Civil War and Its Aftermath.*

Linda Palfreeman, *Spain Bleeds: The Development of Battlefield Blood Transfusion during the Civil War.*

Isabelle Rohr, *The Spanish Right and the Jews, 1898–1945: Antisemitism and Opportunism.*

Gareth Stockey, *Gibraltar: "A Dagger in the Spine of Spain?"*

Maria Thomas, *The Faith and the Fury: Popular Anticlerical Violence and Iconoclasm in Spain, 1931–1936.*

Dacia Viejo-Rose, *Reconstructing Spain: Cultural Heritage and Memory after Civil War.*

Dedicated to Paul Allatson,
without whom this book would never have seen the light of
day; and to all the victims of political violence in the
history of the Spanish state. May you rest in peace.

Las dos Españas

Terror and Crisis in Contemporary Spain

NICHOLAS MANGANAS

Cañada Blanch Centre
for Contemporary
Spanish Studies

sussex
ACADEMIC
PRESS
Brighton • Chicago • Toronto

2 4 6 8 10 9 7 5 3 1

First published in Great Britain in 2016 by
SUSSEX ACADEMIC PRESS
PO Box 139, Eastbourne BN24 9BP

and in the United States of America by
SUSSEX ACADEMIC PRESS
Independent Publishers Group
814 N. Franklin Street, Chicago, IL 60610

and in Canada by
SUSSEX ACADEMIC PRESS (CANADA)

Published in collaboration with the Cañada Blanch Centre for Contemporary Spanish Studies, London.

British Library Cataloguing in Publication Data
A CIP catalogue record for this book is available from the British Library.

Library of Congress Cataloging-in-Publication Data
Names: Manganas, Nicholas, author.
Title: Las dos Espannãs : terror and crisis in contemporary Spain / Nicholas Manganas.
Description: Brighton ; Chicago : Sussex Academic Press, [2016] | Series: The Cañada Blanch/Sussex Academic studies on contemporary Spain | Includes bibliographical references and index.
Identifiers: LCCN 2016014370 | ISBN 9781845198497 (pbk.)
Subjects: LCSH: Terrorism—Political aspects—Spain—History. | Political violence—Spain—History. | Spain—Ethnic relations. | Spain—Politics and government—1982–
Classification: LCC HV6433.S7 M346 2016 | DDC 363.3250946—dc23
LC record available at https://lccn.loc.gov/2016014370

Typeset & designed by Sussex Academic Press, Brighton & Eastbourne.
Printed by TJ International, Padstow, Cornwall.

Contents

The Cañada Blanch Centre for Contemporary Spanish Studies

In the 1960s, the most important initiative in the cultural and academic relations between Spain and the United Kingdom was launched by a Valencian fruit importer in London. The creation by Vicente Cañada Blanch of the Anglo-Spanish Cultural Foundation has subsequently benefited large numbers of Spanish and British scholars at various levels. Thanks to the generosity of Vicente Cañada Blanch, thousands of Spanish schoolchildren have been educated at the secondary school in West London that bears his name. At the same time, many British and Spanish university students have benefited from the exchange scholarships which fostered cultural and scientific exchanges between the two countries. Some of the most important historical, artistic and literary work on Spanish topics to be produced in Great Britain was initially made possible by Cañada Blanch scholarships.

Vicente Cañada Blanch was, by inclination, a conservative. When his Foundation was created, the Franco regime was still in the plenitude of its power. Nevertheless, the keynote of the Foundation's activities was always a complete open-mindedness on political issues. This was reflected in the diversity of research projects supported by the Foundation, many of which, in Francoist Spain, would have been regarded as subversive. When the Dictator died, Don Vicente was in his seventy-fifth year. In the two decades following the death of the Dictator, although apparently indestructible, Don Vicente was obliged to husband his energies. Increasingly, the work of the Foundation was carried forward by Miguel Dols whose tireless and imaginative work in London was matched in Spain by that of José María Coll Comín. They were united in the Foundation's spirit of open-minded commitment to fostering research of high quality in pursuit of better Anglo-Spanish cultural relations. Throughout the 1990s, thanks to them, the role of the Foundation grew considerably.

In 1994, in collaboration with the London School of Economics, the Foundation established the Príncipe de Asturias Chair of Contemporary Spanish History and the Cañada Blanch Centre for Contemporary Spanish Studies. It is the particular task of the Cañada Blanch Centre for Contemporary Spanish Studies to promote the understanding of twentieth-century Spain through research and teaching of contemporary Spanish history, politics, economy, sociology and culture. The Centre possesses a valuable library and archival centre for specialists in contemporary Spain. This work is carried on through the publications of the doctoral and post-doctoral researchers at the Centre itself and through the many seminars and lectures held at the London School of Economics. While the seminars are the province of the researchers, the lecture cycles have been the forum in which Spanish politicians have been able to address audiences in the United Kingdom.

Since 1998, the Cañada Blanch Centre has published a substantial number of books in collaboration with several different publishers on the subject of contemporary Spanish history and politics. An extremely fruitful partnership with Sussex Academic Press began in 2004. Full details and descriptions of the published works can be found on the Press website. The present volume deals with the centuries-old notion of a divided Spain epitomised by the country's numerous civil wars. Dr Nicholas Manganas adopts a controversial multidisciplinary approach in an endeavour to understand the survival of the notion of the 'two Spains'. To do so, he analyses narratives both of terrorism and of economic crisis in contemporary Spain.

Acknowledgements

Las dos Españas: Terror and Crisis in Contemporary Spain is based on my doctoral research I undertook with the former Institute for International Studies at the University of Technology (UTS), Sydney. I would like to profusely thank the Institute for the opportunity and support it gave me throughout the years. First and foremost, Paul Allatson who not only dedicated his time but helped guide the project from its conception until the final product that you hold in your hands today. Thank you also to the wonderful International Studies scholars at UTS, both former and current, from whom I learnt a great deal: Murray Pratt, Jo McCormack, Ilaria Vanni, Elena Sheldon, Antonella Biscaro, Kiran Grewal and Mariana Rodríguez among many others. A big thank you also to Margarita Alonso and the University of Cantabria for giving me the opportunity to teach and research in Spain, a wonderful experience that allowed me to gain a deeper understanding of contemporary Spanish politics and culture.

I owe immense gratitude to the fantastic Spanish Studies scholars in different parts of the world who I quote extensively in the pages of this book. Their work laid the groundwork for my own investigation and analysis. Thank you to Joseba Zulaika, Kathryn Crameri and Pamela Radcliff for reading the original doctoral thesis; Paul Preston for his scholarship and the opportunity to include my work in the Cañada Blanch Studies on Contemporary Spain series; and to the late Begoña Aretxaga whose scholarship inspired me to research narratives of terror in contemporary Spain.

Finally, I would like to express my gratitude to Anthony Grahame and the staff at Sussex Academic Press for their professionalism and assistance throughout the publication process of this book and to Ramón Fernández and my friends and family for their patience and support throughout the years.

The cover design 'Las dos Españas' is part of a series of paintings titled *Tauromaquia* painted in Carlos Andino's typical surrealist and symbolist style. Andino's aim was to represent Spanish poet Antonio Machado's two Spains: *Una de las dos Españas ha de helarte el corazón* (One of those two Spains will freeze your heart). The red bull represents the traditional left, charging towards the blue bull, representing the traditional right, both with equal strength and determination.

Glossary

Abertzale   Basque Nationalist, from the Basque word for "patriot."

Alianza Popular (AP)   See Popular Alliance.

Atocha Massacre   The 1977 Massacre of Atocha was a neo-fascist attack during the Spanish transition to democracy after Franco's death in 1975, killing five and injuring four. It was committed on January 24, 1977, in an office located on 77 Atocha Street near Atocha railway station in Madrid, where specialists of labour law, members of the Workers' Commissions trade union (CCOO), and of the then clandestine Communist Party of Spain (PCE), had gathered.

Autonomous Community   A term that refers to a regional government in Spain. Since 1982, the Spanish state has created 17 different Autonomous Communities, each governed by 17 different Statutes of Autonomy.

Basque Nationalist Party (PNV, Partido Nacionalista Vasco)   The dominant Nationalist party in the Basque region. Presided over Basque regional autonomous government from 1980 to 2009.

Basque Spanish Battalion (BVE, Batalión Vasco Español)   Main protagonists of first dirty war against ETA, 1975–81.

CESID Centro Superior de Información de la Defensa (Higher Information Centre for Defence)   Spanish military intelligence service created in 1977. CESID was replaced by Centro Nacional de Inteligencia (CNI, National Intelligence Centre) in 2002.

CiU Convergència i Unió (Convergence and Union)   Catalan Nationalist Party.

Ciudadanos (Ciutadans in Catalan)   Centrist, postnationalist political party formed in Catalonia in 2005.

Comisiones Obreras (CCOO, Workers' Commissions)   Spain's largest trade union. It has more than one million members.

ERC Esquerra Republicana de Catalunya (Republican Left of Catalonia)   A left-wing Catalan independist political party campaigning for the independence of Catalonia from Spain.

Ertzaintza   Police force controlled by the Basque Autonomous government.

Españolisto/a   Pejorative term for Basques whose primary loyalty/identification is to Spain rather than the Basque Country.

ETA   Euskadi Ta Askatasuna (Basque Homeland and Freedom). Radical terrorist group campaigning for Basque independence since 1959.

Etarra   Member of ETA.

Euskadi   The Autonomous Community of the Basque Country.

Euskal Herria   Basque term that refers to the "imagined" Basque nation, comprising of seven traditional regions: Álava, Vizcaya, Guipúzcoa and Navarra (in Spain) and Basse-Navarre, Labourd and Soule (in France).

Fuero   Medieval charter of special rights, usually granted by the monarch, to villages, cities, provinces and regions.

GAL Grupos Antiterroristas de Liberación (Anti-terorrist Liberation Groups)   Protagonists of second dirty war against ETA, 1983–87.

Guardia Civil   Formed in 1844, the Guardia Civil is a security force regulated by military discipline but has a major police function, particularly in counterterrorism.

Herri Batasuna (HB, Popular Unity)   Political coalition which supports ETA's objectives. The party was banned in 2003.

Incontrolado   Refers to ultra-right elements, inside and outside the security forces, who carried out terrorist attacks against democrats and regional nationalists during the late Franco period and the transition to democracy, without the authorization of the state.

Iparretarrak   French Basque separatist group which has carried out several sporadic terrorism campaigns.

Kale borroka (Street fighting)   Part of a strategy adopted by ETA supporters from the late 1980s. Teenagers were encouraged to conduct a permanent campaign of political vandalism, burning buses, phone boxes, ATMs and rival political offices, creating a permanent social tension in the Basque Country.

Lehendakari   Regional Basque premier.

Nafarroa Bai (Navarre Yes)   Coalition of both left and right wing Basque nationalist parties which was created for the 2004 Spanish General election.

Podemos (We Can)   Left-wing political party formed in 2014 in the wake of the 15-M *indignados* movement.

Popular Party   Spain's dominant centre-right party. Formed in 1989 under the leadership of José María Aznar.

PNV   See Basque Nationalist Party.

PSOE   See Socialist Party.

Popular Alliance (AP, Alianza Popular)   Right-wing party founded by Manuel Fraga in 1976 along with other Francoist ministers. The Popular

Alliance was refounded as the Popular Party (PP, Partido Popular) in 1989.

PP See Popular Party

Socialist Party (PSOE, Partido Socialista Obrero Español) Spain's dominant centre-left party.

UCD Unión del Centro Democrático (Union of the Democratic Centre) Alliance of former Francoists and Christian Democrats. Political party through which Adolfo Suárez steered the transition to democracy, winning elections in 1977 and 1979, collapsing after PSOE victory in 1982.

United Left (IU, Izquierda Unida) Coalition dominated by the Communist Party of Spain. Declining in influence.

Introduction

On March 11, 2004, ten bombs exploded in and around Madrid's Atocha station, killing 191 people and wounding another 1,500. The March 11 attacks were executed by 13 Islamic terrorists 911 days after 9/11 whose *modus operandi* was imitated (four trains, four planes) (Gil Calvo 2005, 9). The attack occurred three days before the March 14 national election when it was generally believed that José María Aznar would lead the Partido Popular (PP, Popular Party) into its third term in office. In a narrative of events that will be long remembered in popular Spanish history, the PP promptly blamed the attack on the Basque Separatist group *Euskadi Ta Askatasuna* (ETA, Basque Homeland and Freedom), despite evidence indicating that an Islamist group had most likely perpetrated the attack in the context of the wider global War on Terror. Three days later, in a climate of civil division and suspicion, the Spanish people unexpectedly ejected the government from power and elected the Partido Socialista Obrero Español (PSOE, Spanish Socialist Workers' Party) under the leadership of José Luis Rodríguez Zapatero. The PSOE, in turn, immediately withdrew Spanish troops from Iraq and in the process was perceived by many political commentators around the world to have sabotaged its relations with the world's sole superpower—the United States of America.

The year 2004 could possibly join 1492 (the year Columbus encountered the Americas) and 1898 (the year Spain lost the Spanish-American War and its remaining four American and Asian colonies in what Spanish elites at the time referred to as *"El Desastre"*) as one of the most significant years in the history of Spain. Those three days in March 2004 amply demonstrate the significance of terrorist attacks not only in modern political society but also for political discourse. While much of the world understood the Spanish people's actions as capitulation or surrender to terrorism, the undeniable fact was that in order to understand the Spanish reaction to the attacks of March 11, 2004, one had to first understand Spanish history.

It is no exaggeration to suggest that the issues of terror and violence have, since the September 11, 2001, attacks in the USA, become a prominent area of study in the humanities and social sciences. As Andrew Strathern and Pamela Stewart suggest in *Terror and Violence*, terrorist acts in recent years "have given rise to seismic shifts of perceptions, policy and ideological responses, as governments and peoples attempt to encompass such events within their imaginations" (2006, 1). Given, however, that the issues of terror and violence are deeply emotive, the vocabulary, assumptions, labels and narratives used to describe terrorist discourses have also become an important area of study within the broader area of studies of terror and violence. The chapters to follow are anchored in this arena. As Joseba Zulaika and William Douglass argue in their seminal work *Terror and Taboo* (1996), there is no need to deny or diminish the atrociousness of terrorist events. Rather, what must be called into question is "the absolutist framework within which terrorism discourse casts its characters and networks, that is, its assumptions of all-encompassing discursive coherence" (4). Indeed, as Zulaika later elaborated, "Terrorism provides a textbook case of the reality-making power of discourse" (1998, 94). Building on that argument, this book is thus interested in delineating the process in which narratives of terror create a "reality-making power" and how that discursive power intersects with long-standing historical narratives formed and formulated in specific national settings—in this case, contemporary Spain.

The aim is to contribute to the broader field of Spanish studies by exploring the historical trajectory of terrorism discourse and its dialogical and symbiotic relationship with contemporary Spanish politics. Although a number of significant studies have dealt with ETA terrorism, state terrorism in Spain, and the social terror of the Franco regime, no scholarly work has yet to synthesize the mass-mediated narratives that emerge from terror discourses in Spain and to situate these narratives in a relevant and historic context. This study thus builds on extant studies of terrorism, particularly the work of Joseba Zulaika and William Douglass (1996) and Begoña Aretxaga (2005). The work of Zulaika, Douglass and Aretxaga challenged many of the assumptions and rhetoric that dominate terror-related discourse not only in the mass-media but also in academia since the 9/11 attacks in the USA. I seek to continue that approach. However, by taking a historical *and* narratological approach, this study departs from other extant studies on terrorism in Spain. No previous study has explored the political narratives that terror-related events spur in contemporary Spanish politics. A historical and narratological approach helps understand how the ritual of Spanish politics is in a constant dialogical and symbiotic relationship with terror-related events. No previous study, moreover, has traced the historical trajectory of these narratives dating from the Spanish Civil War up to the post 9/11 and post 3/11 eras.

The study also contributes to the emerging field of critical terrorism studies, which aim to foster a more self-reflective, critical approach to the study of terrorism. As the editors of the inaugural issue of the journal *Critical Studies on Terrorism* suggest:

In the first case, critical terrorism studies is understood as a research orientation that is willing to challenge dominant knowledge and understandings of terrorism, is sensitive to the politics of labelling in the terrorism field, is transparent about its own values and political standpoints, adheres to a set of responsible research ethics, and is committed to a broadly defined notion of emancipation. (Breen Smyth et al. 2008, 2)

By exploring narratives of terror in Spain my aim is to understand the direction and purpose of terror narratives when at first they may seem too complex and directionless, to find continuity where others see discontinuity, and to identify purpose and structure where others see incoherence. The study thus takes a multidisciplinary approach in understanding narratives of terror in contemporary Spain, in an attempt to contextualize terrorism socially and politically, as well as ideologically.

Investigating mass-mediated narratives when there are so many vested interests at stake is thus a daunting, but highly topical, indeed necessary, task. Accordingly, I am interested in considering the politicization of terror narratives as intrinsically linked to the constitutive historical narratives of the modern Spanish state. Rather than providing an exhaustive account of all the key stakeholders in Spanish political society, the study aims to demonstrate that political terror in Spain is caught between a violence that redresses the past and a violence that addresses the future. As such the Spanish state is, to use Allen Feldman's words, "haunted by a crisis in memory, by its inability both to compensate for the past and to fashion a sustainable memory of the future it seeks to create" (2003, 66). Given the complex nature of the historical and discursive terrains dealt with herein, I propose that the study of narrative is the best methodological tool to understand how terror and violence function in Spain, and to reveal how certain forms of political rhetoric and language are linked to structures that make those actions intelligible and legitimate. The employment of an interpretive rather than a causative logic, therefore, assists understanding how these narratives render acts of terror and violence as plausible or implausible, acceptable or unacceptable, conceivable or inconceivable, and respectable or disrespectable (Yee 1996, 97).

In this study I explore the constitutive cultural or political narratives of the Spanish state that have been destabilized or undermined since the consolidation of Spain's transition to democracy in the early 1980s. I argue that two key narratives drive the historical trajectory of terrorism discourse in Spain. The first is the narrative of *las dos Españas*. The idea of two Spains, one conservative and one liberal, can be traced to the early nineteenth century. But since the late 1990s, the narrative of *las dos Españas* has become a vehicle for political elites to settle political scores and to narrativize their respective national histories. The constitutive narrative of *las dos Españas* is evident across many political and historical debates operating in the Spanish state, and it shadows and informs national issues from immigration and Spain's State of Autonomies, to the teaching of history in schools. The narrative is most polemical, however, in debates concerning the issue of terror in all its manifestations, regardless of whether that terror is linked to Islamic groups or ETA in the Basque Country. The second constituent narrative is the metanarrative of terror that has been articulated since the September 11 attacks in the USA as a global War on Terror. The metanarrative of terror is thus itself global in that it presumes that terror(ism) can no longer be contained on a local scale. In considering these constituent narrative drives I demonstrate that there is a fundamental tension at play in terror politics. That is the tension between the projection of a global metanarrative, the US-led War on Terror and the national historical debates of terror that remain state-based and domestically mass-mediated. The study therefore seeks to understand the Spanish response to the March 11 attacks and other terror-related events in terms of the constraints emanating from the Spanish state's historical narratives.

As event, news story, and social drama, terrorism is a mode of "emplotted" action in which narrative sequence is a moral and discursive construct. Moreover, as Feldman notes, "the event is that which can be narrated" rather than what actually happens (1991, 14). Accepting Feldman's proposition, I attempt to escape the confines of descriptive narratives. My aim here is to explore multiple genealogies of mediated terror by considering *all* violence as expressive, and thus as having a structuring and constitutive power over political narratives. In the form of official political discourse, the discourse of the mass-media, political ephemera and informal everyday conversations, Spanish narratives about political violence are a pervasive component of sociopolitical cultures in that country.

My focus is on a range of terror narratives in contemporary Spain. The book thus has a significantly broad historical scope, necessarily including in its panorama the aftermath of the Spanish Civil War, the end of the Franco era and the Spanish transition to democracy. But it pays particular attention to the democratic era from the early 1980s to 2015. That large ambit is necessary in order to situate the "tattered" narratives that concern me in a suitable historical context and to effectively delineate their historical trajectory. The study is more concerned with the effects of terrorism and violence rather than the acts of terror themselves. This is why the book is selective in its case studies and focuses exclusively on those acts of violence that have had the greatest influence in shaping mass-mediated narratives of terror in Spain. The study, therefore, does not investigate every terrorist group active in Spain in the last few decades. For example, I do not investigate one of the most active terrorist groups in post-Franco Spain, the anti-fascist *Grupos de Resistencia Antifascista Primero de Octubre* (GRAPO, First of October Anti-Fascist Resistance Group).[1] The reason for not attending to the violent attacks by GRAPO is that they were not narrativized by the central Spanish government as threats to the existence of the Spanish state. However, attacks by the Basque separatist group ETA, and the March 11, 2004, attacks, were, and continue to be, key discursive sites of political and social tension. This approach thus provides not a genealogy of terror in Spain but rather an investigation into the relationship between acts of violence and the narrativization of those acts of violence. My investigation highlights how violence disrupts systems of interpretation and leads to the proliferation of discourses about Spanish history and the Spanish nation.

This study both builds on and departs from extant studies on terrorism in contemporary Spain. Recent scholarship in and/or on Spain has tended to over-emphasize what has been occurring within the so-called national periphery (Catalonia, Basque Country, Galicia) and ignore the centre. I am concerned to address the debates and issues associated with terrorism in Spain and thus inquire into the processes in which terrorism has been narrativized by the state apparatus. In particular, the book has two parallel aims. First, to assess to what extent the narrativization process to do with terror has been used to achieve the political ambitions of the national government (irrespective of its ideological position). And second, to determine to what extent the narratives of terror have been informed by the traditional concerns of Spanish studies and the relatively recent influx of collective memories of the Civil War and the Franco era into Spanish public discourse.

Where this book differs from much recent scholarship on terror is the degree of significance it gives the September 11, 2001 terrorist attacks in the USA in purportedly refashioning a new global order. Although scholars such as Michael Hardt and Antonio Negri (2004) argue that 9/11 represented a paradigm shift from a post-Cold War era to an era of "total" or "perpetual" war, their argument is neither confirmed nor sustained by the

---

[1]   GRAPO was created in 1975 as the armed wing of the then-banned Communist Party during the last year of the Franco regime. Its goal was to overthrow the dictatorship and replace it with a Marxist-Leninist regime, although Franco's death later that year did not deter it from continuing its activities. GRAPO is listed as a terrorist organization by the USA and the European Union, with 84 killings and 25 kidnappings to its name.

Spanish experience. Spain has been dealing with terrorism as one of its principal national and existential concerns since the late 1950s. During the Spanish state's transition from the Franco dictatorship (1939–1975) to democracy, terrorism arguably posed a greater threat to democratic stability than it does today. Toward the end of the millennium's first decade, terrorism in Spain can be considered "a protracted violent phenomenon that systematically violates fundamental rights and impairs the free exercise of civil and political liberties," rather than a grave threat to the state's existence (Alonso & Reinares 2005, 265). That said, it is clear that the Spanish state inevitably adapted to the new post 9/11 international context while simultaneously fighting an old internal enemy: ETA.

Noting those historical processes and adaptations, the argument put forward is that the issues of violence and terrorism in Spain are largely mass-mediated narratives that are politically driven by elites in order to situate terror at the centre of national political discourse. This argument does not deny the horrific consequences of terror attacks, particularly on those directly affected. Rather it attempts to understand how terror and violence is usurped both by governments and other key stakeholders to advance their ideological causes, a process that almost always relies on the repetition of certain narratives in mass-mediated discourse. Given that more pressing issues in Spain, such as the housing crisis, precarity in the labour market, and the rising cost of living are too difficult for politicians to solve or use as electoral leverage, it is not surprising that the more "abstract" problems of terrorism, and to a lesser extent peripheral nationalisms, are elevated into the most pressing issues confronting the Spanish state. As sociologist and *El País* columnist Enrique Gil Calvo (2007) suggests, the manipulation of these issues creates a false reality that is much more attractive for the Spanish mass-media, increasing its capacity for drawing in more viewers and readers. Gil Calvo argues that this new "reality" is a complete falsification, a "virtual" reality that comes to be perceived as the natural order of things (2008, 49). News frames, manipulated by partisan media groups, create a new reality by selectively editing the news narrative. The March 11, 2004 attacks in Madrid are the most notable example of the uses made of these framing devices. Between the attacks in Madrid and the subsequent general election three days later, Spaniards apparently knew what was occurring on a day-to-day and minute-to-minute basis from the news media, but the news frames completely manipulated and distorted the narrative about what was true and thus "real" (50).

Although most of the book deals with terror-related events in contemporary Spain, the final chapter details the process in which dominant mass-mediated narratives have shifted away from terror narratives towards narratives of crisis. The 2008 global economic crisis hit Spain particularly hard. The crisis also coincided with other key events which I refer to as "institutional crises." These events include the definitive cessation of ETA violence; the emergence of the 15-M movement; and the renewed drive for Catalan independence. In my reading of these events, I suggest that both narratives of terror and crisis circulate and are manipulated in Spanish political discourse in similar ways. The shift from terror to crisis thus points to a continuity in Spanish political narratives rather than a rupture. That said, it is clear that in 2016 Spain is at a crossroads. The shift from terror to crisis has provoked a fragmented bipolarism in Spanish politics, the consequences of which are yet to be played out.

Chapter outline

Chapter One, "Narratives of Political Violence," posits that the two funda-mental, constituent narrative drivers that have had a significant impact on the issue of terror and its subject-position in the Spanish state in the new millennium are the narrative of *las dos Españas* and the global metanarrative of terror. These two constituent narratives, one global and the other internal, often converge; at other times they contradict each other. As I argue, the two narratives shape and articulate narratives of terror in Spain in the post-2001 epoch. Understanding narratives of terror in Spain, I suggest, is therefore impossible without first understanding the constituent narrative of *las dos Españas*. That narrative is a story of two Spains, and has been used to explain the course of Spanish history since the early nineteenth century. The chapter argues that although the significance of the narrative of *las dos Españas* has probably been overstated, it has attained almost mythological ubiquity in contemporary Spanish political and public discourse. The chapter then evaluates the role of "memory" research in the social sciences as a prelude to discussing the pacts of "forgetting" and "silence" agreed by political elites during Spain's transition to democracy. The chapter highlights how the recent "explosion" of interest in the Spanish Civil War from both civil and political society has broken down these unof-ficial pacts. Consequently, a new set of memory battles has emerged in public discourse, paradoxically framed in terms of the older theory of the two Spains. In this chapter, then, I argue that the constitutive narrative of *las dos Españas* is evident in many political and historical debates circulating in Spanish political discourse, but it is at its most polemical in debates concerning the issue of terror in all its manifestations, and regardless of whether it is linked to Islamic groups or ETA.

If the narrative of *las dos Españas* is a fundamental internal narrative used to explain the trajectory of Spanish history in terms of its histories of confrontation and violence, the second part of Chapter One investigates the global metanarrative of terror, a narrative that positions terror and terrorism at the centre of global political discourse. This part of the chapter discusses the global impact of the September 11, 2001 attacks in the USA and considers how the attacks, and the subsequent War on Terror as articulated by the USA (and in such staunch allies as the UK and Australia and, at the time, Spain under Aznar), impacted on, and intertwined with, narratives of terror in Spain. In this section, therefore, I investigate three related debates and situate them in a Spanish context. The first is the shift from what has been termed "classical" terrorism to "global" terrorism, and what the shift implies for local national terror groups such as the Basque separatist group ETA. The second debate concerns the usefulness and appropriateness of conceptualizing terror as a narrative, or even as a metanarrative. The third debate relates to the role of the mass-media in projecting that metanarrative and what that mediatization implies for local political groups and the national histories that sustain them.

Chapter Two "History, Terror and Myth: ETA, Spain, the State, and the Nation," considers the constituent narrative of *las dos Españas* and the metanarrative of terror in terms of the long-running struggle in the Basque Country. The chapter explores the phenomenon of Basque terrorism and suggests that ETA was positioned in Spanish political discourse as the most urgent and pressing threat to the Spanish state. The chapter examines the emergence of ETA and Spain's transition to democracy in order to highlight how unresolved questions of the nation (centre-periphery, centrist or federalist) have been constructed as a narrative device to legitimize the Spanish "state" while minimizing the potential disturbance of regional nationalism to the unity of the Spanish "nation." The chapter concludes by looking at how these narratives have evolved in the post-9/11 era and argues that the narratives of violence that emerged from the Basque Country clashed with the prevailing narrative scripts of the Spanish state in the post-Franco era. Here I argue that those narratives were ultimately delegitimated, if not illegitimated, after September 11, 2001.

Chapter Three, "Terror and the State: The GAL, Fantasy, and the (Un)imaginable," takes a different perspective of the Basque conflict. Here I discuss the nature of state terrorism in Spain by tracking the GAL scandal of the 1980s. Over the course of four years (1983–1987), the *Grupos Antiterroristas de Liberación* (GAL, Antiterrorist Liberation Groups) claimed twenty-seven mortal victims, nine of whom were confirmed as having no connection with ETA. The chapter argues that far from hurting the credibility of the state, the GAL scandal actually helped to legitimate the state and state power. The GAL scandal not only demonstrated how issues related to terror converged with the narrative of *las dos Españas*; it also reminded Spaniards that the recollection of past violence feeds the violence in the present. The GAL scandal also confirmed how the debate about state terror was neatly adopted by both sides of Spanish politics and used as a vehicle to promote many discourses that form part of the narrative of *las dos Españas*, whether from the left or the right. The GAL, as an antiterrorist discourse, confused more than it clarified many of the complex political narratives that were still functioning in Spanish political discourse in the 1980s and early 1990s.

Chapter Four, "The Aznar Years (1996–2004): History, Politics and Narratives of the Spanish 'Nation,'" argues that the narrative of *las dos Españas*, which was more or less neutralized in the face of the Spanish transition to democracy, and its attendant myths of compromise and forgetting, again resurfaced during the Aznar years. The chapter studies the potency of the narrative of *las dos Españas* and the scholarly debate circulating around "Spanish" nationalism. I posit that both the Spanish left and right utilize their respective narratives of the "Spanish nation" in an attempt not only to appeal to the Spanish electorate but also to synthesize their modern electoral platforms with their constituent ideological histories. The chapter examines the narrative battles between the two major Spanish political parties, the PP and the PSOE, during the Aznar years and is concerned with reading the narrative of *las dos Españas* not in terms of ideological conviction but rather as a saga of rival political manipulations and electoral gains.

Chapter Five, "Blame Games and Narrative Battles: The March 11 'Terror' Attacks and the March 14 General Elections," argues that the events of March 11, 2004, instigated a narrative battle between the two major political parties. The PP promoted the narrative that ETA was responsible for the attacks while the opposition PSOE projected a counter-narrative that accused the government of misinformation and blamed the attacks on Islamists. The chapter thus explores the clash between the global metanarrative of terror and the local/national narrative of *las dos Españas*, as it was played out during those three fateful days in Spain. I argue that the narrative battle was won by the opposition PSOE because its narrative promoted continuity with the historical pacts of compromise negotiated during Spain's transition to democracy. The PP narrative ultimately failed because while it attempted to undermine those historical pacts, it raised the ire of many Spaniards due to the perception that the PP narrative was authoritarian and manipulative, and thus evocative of the Franco era.

Chapter Six, "The Zapatero Years (2004–2011): *Crispación* and the Return of *las dos Españas*," looks at the mass-mediated divisions and narrative battles that emerged with the Socialist Party victory in 2004. The years from 2004 to 2008 witnessed perhaps the most partisan polarization in Spanish society since the restoration of Spanish democracy. The chapter details the process of *crispación* (best translated in English as polarization) in two main areas: the polarization of political discourse that stemmed from the March 11, 2004 attacks in Madrid; and the polarization that emerged from the narrative projected by the PP that *España se rompe*. That is, Spain was in danger of being broken up. The chapter argues that *crispación*, as it was and is dubbed by the Spanish mass-media, is an updated version of the narrative of *las dos Españas* that has plagued Spanish political and public discourse since the early nineteenth century. This key constituent narrative of Spanish political life drives narratives of terrorism in mass-mediated discourse. As such it provides a vehicle for the two major political parties in Spain to project their ideological positions. The repetition of certain narratives of terror by both the PP and the PSOE during Zapatero's first legislature had the effect of creating a "reality-making power" for their respective support bases.

Chapter Seven, "The Beginning and End of the ETA Peace Process: Between Dialogue and *Engaño*," relates the mass-mediated narratives in Spanish political discourse generated by the peace negotiations between ETA and the Spanish government in 2006 and 2007. The chapter posits that since political and media elites perceived the peace process in the historically contested terms of the narrative of *las dos Españas*, those perceptions make evident how the ETA peace process was not just about the dissolution of a terrorist group. Rather, the process was concerned with the dissolution of a spectral enemy that the state had utilized for decades to construct, and imagine, a unified Spanish "nation."

Chapter Eight, "The Semantics and Rhetoric of Victims of Terrorism Groups," responds to the dearth of extant analysis on groups formed by victims of terror. Here I discuss the role of victims' groups in Spanish society and how the mass-mediated debates surrounding them are, again, linked to long-standing historical narratives. In Spain victims' groups have widespread influence in the national political arena; more tellingly, the groups are not only numerous but divided by political allegiances. In Spain there are several associations, organizations and foundations for victims of terrorism and their families. Each one has a specific, if undeclared, political allegiance. Victims of ETA terrorism tend to gravitate toward the Popular Party (PP) because of its hard-line stance against the Basque organization. March 11 victims tend to favour the Socialists, believing that the PP manipulated the 2004 bombings for political gain. Although part of the remit of this chapter is to explore the partisan interests of victims of terrorism groups in Spain, and their influence on Spanish mass-mediated narratives, the chapter also seeks to question the semantics and rhetoric of guilt and innocence surrounding terrorism's victims, and understand how victim narratives also shape and inform contemporary Spanish politics.

Chapter Nine, "From Terror to Crisis," explores the shift away from terror narratives towards crisis narratives with the onset of the global economic crisis which hit Spain in 2008. First I examine the extraordinary impact that the crisis had on Spanish society and the attempts by scholars and media commentators to understand the crisis. The chapter then considers three key events which unfolded during those important years (2008–2016): the definitive end of ETA; the emergence of the 15-M movement; and the renewed drive for Catalan independence. I argue that the economic crisis and the impact of those three events heralded a new era in Spanish politics characterized by bipolar fragmentation. The emergence of the new political parties Podemos and Ciudadanos thus led to a political stalemate in the aftermath of the general elections in December 2015. This chapter reads these events through the lens of *las dos Españas* and suggests that although there are many continuities from previous eras, there are also many new factors which could lead to further political destabilization. I note, however, that the future of the Spanish state is not as bleak as many political commentators suppose.

The study thus takes a multidisciplinary approach to understanding narratives of terror and crisis in Spain. The book contributes to the wider field of Spanish studies and critical terrorism studies by exploring the complexity of terrorism discourses in a state which has dealt with a long-running terrorist struggle (ETA), while simultaneously coming to terms with a "global" terrorist attack on March 11, 2004. As such, the study argues that there is a dialogical and symbiotic relationship between discourses of terrorism and the ritual of contemporary Spanish politics. I posit that two key constituent narratives drive terror related discourses in Spain: the narrative of *las dos Españas* and the global metanarrative of terror. The partisan manipulation of these two narratives in mass-mediated discourse serves to situate terrorism at the centre of Spanish political discourse. Indeed, understanding the historical trajectory of these constituent narratives is an important, and necessary, task in understanding discourses of terror in Spain.

The following chapters will evaluate the process in which terror events in Spain, particularly the March 11, 2004 attacks in Madrid and the peace process with ETA, intersect with the constitutive narrative of *las dos Españas* and the global metanarrative of terror. The remit of this study is to understand these constituent narratives. Why did the March 11, 2004 attacks re-energize the theory of the two Spains? And why is it that the peace negotiations with ETA were framed by both Spanish conservatives and liberals as a struggle between two different understandings of what Spain is? The narrative script of "winners" and "losers" emerges in these history battles as a sore point for both sides of Spanish politics.

CHAPTER ONE

Narratives of Political Violence

The Narrative of *las dos Españas* and the Global Metanarrative of Terror

> It seems clear that, one way or another, Spanish society has entered the early 21st century having to face the unexpected and uncomfortable ghosts of the 20th. (Ferrándiz 2006, 12)

Spain's transition from the Franco era after 1975, and its subsequent democratic consolidation, successfully transformed the country into a stable democracy and a respected member of the European Union and NATO. But, in the early twenty-first century, it is still necessary to ask: What is "Spain?"[1] In recent years, it has become highly problematical for scholars to assume that there is such a thing as a coherent Spanish identity, and indeed to assume that the transition is, in fact, complete. Spanish theorists such as José Álvarez Junco (2002) have pointed out that although some kind of "Spanish" identity can be traced to the late Middle Ages, the Spanish "nation" and its accompanying "nationalism" are relatively new phenomena. Similar arguments, of course, can be made with respect to Catalan, Basque, and Galician "national" identities, and more recently with the emergence of Andalusian and Valencian (and even Aragonese and Balaeric) regional identities. This situation is not unique to the Spanish state. What is perhaps distinct is that these conflicting (or complementary) identities are very much prominent in Spanish public and political discourse, so much so that it is common to read opinion pieces on the "national question" in Spanish national newspapers such as *El País* and *El Mundo* on a weekly, or even daily, basis. In recent years, the renewed drive towards Catalan independence has become one of the most urgent issues in Spanish political discourse (see Chapter Nine). Identity debates are thus

---

[1] Thanks to Paul Allatson for allowing me to reuse the driving question in his subject Contemporary Spain, at the University of Technology, Sydney.

hotly contested in Spain, overflowing on to the streets of major cities and manifesting themselves in a variety of forms, sometimes directly and other times in a more veiled fashion, a case in point being the conflict between the Catalan and Valenciano languages.

Spain's constitutive cultural and political narratives are thus complex, and they vary significantly according to time and place. However, some official narratives that emanate from the Spanish government are crucial in understanding recent developments in Spanish political culture. This is particularly so when they relate to discourses of terror and crisis, even if those discourses are not always coherent and can be arbitrary and contested. I work, then, from two sets of assumptions. First, societies and individuals need narratives to make sense of themselves, the media plays a role in these narratives, and regimes of terror and political parties alike benefit from these narratives. Second, the mass-mediated narratives of terror that emerged in the aftermath of the March 11, 2004 attacks in Madrid can be understood as a discursive site of struggle both for negotiating current political battles over national identity and for renegotiating previous narratives of national identity. Prominent among the latter are the narratives that emerged from the Franco dictatorship, which constructed national identity in another context of social terror.

With those qualifications, this chapter discusses the dialogical relationship between history, memory and narrative in contemporary Spain. The chapter first discusses the usefulness of narrative as a mode of theory in the social sciences and then posits that the two key narrative drives in contemporary Spanish history are the narrative of *las dos Españas* and the global metanarrative of terror. The narrative of *las dos Españas* is domestic and state-based, and has been used by historians, journalists and politicians to explain Spain's violent and conflictive history since the early nineteenth century. The metanarrative of terror is a global narrative that stemmed from the 9/11 attacks in the USA, and that re-articulated the global security discourse. In Spain, these two constitutive narratives are sometimes complementary, but also often in conflict with each other. In the analysis that follows, I query what function the two constitutive narratives serve, and what each narrative disguises, displaces, enforces, and mobilizes in the context of understanding terror and political violence in contemporary Spain.

Conceptualizing narratives of terror

In *Terror and Taboo*, Zulaika and Douglass argue that "stories" provide a context (religious, cultural, national) in which to situate terrorist behaviour

(1996, 109). Discourses on terrorism, they argue, "conform to, and borrow from, some form of fictionalization" (109). By this they mean the crafting of a narrative, where terrorist related events are frequently perceived as a kind of fictional reality. Yet, the reporting about the "innocent victims" that are killed in a terrorist attack, they suggest, is so brutally factual that no possible explanation makes sense: "indeed it is so 'real' that it requires no frame, so 'true' that no interpretation is necessary, so 'concrete' that no meaning need be inferred" (5). Nonetheless, the really challenging issues, posit Zulaika and Douglass, "have more to do with the ways in which the popular media, scholarly treatises, and official reports employ narrative strategies to anticipate, relate and interpret such events" (11). The deep impact of terrorism, they argue, goes far beyond the shattered bodies or buildings, for it is manifested in terrorism's resonance "in the halls of the collective imagination" (11). Perceptions of terrorism, therefore, constitute one of the many discursive fields by which social actors understand and explain the contradictions and paradoxes of their society and historical moment.

Given that social processes are constituted through, and guided by narrativity, as Margaret Somers argues, in that all social processes and interactions are narratively mediated, the complexities of terror are also mediated through narrative (2003, 364). When confronted by the 2004 terrorist attacks in Madrid, critical theorists need to ask how they might understand this historical event if not through, on the one hand, a narrative (ten bombs exploded, killing 191 people, leading to the government being voted from office three days later), or, on the other hand, as memory (memory in this case being the raw material of history, that is, the essential element that constructs individual and collective identity) (Le Goff 1992, 98). Through narratives (our life stories) we come to know and make sense of the social world. Our social identities are inscribed within these narratives, as is our memory of them. Irrespective of the fact that terror might be directed from the state, or from non-state actors, we need narratives to make sense of the world around us, as does the state itself. Narratives, then, can circulate in society in different ways, can be contested and are not always exclusionary.

The concept of narrative as a mode of theory has become prominent in a range of disciplines, though it has been defined differently. According to M. C. Lemon, narrative as a mode of theory is inherently "messy" for philosophical or scientific purposes (2003, 110). This is because narrative lacks the coherence of philosophy; its practitioners rarely examine their own premises, and it also lacks science's laws of causality, determinateness and inevitability. In social theory, particularly in the work of Somers (1994) and

Somers and Gibson (1995), narrative is conceived as *the* principal and inescapable mode by which we experience the world. Narratives in this view are public and personal "stories" that we subscribe to and that guide our behaviour. They are the stories we tell ourselves, not just those we explicitly tell other people, about the world(s) we live in. It also follows from this that a narrative, in the social theory sense, is not necessarily traceable to one specific stretch of text. Rather it is more likely to underpin a whole range of texts and discourses without necessarily being fully or explicitly articulated in any one of them. According to Somers, we come to know, understand and make sense of the social world through narrativity, and it is through narratives that we constitute our social identities: "we come to *be* who we *are* (however ephemeral, multiple and changing) by our location (usually unconsciously) in social narratives and networks of relations that are rarely of our own making" (2003, 360). In other words, we are always embedded in social narratives. Whether we recognize it or not, our social identities are constituted through narrativity.

Somers and Gibson (1995) distinguish between ontological, public, conceptual and metanarratives. I am particularly interested in public narratives and metanarratives. Public narratives, as their name suggests, are stories elaborated by and circulating among social and institutional formations larger than the individual, such as the family, religious or educational institutions, political or activist groups, the media, and the nation. Somers and Gibson give as an example of public narratives stories about US social mobility involving the "freeborn Englishman" (62). A more recent example might be the numerous competing public narratives about the March 11, 2004 terrorist attacks in Madrid: who is responsible, why did it happen, could it have been avoided, and how many died?

Metanarritivity refers to the "master narratives" in which we are embedded as contemporary actors in history and as social scientists (Somers 2003, 362). Our sociological theories and concepts are encoded with aspects of these master narratives—Progress, Decadence, Industrialization, Enlightenment—even though they usually operate beyond our awareness. These narratives can be the epic dramas of our time: Capitalism versus Communism, or, the Individual versus Society. They may also be progressive narratives of teleological unfolding: Marxism and the triumph of class struggle; Liberalism and the triumph of liberty; the Rise of Nationalism or of Islam (362). Indeed, the global US-led War on Terror can also be embodied in the theory of metanarrativity since it, too, has become one of the epic dramas or "grand narratives" of our time. Metanarrativity explains that a war cannot be simply won; rather it has to be won in a narratorial sense again each day. The social and political ramifications of terror can only be understood in narrative form. Extant theories are yet to adequately explain the process whereby the unending nature of the war against terrorism becomes a permanent social relation. Narrativism, on the other hand, is better positioned to understand which public discourses are socially predominant, based on the existing distribution of power, and which discourses are politically contested.

Slavoj Žižek points out that we live in a "postmodern" era in which truth-claims as such are often dismissed by critical theorists as expressions of hidden power mechanisms (2006, 240). What we get, instead:

> is a multitude of perspectives, or, as it is fashionable to put it today, 'narratives'—not only literature, but also politics, religion, science, they are all different narratives, stories we tell ourselves about ourselves, and the ultimate goal of ethics is to guarantee the neutral space in which this multitude of narratives can peacefully coexist, in which everyone, from ethnic to sexual minorities, will have the right and ability to tell his/her story. (240)

I agree that truth-claims often do express hidden power mechanisms. Narratives most certainly do operate in society *as if* they are based on truth. This is not a radical supposition since political parties, for example, consciously narrate a convincing story to sell themselves to the electorate and in the process their "story" becomes regularized, usually by the mass-media, as one of many "truths" that we, as consumer-citizens, either accept or reject. However, the concept of universal truth still merits serious consideration in the contemporary world. After all, a master narrative is a narrative that is projected *as* universal truth. The point is not whether universal truth exists or not, but rather whether a narrative is (or can be) mediated in a universal way, and why.

Žižek suggests that one should subvert the standard self-enclosed linear narrative "not by means of a postmodern dispersal into a multitude of local narratives, but by means of its redoubling in a hidden counter-narrative" (2006, xxv). To a point this is a useful argument. However, I argue that the study of political narratives of terror often intersects with multiple histories and desires, hence it is inevitable that a postmodern dispersal of the linear narrative (or in this instance the master narrative) will occur. With that caveat, I attempt to locate the hidden Spanish counter-narrative and investigate its role in shaping and determining the multitude of local Spanish narratives it encompasses. I posit that the hidden counter-narrative in much Spanish political discourse is the narrative of *las dos Españas* (the two Spains). This narrative refers to liberal and conservative "Spains," two antagonistic visions of Spain that eventually clashed in the 1930s, leading to civil war. Since the 1930s, the long lasting theory of the two Spains has continued to be one of the key narratives deployed in Spanish public discourse to explain not only the Spanish "nation," but also the long trajectory of violent and discursive conflict in the Spanish state. In their preface to *The Reinvention of Spain* (2007), Sebastian Balfour and Alejandro Quiroga suggest that the power of national narratives "[. . .] does not have to rest on veracity; they are real in the sense that they are unquestioned presuppositions embedded in identities and views of the world" (v). I posit that the narrative of *las dos Españas* is one of the key mass-mediated drivers of the issues of terror and violence in Spanish political and public discourse. The Two Eternal Spains: forever at odds; always the same timeless story. This is not a revolutionary idea, since the narrative of *las dos Españas* has existed in Spanish cultural discourse, and inflected debate about what Spain is, since the early nineteenth century. However, the narrative of *las dos Españas* is the often overlooked counter-narrative that shadows almost every other political narrative in Spain. This hidden narrative *regularizes* and shapes the potency and effectiveness of other more localized political narratives. Although the narrative of *las dos Españas* is arguably not very well "hidden" in Spanish political rhetoric and discourse, I demonstrate that it is a key national narrative whose operations are at once silent and ambiguous, present and ghostly.

The narrative of *las dos Españas*

If one of the overwhelming drivers of contemporary Spanish politics and history is the struggle to come to terms with multiple identities, another driving force is the struggle to come to terms with the Spanish state's multiple violent histories. The idea that political problems are best settled by violence is a commonplace of Spanish history and literature. Paul Preston, one of the most eminent historians of modern Spain, highlights that Spanish historical writing by Spanish émigrés after the Civil War, but also in Spain itself since the death of Franco, has involved "an all-consuming quest for an explanation for the country's plethora of civil wars, conflicts, and violent regime changes since the late eighteenth century" (1990, 30). He adds: "the consequent cultural/national character interpretations [in this historical trend] provided implicitly, and sometimes explicitly, teleological versions of Spain's history, characterising the national past in terms of a propensity to pitiless blood-lust and savage discord" (30). A desire to reconcile national identity, even humanity, to the excesses of civil war and violence is not unique to Spain. What is unique, however, is that since Spain was denied liberation in 1945, as other European states were, "the question of coming to terms with the past has been rendered difficult by the fact that 'the past' continued for nearly forty years after the war's conclusion and indeed beyond" (33). Preston is referring here to how the Franco dictatorship promoted a one-sided view of history and stumbled into the 1970s with the same rhetoric and epithets it had used in the 1930s.

Since the Spanish state never experienced a clean "break" with the politics of the 1930s until Spain's transition to democracy in the late 1970s and early 1980s, certain constitutive narratives remained discernible in Spanish political and public discourse. The most important of these constitutive narratives is that of *las dos Españas* (conservative and liberal Spains). The epithet *las dos Españas* is taken from a short untitled poem (number LIII) by the Spanish poet Antonio Machado in his *Proverbios y cantares* (Proverbs and Songs), originally published in 1909. Here he refers to the left and right division in Spain as one national half that dies and another national half that yawns (1983, 113):

Ya hay un español que quiere
vivir y a vivir empieza,
entre una España que muere
y otra España que bosteza.
Españolito que vienes
al mundo, te guarde Dios.
Una de **las dos Españas** [my emphasis]
ha de helarte el corazón.

(There is a Spaniard today, who wants
to live and is starting to live,
between one dying Spain,
and another Spain yawning.
Little Spaniard just now coming
into the world, may God keep you.
One of those two Spains
will freeze your heart).

The idea of a divided Spain, however, where one half is antagonistic to the other half, dates back at least to the 19th-century Spanish satirist Mariano José de Larra who, in his essay *Día de difuntos de 1836* ("All Souls' Day 1836") wrote "Aquí yace media España; murió de la otra media" (Here lies half of Spain. It died of the other half) (1836). But historians trace the idea still further back, to the seventeenth and eighteenth centuries and the formation of the purported "Spanish" character.

According to Spanish historian Santos Juliá in his book *Historias de las dos Españas* (2004), public discourse by Spanish intellectuals over the last one hundred-and-fifty years presents a mythical vision of Spanish history with a dual character, opting for antagonism over consensus and promoting a vision of national history as conflictive, tragic and heroic. Whether they comprise Liberals, Catholics, communists, Francoists or antifascists, argues Juliá, Spanish intellectuals are defined by "la proyección hacia el pasado de un momento de grandeza y la promesa del futuro como regeneración o resurrección de lo que ya fue realidad en otro tiempo" (The projection towards a past moment of grandeur and the promise of a future of regeneration or resurrection of what was once a previous reality) (45). The division of society between one side that is conservative, reactionary and resistant to change, and another side that is reformist and progressive, is not such a radical idea. The division could be applied to many countries that have been divided ideologically between left and right. The narrative of *las dos Españas*, however, is more than just a catchphrase that describes two different political ideologies. In Spain, the concept of *las dos Españas* is part of mass-mediated narratives of the state and it is linked controversially to almost every major debate of national significance in the country.

Although the narrative of *las dos Españas* implies two distinct political, economic and even cultural sensibilities, it also encompasses two very different approaches to Spanish history. In *The Archaeology of Knowledge* (1972), Michel Foucault highlighted how the idea of discontinuity has assumed a major role in the historical disciplines. According to Foucault, "for history in its classical form, the discontinuous was both the given and the unthinkable: the raw material of history, which presented itself in the form of dispersed events—decisions, accidents, initiatives, discoveries; the material which, through analysis, had to be rearranged, reduced, effaced in order to reveal the continuity of events" (9). Discontinuity, he adds, "was the stigma of temporal dislocation and it was therefore the traditional historian's task to remove the discontinuous from history" (9). According to Foucault, discontinuity has now become one of the basic elements of historical analysis. Foucault was thus rather prescient in the early 1970s when he stated that: "The cry goes up that one is murdering history whenever, in a historical analysis—and especially if it is concerned with thought, ideas, or knowledge—one is seen to be using in too obvious a way the categories of discontinuity and difference, the notions of threshold, rupture and transformation, the description of series and limits" (15). Indeed, Foucault was referring specifically to the disciplinary production of ideas, (the history of science, knowledge), disciplines that were more or less self-contained in an academic context. But in the early twenty-first century the role of discontinuity in history is more controversial than ever (at least in Spain), if only because the debate has extended beyond the academic frontier and into popular mass-mediated narratives that tell the story of the "nation" to the Spanish electorate. Indeed, in the Spanish state the battle lines between conservative and progressive views of history have been drawn exactly as Foucault foretold. On the one side, the Spanish left and regional nationalists are attempting to highlight the discontinuities of historical narratives that have until recently remained unchallenged. On the opposing side, conservatives and the Popular Party argue, in a sense, that the left is "murdering" history by challenging long-standing historical narratives and the pacts of compromise that were enacted during Spain's transition to democracy.

In contemporary Spanish cultural and historical studies the concept of *las dos Españas* has thus been ascribed almost mythological significance. As Juliá argues, since the early nineteenth century Spanish intellectuals have tended to use a series of myths and metaphors to refer to Spain:

> El pueblo en Guerra por su independencia y su libertad; la anomalía y decadencia; la muerte y resurrección de España; la nación dormida, inconsciente de que un poder ajeno le impide crecer; la vieja y nueva España; el romance del pueblo en Guerra contra invasores y traidores; el mito de la única verdadera España contra la Anti-España espuria y extranjera, son algunos de estos relatos que han gozado de particular vigencia. (The nation at war for its independence and liberty; anomaly and decadence; death and resurrection of Spain; the nation asleep unaware that a foreign power impedes its growth; old and new Spain; the romanticism of the nation at war against invaders and traitors; the myth of a unified and true Spain against a spurious and foreign anti-Spain, are some of the discourses that have enjoyed particular prominence). (2004, 18)

These myths were oft-repeated throughout the nineteenth and twentieth centuries, especially during the Franco era, particularly the trope of an authentic "true" Spain struggling against an "anti-Spain." The repetition of these myths in public and political discourse projects the idea that the Spanish state has a long and violent history that can be traced back to the Spanish Reconquest and beyond. This revisionist reading of history links a whole series of Spanish conflicts into a neat historical trajectory of violent conflict, including Spain's War of Independence (1808–1814), three Carlist Wars (1833–1876), the Spanish-American War (1898), the Spanish Civil

War (1936–1939), as well as a series of smaller conflicts and uprisings. It is therefore easy for theorists, historians and commentators to narrativize this violent trajectory as a struggle between two anthropomorphized equals with corresponding and unambiguous values. Liberal Spain is accorded the values of the French Revolution and is described as anti-monarchical and pro-European. Conservative Spain is branded as traditionalist, centralist, pro-monarchical, anti-regionalist and parochial. Liberal Spain's moment of glory was the Second Republic (1931–1939), which established unprecedented political and intellectual liberty, separated the Church from the State, successfully initiated Catalan autonomy as a first step in recognizing the culturally diverse nature of Spain as a nation, enshrined labour rights, and initiated land reform despite opposition from the traditional ruling and land-owning classes. In popular history, the clash between two distinct "Spains" led to nearly four years of civil war (1936–1939), and culminated in almost forty years of dictatorship under the Franco regime (1939–1975). That regime has been cast as the epitome of "conservative" Spain: it is the logical conclusion of traditionalist values that are at once illegitimate, oppressive and undemocratic. The problem with this narrative is that it is overly deterministic and simplifying, and it assumes that every Spanish citizen can be neatly situated on one side or the other, with undivided loyalty to the values of either conservative or liberal Spains. Sebastian Balfour and Alejandro Quiroga argue that "this Manichean conception of the nation helped to create the myth of the existence of two Spains, a myth that Franco was later to institutionalize during his forty-year-long dictatorship" (2007, 21). Nonetheless, this is a potent narrative and for the families that lost loved ones on both sides of the Civil War, this Manichean division is very much real.

Memory politics

In recent years, memory, particularly the area of collective memory, has flourished as a field of study in the social sciences. This has also been the case in contemporary Spanish Cultural Studies. The study of memory, according to Michael Richards, "explains how recollections of events are acquired and subsequently altered in the constant forming and reforming of identities" (2002, 93). Collective memory, argues Jeffrey Olick, often plays an important role in the configuration and evolution of politics and society in particular historical moments and places (1999). In Spain, collective memories of social terror can signal a struggle to negotiate current political battles of (national) identity, and simultaneously a desire to renegotiate the historical pacts that emerged from regimes of social terror such as the Franco dictatorship. But the term collective memory raises an important challenge to scholars interested in using the term in their social research. The key concern, according to Olick, "is not with the term itself, but with the ways in which the label structures (that is, both enables and constrains) conceptual and empirical work" (1999, 334). What are the advantages and disadvantages of using "collective memory" in comparison to other terms, like commemoration, tradition, myth, and so forth? What does it mean to say that the memories of individuals are "influenced" by the groups to which they belong (334)? If the constitutive narrative of *las dos Españas* is to a great extent mass-mediated, it is therefore logical to also assume that individual memories are "influenced" by the groups to which they belong and the communications industries in which they operate. I thus agree with Winter and Sivan who consider collective memory as constructed through the actions of groups and individuals: "When people enter the public domain, and comment about the past—their own personal past, their family past, their national past, and so on—they bring with them images and gestures derived from their broader social experience" (2000, 6).

According to French historian Jacques Le Goff, since memory is the raw material of history, the historian must render an account of these memories and of what is forgotten, "to transform them into something that can be conceived, to make them knowable" (1992, xii). This is because history is still at risk of conscious manipulation on the part of political regimes that oppose the "truth." The recent pursuit, rescue and celebration of collective memory in the spoken word, images, gestures, rituals and festivals amounts to what Le Goff describes as the public's obsession and "fear of losing its memory in a kind of collective amnesia" (95). Collective memory, according to Le Goff, is "one of the great stakes of developed and developing societies, of dominated and dominating classes, all of them struggling for power or for life, for survival and for advancement" (1992, 98). In contemporary Spain, the re-emergence of the victims from the Spanish Civil War and Franco eras into the media spotlight, has thrown the country, according to Spanish anthropologist Francisco Ferrándiz, "into an unexpected public debate that exposes a range of conflicting political cultures, not only between ideological groupings but also between generations" (2006, 10). The new Spanish history and memory battles are instruments and objectives of power that seek to advance a particular narrative, often linked to the past, and almost always linked to the particular ideologies of either conservative or liberal Spains.

If there are two Spains, there are also, according to Le Goff, at least two modes of history making; that of collective memory, and that of historians (1992, 111). Collective memory, according to Le Goff, is essentially mythic, deformed, and anachronistic, but it nonetheless "constitutes the lived reality of the never-completed relation between present and past" (111). It is the role of professional historians and the mass-media to correct this false traditional history: "History must illuminate memory and help to rectify its errors" (111). In English-language contemporary Spanish cultural studies, two publishing events have been crucial in bringing the study of memory to prominence: the collection of essays in *Disremembering the Dictatorship* edited by Joan Ramon Resina in 2000; and the journal *History and Memory*, which dedicated a special issue to "Spanish Memories: Images of a Contested Past" in 2002. The essays included in both publications overwhelmingly argued that the Spanish state in the post-Franco era has been unable to reconcile itself with its authoritarian and traumatic past. It is difficult, however, to "correct" traditional Spanish history when the narrative of *las dos Españas* is functioning discursively in the public sphere. Historians and the mass-media in Spain tend to complicate these constitutive narratives rather than help "correct" them. Any attempt to recover collective memory is burdened by the narrative of *las dos Españas* since the recuperation of public memory inevitably intersects with competing liberal and conservative ideologies. As Ferrándiz phrases it: "Is there a 'tolerance threshold' in Spanish society for how much of the traumatic past can be dug up and aired before it becomes a nightmare?" (2006, 12). Any attempt to recuperate collective memory, including exhuming mass burial sites, is bound to influence the ways in which Spaniards perceive themselves and their past (12). This presents enormous challenges to social researchers attempting to understand historical narratives in Spain. Nonetheless, despite the complexities of Spain's multiple competing histories, the fact that both Spains are attempting to grapple with these narratives in a self-reflective manner could be regarded as a positive development.

In this context, Le Goff cynically wrote that "memory has [. . .] become a best-seller in a consumer society" (1992, 95). His claim remains particularly pertinent for understanding Spain in the early twenty-first century given that Spanish society has yet to reach a "tolerance threshold." Spain's post-democratic transition period has coincided with a wealth of publications including memoirs, popular histories, as well as documentaries and films, all dealing with specific hidden histories of the Spanish Civil War and the Franco era, from prisons and labour battalions, to guerrillas and the lost children of Francoism. Many of these books, such as *Las fosas de Franco* (Franco's Graves) by Emilio Silva and Santiago Macías, which sold nearly 20,000 copies in the first two months after its publication in March 2003, have been bestsellers. But a familiar pattern with the trend is also clear: the more polemical the book, the more it sells. Often, instead of illuminating the tragedy of the Spanish Civil War, suggests Ferrándiz, "the publications tend to engage with a tortuous debate into which side initiated the war, who was responding, who was more systematic, and who was crueller" (2006, 8).

On the other hand, since the 1990s, a plethora of publications has also chronicled the histories of the losers of the Civil War, histories that were at risk of being forgotten. The new history of the repression of the Franco regime, told with real names, and counting the dead from municipal registers and cemetery lists, "is, in a very real sense, the equivalent of war memorials for those who never had them, for those who were not liberated in 1945" (Graham 2004, 323). Much of the empirical historical research and the ensuing publications are themselves "an act of commemoration for whole groups of Spaniards who could never be mourned publicly when they died … they are an act of reparation [and] restitution in the work of collective memory" (323). The overwhelming motivation, according to Georgina Blakeley, is "not revenge, or even justice if we understand the latter as entailing the holding to account of those responsible; rather the key desire is to achieve the public acknowledgement and recognition that the winning side of the Civil War has always enjoyed. In short, the recovery of historical memory is in itself a kind of justice" (2005, 49).

Such textual events have coincided with other prominent events in recuperating memory in Spain. The best known examples are: the campaign to exhume common graves and identify the remains of the men and women murdered by the Francoist forces before and after the Civil War; the campaign for compensation by those used as forced labour by the regime; and widespread debate about the lost children of Francoism who were taken forcibly from Republican women prisoners and adopted by Francoist families (Graham 2004, 314). These campaigns have exposed an undercurrent of repressed memories dating from the Spanish Civil War, mirroring the tragic events that unfolded in Latin American states such as Argentina and Chile in the 1970s and 1980s. Unlike those countries, however, Spain has been surprisingly slow in recovering and coming to terms with its tragic past. This is because Spain's transition to democracy was characterized by an unofficial *pacto del silencio* (pact of silence) or *pacto del olvido* (pact of forgetting). The pacts meant that the dominant narrative of Spain's transition to democracy was of compromise and consensus, a discursive and rhetorical means of marginalizing extreme left and right ideologies. Only in the beginning of the twenty-first century was the movement to reclaim what has been termed Republican memory reinvigorated by the grandchildren of the dead, and galvanized support in many sections of Spanish society while inevitably meeting opposition in others. The grandchildren of those who experienced the war are speaking now, because, according to history professor Paloma Aguilar, "they can't be accused of conniving with the Franco regime, and they don't suffer from the fear of repression that paralysed those who suffered the dictatorship. They have a much freer vision of events" (quoted in Rojo 2004, 2).

Despite the Franco dictatorship's efforts to erase the legacy of liberal Spain, the narrative of *las dos Españas* remained in the consciousness of the regime. One of Franco's first orders was to abolish the nascent federal structures of the Second Republic, together with banning political parties and independent trade unions. The historic regions were, according to Omar Encarnación, "stripped of their autonomy and a comprehensive and oppressive policy of cultural homogeneity aimed at erasing the distinct linguistic heritage of many regions was implemented" (2004, 64). Franco's attempt to homogenize Spain included a ban on the use of Catalan and Euskera in schools, government offices, and other public places. The enactment of these policies, suggests Encarnacón, "corresponded to the myth sustained by the Franco regime that Spain's multiple nationalities were at the root of the nation's proclivity for anarchy and separatist violence" (2004, 64).

In the early years of Franco's regime, Helen Graham notes, the military actively recruited thousands of civilian vigilantes to carry out a dirty war against the defeated Republicans (2004, 315). For Graham, "this was the beginning of the 'fellowship of blood,' of the complicity of whole sectors of Spanish society, 'ordinary Spaniards' who became enmeshed in the murder of their compatriots" (315). The violence brought down against those associated with the Republicans usually stemmed from a need to humiliate or to break the enemy, publicly or otherwise. Graham argues that these forms of violence functioned "as rituals through which social and political control could be re-enacted" (318). When the Francoists murdered the "enemy," they were murdering the threat of change. Borrowing from a Manichean brand of Catholicism, the assumption was that a "new" Spain could only be reborn through a blood sacrifice, a process of purification (318). This process was legitimized through the creation of categories of the anti-nation or "Other." Although these categories included ethnic groups such as Jews, the most powerful and salient epithet was that of "red" (320). The amorphous and generously applied term "red" not only included wartime political opponents, but whole constituencies of people, such as urban workers, Republican identified intellectuals, liberal professional sectors, non-Catholics and women who did not conform to the rigid gender norms deemed appropriate by Francoism (320). The sum of this politics of retribution was that the Republican dead could not be publicly mourned. As Graham states: "the defeated cast no reflection. No public space was theirs" (321). The result was a devastating schism between public and private memory in post-Civil War Spain.

Franco's authoritarian rule endured, argues Encarnación, "because the Spanish people had been socialized to believe that Spain was different, that it was an inherently anarchic country in need of a strong hand" (2001/02, 35). Franco's death in 1975, however, ended thirty-six years of a military dictatorship that had, for the most part, been stable, notwithstanding its brutality. But according to the Spanish scholar, José Amodia, writing after Franco's death: "It is naïve to expect Franco's death to work a miracle. In the political future of Spain I see a great deal of darkness and hardly any light; my forecast must be pessimistic" (1976, 204). As Encarnación reminds us, the Francoist parliament legalized political parties, trade unions and scheduled elections for June 1977 when Adolfo Suárez and his centre-right party (UCD) won the first free elections in four decades (2001/02, 36). The new Spanish Constitution was ratified in 1978 "officially completing the transition to democratic rule" (36).

With Franco's death and Spain's transition to democracy it seemed that the ghosts of the past would be unleashed and a formal process of reconciliation would somehow be addressed. Instead, Spanish society agreed to what various historians have called unofficial pacts ("pact of silence" and "pact of forgetting"), which were fundamental to Spain's successful transition to democracy. The "pact of silence" was agreed to by the Francoist elites in return for a *de facto* political amnesty, meaning that no Francoist would be called to judicial account (Graham 2004, 322). The anti-Francoists and former Republicans who had been obliged to be silent for nearly forty years were, according to Graham, "told that there could be no public recognition of their past lives or memories" (323). More controversially, the "pact of silence" was necessary because much of the political repression was undertaken by "ordinary Spaniards" (323). The widespread social unease that underwrote the "pact of silence" was a fear of reopening old wounds that "the social and cultural policies of Francoism had [. . .] expressly and explicitly prevented from healing" (324). Amnesty was conceived, according to Ferrándiz, "as an act of closure for the open wounds of the Civil War and the dictatorship, and also as an end to the enduring myth of the two Spains" (2006, 11). It did not mean that the excesses carried out by both parties during the Civil War were forgotten. Rather, as Santos Juliá points out, they were deliberately "thrown into oblivion" (quoted in Ferrándiz 2006, 11).

In Stephanie R. Golob's study of pacted democracy, and the legal case involving the ex-Chilean dictator Pinochet, she argues that "pacting [. . .] involves both the construction of a new future-oriented post-authoritarian 'constitutive story' and what might be called a non-story, a 'pact of silence'" (Golob 2002a, 32). Thus, the process of pacting can be described as a form of national narrativization. In the Spanish case, the pacting elites purposefully chose the narrative of peace, stability and prosperity, instead of truth, reconciliation and justice. According to Golob, these choices were made in order to reconceive the Spanish state in ways that appeared more inclusive (2002a, 32). Instead, the elite narrative was exclusionary in its denial of the past: "it symbolically narrowed the contours of national identity to include only those 'safe' feelings sanctioned by the official post-authoritarian narrative" (32). Blakely argues that the actors in civil society were not duped into "forgetting" (2005, 52). Rather, she argues, pacts can only succeed with the support of public opinion. In the Spanish case the majority of people clearly wanted a transition based on consensus and moderation. The transition, therefore, was an interactive process with both the elites and civil society taking cues from each other. But as Golob points out, "pacts are not forever" and "even 'successful' transition pacts sometimes have to be renegotiated or amended" (2002b, 47). What has clearly occurred, suggests Blakeley, is that the balance of power existing at the time of the transition did not remain static but shifted as democratization progressed (Blakeley 2002, 50). With the strengthening of Spanish civil society throughout the 1980s and 1990s, these pacts were once again up for renegotiation.

The pact of forgetting was quite literal in the sense that for many years relevant debates about the Civil War and the Franco dictatorship were not part of the mainstream political narratives of the Spanish state. But as Blakeley points out, the "pact of forgetting" is also a misnomer in the sense that "nothing was, or has been, forgotten" (2005, 51). Indeed, what stands out from the many newspaper accounts of the exhumation of the Civil War graves is "the extent to which people have always known, not only of their [the graves'] existence, but often of their exact location" (51). The process of forgetting, therefore, was never absolute; the success of the pacts rested on the need for Spaniards to remember the dangers inherent to their shared histories. Forgetting was more an official state policy, rather than an individual one. Assessing more recent developments, Golob is rather cynical of the "explosion" of public memory in Spain by considering it a "quasi-remembrance" (2002a, 34). Although she admits that the former dictatorship and the legacy of the pact of silence have been more openly discussed in recent years, the discussion of criminal liability or moral responsibility remains conspicuously and paradoxically absent in a country whose own judicial system initiated proceedings against the Chilean former dictator General Pinochet (2002a).

But with the election of the Socialist Zapatero government in 2004 and the implementation of the Historical Memory Law (2007) that the Zapatero government spearheaded (see Chapter Six), Spanish society has, in the new millennium, sought to address historical injustice and "return" to the past. Encarnación argues that Pinochet's arrest was the catalyst behind the return to the past: "the Pinochet affair crystallized what the social movement theorist Sidney Tarrow has referred to as "political opportunity structure" or a change in the political environment of collective action" (2007/08, 40). The Spanish public overwhelmingly supported Pinochet's arrest. According to Madeleine Davis, there was "some kind of psychological transference factor at work—the impulse to do to Pinochet what was not done to Franco" (2005, 869). Encarnación, however, argues that the Pinochet case highlighted the irony of Spain forcing another new democracy to face its authoritarian past while refusing to face its own and launched "a vigorous movement devoted to 'recovering' Spain's own historical memory by exposing the political excesses of the old Franco regime" (2007/08, 40). Domestic factors were also crucial. The timing of this process coincided with an astonishing string of public anniversaries: 2000, the 25th anniversary of the death of Franco; 2001, the 20th anniversary of the failed military coup of 23 February 1981; January 2002, the 25th anniversary of the Atocha massacres (where seven lawyers belonging to *Comisiones Obreras*, the syndicate of the Communist Party, were killed by extreme right-wingers); April 2002, the 25th anniversary of the legalization of the Spanish Communist Party; June 2002, the 25th anniversary of the first democratic elections since 1936; and October 2002, the 20th anniversary of the first Socialist government in post-Franco Spain. The official commemorations continued in 2003 with the 25th anniversary of the Spanish constitution (46). All of these commemorations received extensive coverage in the Spanish print and broadcast media.

During Spain's rapid, but at times fraught, transition to democracy, the Spanish media played the important role of erasing the memory of Franco and recreating the idea of a Franco regime without supporters. Fernando León Solís's criticism of the Spanish media's coverage of the anniversary of Franco's death in the Spanish daily *El País* indicates how the official narratives favoured by the media attempted to establish a clear break between Spain's "murky" past and its glorious democratic future by creating a "sense of closure" about anything related to the Spanish state's authoritarian history (2003b, 50–54). Indeed, in the post-Franco era the media contributed to the Spanish state's narratorial re-branding of itself as a peaceful and democratic state with a rightful place of belonging in "civilized" Western Europe. Since it joined the European Union in 1986, Spain has been one of the EU's most enthusiastic supporters. The "murky" Francoist past is thus recast inside Spanish political borders, and beyond them in a European setting, as a mere historical glitch, an anomaly in the trajectory of Spain's "true" progressive and emancipatory history. Many Spanish people today view any events that challenge this narrative with suspicion. For example, popular opinion turned against ETA in the 1980s, even though until Franco's death some Spaniards regarded ETA as engaging in a legitimate fight against a fascist regime (Woodworth 2001, 38). Even public revelations in the 1980s that the Spanish state was using terrorist tactics to fight Basque separatists failed to send the anticipated shock waves across Spanish society that many political elites expected (Woodworth 2001). This may also explain why, in my view, Spain had the highest number of people of any congruent country opposed to the invasion of Iraq in 2003 (up to 91 percent according to some polls) (Tremlett & Arie 2003, 9). Perhaps no other state except Japan and Germany in the post-war era has so successfully erased violence from its popular state narratives. The process of political compromise on issues ranging from counterterrorism to immigration continued into the 1990s and only began to break down with the PP's second term in office (2000–2004). Thus, although the concept of *las dos Españas* has always been present in post-Franco Spain it has not been fully disarmed by Spanish political realities.

The constitutive narrative of *las dos Españas* was therefore effectively relegated to the margins of Spanish society during Spain's transition to democracy, which was sustained by the future-oriented narrative scripts of the "pact of forgetting" and "pact of silence." In 1982, when the Socialist Party won the national elections, bringing the left back to power for the first time since the Second Republic, the prevailing fear was that the narrative of *las dos Españas* and the accompanying extremisms of the 1930s would once again haunt and divide Spanish politics. But under the leadership of Felipe González (1982–1996), the PSOE pursued a centrist platform by modernizing Spanish capitalism, decentralizing the Spanish state, placing the military under civilian control and strengthening the market economy. The politics of compromise that have dominated the post-Franco era ensured that the concept of *las dos Españas* was more or less neutralized because of the general antipathy of Spanish citizens towards extreme ideologies of whatever political persuasion. The narrative scripts of the pacts of "forgetting" and "silence" were so successful, Preston argues, that the attempted military coup on 23 February, 1981, where King Juan Carlos risked his throne and his personal safety in the cause of a democracy for all Spaniards, "demonstrated that the cherished Francoist divisions between victors and vanquished, Spain and anti-Spain, were finally exposed as meaningless" (1990, 47). In hindsight, the claim was premature. As I have been arguing here, the divisions Preston identifies became benign in the early 1980s, their import repressed rather than made permanently meaningless. After all, these divisions are part of historical and constitutive narrative scripts; meaning is derived from the people who seek to manipulate those scripts. If they were truly meaningless then those narrative divisions and disputes could not have been so successfully reconstituted by the PP in the aftermath of the March 11, 2004, attacks in Madrid (see Chapter Five).

Yet, Preston also highlights in *The Politics of Revenge* (1990) that the contours of the Spanish right effectively shaped the trajectory of modern Spanish history:

> During several years living in Spain it was impossible not to be led by my own research into the political conflicts of the Second Republic, and by my everyday observations, to see a Spanish right which seemed, harsh, rigid and obstinate, in comparison with the relatively flexible conservatism that then still apparently prevailed in England. I was also much struck by the extent to which the right, in the starkest possible contrast with the left and despite the considerable ideological, strategic and tactical discrepancies between its component groups, tended to act with unity of purpose. [. . .] The particular development of Spanish history in the twentieth century can be traced in large measure to the right's obstinacy, inflexibility and fear of democracy, just as the country's present progress can in some measure be attributed to the emergence of a modern, moderate and civilized right capable of working within a democratic system. (xiv)

Preston wrote this in 1990, when the fear of the return to violence that characterized the transition to democracy, and which was given credence by the high level of violence during that period (especially by ETA and including the attempted military coup by Lieutenant-Colonel Antonio Tejero on February 23, 1981), was still in Spanish people's consciousness. In the early twenty-first century, although the fear of a return to extreme ideology and violence still exists, it is, according to Blakely, "no longer such an obstacle to action" (2005, 47). Blakely is referring to the recuperation of Republican memory, such as the unearthing of mass burial sites; but recent events in Spanish politics indicate that many other areas that were once off-limits in public discourse have returned to the Spanish public sphere. While these returns to public debate include liberal Spain's recuperation of its collective memories, they also encompass the Spanish right's recuperating of much of its former anti-leftist rhetoric.

Although the narrative of *las dos Españas* was, to an extent, sidelined during Spain's transition to democracy, the narrative nonetheless remained part of Spanish political, public and mass-mediated discourse, albeit in more muted ways. The Spanish media is one of the world's most partisan, with Spanish newspapers and radio stations flagrantly voicing their support for or opposition to one of the major parties with little pretence of objectivity. The Socialist Party, which was in power from 1982 to 1996, and which won government again after the March 11 attacks, has been narrativized by more or less all sides of the mass-media as the continuation and representation of "liberal" Spain, whereas the opposition Popular Party is accorded the "traditional" Catholic values associated with the historically "conservative" Spain. These two major political parties are now at loggerheads over countless issues of importance to many Spaniards, including the process by which historical memory is officially articulated and preserved. Since 2015 this process has been further complicated by the emergence of the new political parties Podemos and Ciudadanos into mainstream politics (see Chapter Nine).

Ferrándiz points out that right-leaning historians and politicians generally dismiss the process of recuperating Republican memory as "petty, unnecessary and vengeful, and one that will only lead to the opening up of old wounds and the re-emergence of outworn political discourses" (2006, 11). Some critics accused former Prime Minister Zapatero himself of contributing to destroying the "spirit of the transition" by trying to impose the new "hegemony of the defeated" in place of the "agreement of all." (11) These debates have spilled into numerous other areas in Spanish politics. The Zapatero Socialist government's negotiations for a new Statute of Autonomy for Catalonia were plagued by acrimony, fuelled mainly by the right (see Chapter Six). A speech read in Seville by Lieutenant General Mena during the Christmas military ceremony in 2005, invoked Article 8 of the Spanish Constitution as a pretext for future intervention by the armed forces against the parliamentary institutions, should the proposed new Catalan Statute, approved by the Parliament and by referendum, exceed the "impassable limits" that the Constitution sets upon the regional Statutes of Autonomy (Pradera 2006, 2). Although his comments were roundly condemned by all sides of Spanish politics, their utterance in public was enough to raise the ghosts of the dead.

Many members of the Spanish media elite, including Félix de Azúa, thus argue that the division of Spain into *las dos Españas* has returned:

Slowly, and with understandable caution, we have been moving back toward the eternal order of things in this country, the intransigent division between good and bad, red and blue, Christians and Moors. Recently one of the most lucid of the victims of terrorism, Maite Pagazaurtundua, said that we are back in the two Spains spoken of by the poet Antonio Machado. One of them is supposed to freeze your heart, but now it seems that both are likely to do so. (2006, 2)

According to de Azúa, a chronic tendency toward fanatical dualism plagues Spain for deep-rooted reasons: Spain went through a feeble version of the Enlightenment in the eighteenth century, a narrow industrialization in the nineteenth century, and was absented from modernity in the twentieth century. De Azúa cynically adds that such a peculiarity comes not from ethical reflection, but from obedience to a party line: "If the Popular Party had favoured the segmentation of regional oligarchies, then the left would have been in favour of strong central government" (2). Joaquín Arango, a professor in sociology at the Complutense University in Madrid argues differently: "attitudes have softened, but the two Spains have not disappeared altogether. Party lines are very clearly drawn—far more than in any other European country and this influences every aspect of society" (quoted in Cué 2005, 2).

If the narrative of *las dos Españas* can therefore be considered the key "hidden" counter-narrative in a Žižekian sense (2006, xxv) that explains much of Spain's discursive popular history, this constitutive narrative remains domestically state-based. Narratives of terror and political violence since the September 11 attacks in the USA, however, are now subject to the global metanarrative of terror that has overdetermined terrorist acts in terms of a North American/global hegemony (Gabilondo 2002, 62). The next section looks at the global metanarrative of terror and explores its role in shaping and influencing narratives of terror in the Spanish state in the new millennium.

The metanarrative of terror

What happened there is—they all have to rearrange their brains now—is the greatest work of art ever. That characters can bring about in one act what we in music cannot dream of, that people practise madly for ten years, completely fanatically, for a concert and then die. That is the greatest work of art for the whole cosmos. Against that, we composers are nothing. ("Attacks Called Great Art" 2001, 3)

The above quote, attributed to avant-garde composer Karleinz Stockhausen, caused controversy in the immediate aftermath of the September 11 attacks in the USA: Stockhausen had dared to compare "horrific hate" to "art." According to Sam Frank, Stockhausen's statement offends us because it is true: "When America was attacked, it was an aesthetic attack as well as a political one—an act born out of aesthetic politics, on politic aesthetics" (2001). Or as Žižek remarked, "one can effectively perceive the collapse of the WTC towers as the climactic conclusion of twentieth century art's 'passion for the real'—the terrorists themselves did not do it primarily to provoke real material damage, but *for the spectacular effect of it*" [original emphasis] (2006, 269). The symmetry between large-scale international terrorist attacks and Hollywood was readily seized upon after 9/11 by many theorists who highlighted the hyperreality of the real and—impossible to imagine—terrorist attack. In "Terror as Thrill," Begoña Aretxaga argues that in the USA after the Cold War terrorism became "the object of obsessive publishing by the state department, replacing the old figure of communism as the spectral enemy" (2002, 139). Meanwhile, in Hollywood, films depicting apocalyptic anxieties began to saturate popular culture in the 1990s, as exemplified by *Independence Day* (Emmerich 1996) and *Armageddon* (Bay 1998), prompting Aretxaga to suggest that the 9/11 attacks was like watching a movie, and thus, eerily familiar (139).

After 9/11, then, few, if any, terms are as loaded with ideological and symbolic meaning, and yet are as difficult to pin down, as terrorism. Belinda Davis points out that despite numerous attempts, the United Nations remains unable to compose an operational definition (2003, 38). A typical rejoinder is that terrorism is like pornography—you know it when you see it (Zulaika and Douglass 1996, 22). Hardt and Negri in *Multitude* rightly argue that the concept of terrorism does not provide a solid foundation for understanding the current global state of war (2004, 17). This is because the term terrorism has become a political concept, one that Hardt and Negri claim refers to different phenomena that are sometimes separated and at other times conflated. Indeed, as they aptly point out, the crucial question remains as to who defines these phenomena? Who determines what a legitimate government is, what human rights might be, and what the rules of war consist of? More importantly, what useful purpose might such a definition serve? As Strathern and Stewart suggest, for the purposes of any given participant in a conflict "it may be vital to define what constitutes a terrorist act and terrorism in general" (2006, 3). Analytically, however, it is clear that "whatever components of specific meaning enter into the definition of terrorism, the application of the term 'terrorist' is relative and situational" (3). The War on Terror is even more problematic than the singular terror/ism on a number of levels. If the goal is to stamp out every terrorist group of global reach, asks Ramazani, "does that extend to separatists in Northern Ireland and militant right-wing fundamentalists in America? Would U.S. military sanctions not also have to apply to Russian atrocities in Chechnya, to Chinese oppression in Tibet and Xinjiang, and to brutal government crack downs against rebels in Indonesia" (2002, 119)?

Terrorism cannot (and should not) be reduced to a terrorist attack, even one of the magnitude of the September 11, 2001, attacks in the USA. Instead, uses of terror as a concept should be more fluid and radical in their underlying presumptions. If the global War on Terror cannot adequately explain the process by which terror narratives operate within individual states, then a better conceptual framework or approach needs to be articulated. This section argues that in order to get beyond the current understanding of the War on Terror, re-conceiving terror as a metanarrative is a more useful way of understanding terrorism. The term metanarrative has the advantage of being applied in global and national contexts and conveniently encompasses the events of classical terrorism (acts of terror that can be defined as either local or inter-national) and global terrorism. Conceiving terror(ism) as a metanarrative is not a new idea. In his *Culture, War, and America's War on Terror* (2006), Stuart Croft attempted to bridge the discipline of international relations with cultural studies by explaining how security crises often unfold through discursive processes that also register in popular cultural productions and receptions. Croft argued that a coherent meta-narrative rapidly emerged as the hegemonic "common sense" that both guided and legitimized the War on Terror.

Terrorism, according to Richard Jackson, "has in a very short space of time become a core concern for policy-makers, and for some critics, is now a central characteristic of modern Western culture" (2007, 241). Suman Gupta in *The Replication of Violence* (2002) highlights what has usually been a fundamental dichotomy: the unassailable division between inside and outside:

> The spectre of "international terrorism," which in its very turn of phrase conjures a threat that cannot be easily managed, that seeps across boundaries and cannot be restrained and may threaten the world eventually, has been anticipated with a sort of horrified thrill by the West as a contamination that may appear (much to the glee of xenophobes and conservatives) from *outside*—from ultra-left groups, from Islamic fundamentalist groups—but still reassuringly *outside* [original emphasis]. (5)

More interestingly, Gupta continues:

That "international terrorist" acts have now *actually materialised with such all-too-tangible* effect within the Western context [original emphasis] is a substantial shock: "international terrorism" appears to have suddenly become more than a xenophobe's or conservative's nightmare or a media fad or a Hollywood fantasy, it appears to have become a serious and urgent and in some sense *within-our-zone* [original emphasis] affair crying out for a renewed academic assessment and a concerted political effort. (6)

International terror is thus like a foreign external virus that has entered *within-our-zone*, defeating what was once a fool-proof immunodefence system.

To what extent, then, has the realm of the real and the tangible become indistinguishable from the fantastical and the far-fetched? Although the remit of this section does not allow for a detailed and fundamental answer to this question, nor of the 9/11 attacks in the USA as a global event or what Jean Baudrillard called the "mother" of all events (2002, 4), this section examines two related debates that have emerged in social science theory since 9/11 and situates them in a Spanish context. The first is the shift from what has been termed "classical" terrorism to "global" terrorism and what this shift implied for local national terror groups such as the Basque separatist group ETA. The second debate concerns the usefulness and appropriateness of conceptualizing terror as a narrative, or even as a meta-narrative.

In considering these debates, I demonstrate that there is a fundamental tension at play in terror politics between the projection of a global meta-narrative, the US-led War on Terror and the national historical debates of terror that remain state-based and domestically mass-mediated. This tension challenges Hardt and Negri's compelling argument in *Multitude* that the September 11 attacks opened a new era of war and that "war is becoming a general phenomenon, global and interminable" (2004, 4). Spain is a particularly interesting and important case study because in that country terror narratives are not new. For decades, the Spanish state grappled with the challenges that Basque terrorism posed to Spanish unity. Thus, the next section argues that while September 11, 2001 might have delivered Spanish attention to the global field of terror, the March 11, 2004 attacks effectively returned the frontline to the Castilian heartland. This section, and the study as a whole, seeks to understand the Spanish response in terms of the constraints of its historical narratives.

The classic/global '(m)other' of all events

The World Trade Centre attacks in New York City and the Pentagon in Arlington on September 11, 2001 effectively positioned the subsequent War on Terror at the centre of global political discourse. The War on Terror is a US-led war that is intentionally broad enough to encompass so-called rogue states, declared failed states, national liberation struggles, remnants of the Cold War apparatus, and any security issues that can be filtered through a terrorism discourse. In effect, any threat or violence that is not state sanctioned—and any perceived threat that may not, in fact, be violent—neatly fits into the War on Terror narrative, at least as articulated by the USA government and its allies. State terror is a significant omission from this discourse: the crimes of states are generally not illegitimate unless they are committed by "rogue" states such as Iraq, Iran or North Korea, or by authoritarian regimes such as govern Zimbabwe or Myanmar. This discourse has also crept into many other issues of global concern: mass migration from developing countries into the west, the difficulties in integrating immigrants with different "values" into western communities, and other issues that are encompassed in national identity debates and struggles. Many political theorists thus argue that 9/11 was a paradigm shift in transnational relations, the start of a new era after a ten-year interregnum period that began with the end of the Cold War (1991–2001). There are notable dissenters to this view, for example Noam Chomsky (2005), who argues that a War on Terror was first articulated by former US President Ronald Reagan and that the only thing that changed on 9/11 was the location of the attack. That is, for the first time, the USA, the world's sole superpower, was under attack; but this was a superpower with the power and communication reach to change the global security apparatus and re-articulate the global security discourse.

However, most scholars and media pundits agree that some kind of ill-defined paradigm shift did begin with 9/11. One of the most controversial interpretations of this change was articulated by Michael Hardt and Antonio Negri in *Multitude* (2004), their follow up to the seminal *Empire* (2000). Hardt and Negri argue that the unending nature of the new war (the global War on Terror) takes on a generalized character with the result that "war has become a permanent social relation" (2004, 12). By updating Foucault's conceptualization of biopower, Hardt and Negri claim that this new type of war has become the general matrix for all relations of power and techniques of domination. Hardt and Negri are not the only theorists who have attempted to articulate the 9/11 paradigm shift. Other critics, such as Joseba Gabilondo (2002), argue that since 9/11, terrorism has ceased to be a national or domestic issue and has become overdetermined by the spectre of global narratives of terror. Gabilondo does not suggest that domestic or national narratives do not influence or shape metanarratives. Rather, he posits that any political violence, regardless of its aim or history, "is today overdetermined by the new North American/global ideology, and thus is equated with terrorism" (2002, 62). Gabilondo thus argues that the global re-articulation of terrorism since 9/11 means it is difficult for a Western terrorist group to resort to violence as a means to achieve political revolution or utopia (from the workers' revolution to national sovereignty). In this respect and in the foreseeable future, any form of terrorist violence against any political target other than the USA is liable to be interpreted and dealt with as a threat to the USA while at the same time being connected to violent Muslim fundamentalism. This is, according to Gabilondo, "the powerful effect of ideological overdetermination" (63).

Since 9/11 and the emergence of deterritorialized groups such as Al-Qaeda, terrorism has been rearticulated as "global" in a radical and unprecedented way. According to Gabilondo, "the terrorist actions of September 2001 close an entire chapter—one we could denominate 'classical terrorism'—in what we might provisionally label a traditional and teleological history of terrorism" (2002, 62). Classical terrorism refers to terrorist acts perpetrated between 1945 and 2001 that were for the most part (though not always) local events. For Gabilondo this does not mean that classical terrorism was not international. In the Basque case, for example, the connections between ETA and the IRA or Libya were generally well established (Domínguez Irribaren 2000). Moreover, many terrorist groups borrowed from each other's historical and theoretical discourses. As Gurutz Jaúregui Bereciártu points out, Mao Zedong, Franz Fanon, and Lenin became important theoretical references when ETA articulated a revolutionary discourse based on the working class and the Third World in the late 1960s (1981, 267–71). Nevertheless, these terrorist groups and practices were ultimately located within a specific state and responded to the local politics of that state. In this sense, terrorism was either national or inter-national (given ETA's bases were located in southern France and Spain). Yet the new terrorism inaugurated by the 9/11 attacks, according to Gabilondo, "is global in the sense that it affects terrorism elsewhere in the world and makes it impossible to contain it on a local scale" (2002, 63).

A plethora of books and articles has been published since 2001 with the aim of distinguishing the novel features of the new terrorism from classical terrorism. According to Wyn Rees, the new terrorism is characterized by religion rather than nationalism. It is an ongoing conflict against the nominal enemies of Islam rather than a struggle over territory, is loosely networked rather than having a hierarchical structure, lacks territorial focus, and eschews traditional political strategy whereby small acts of violence are undertaken in order to generate the maximum amount of publicity (2007, 216–17). But Rees does point out that the extent to which this terrorism is new is subject to reappraisal and dispute. It is possible to argue that the rhetoric of "holy war" obscures the more traditional political motivations of terrorist leaders, such as the removal of authoritarian governments from several Arab states, and expunging the Israeli and US presence from the Middle East (217). Furthermore, the tactics employed in innumerable suicide attacks, namely the use of conventional explosives in vehicles, is far from innovative. However, Rees suggests that the new terrorism "is sufficiently different to distinguish it from the violence of the past; indeed the fact that the USA altered its strategic agenda to focus on this threat has accorded it enormous significance" (217).

The new ubiquitous terrorism-threat narrative of so-called new terrorism has led many EU-based observers to argue that "the nature of terrorism has changed" and that the new kind of terrorism "is willing to use unlimited violence to cause massive casualties" (Jackson 2007, 237). According to the discursive logic of these assumptions, the religious fanaticism at the heart of the new terrorism means that there is no possibility of dialogue or diplomacy as a solution to terrorism. The only options are to eradicate or deter the terrorists through the deployment of superior force, or prevent its emergence by combating the radicalization of certain alienated groups (237). Consequently, Gabilondo argues that bin Laden and 9/11 have "terrorized" any possibility of revolutionary politics based on terrorism:

> There is no longer room for any other form of terrorism than the global one inaugurated by bin Laden. Ironically we can no longer talk about 'terrorist movements' around the world; all of them have been overdetermined—terrorised—by bin Laden's actions. Any terrorist action no longer responds to a local, state-based order, so that it can be read from that local context: global terrorism is always the terrorism of the global Other. (2002, 64)

Determining the effects of this shift from the local to the global is tenuous and difficult, considering that the complexity of the post-9/11 global security apparatus is yet to be adequately understood. But at the very minimum it can be ascertained that groups falling under the auspices of classical terrorism have had to redefine themselves in the face of the global hegemonic discourse of the War on Terror. Thus, Gabilondo argues that "through the retrospective manoeuvre of history-rewriting enabled by ideology, North American/global hegemonic discourse can claim that 'terrorist history' starts in the USA" (2002, 74). Any previous terrorist attempt or enterprise is now part of terrorism's prehistory (74).

It is debatable as to the extent to which the purported division between history and prehistory is useful in this study, which deals with Spain. But these discursive and critical shifts do beg the question: if history has indeed reached a turning point, does the global metanarrative of terror function in the same manner everywhere in the world? Phrased differently, what can we make of the fact that the Spanish state was currently fighting a "prehistoric" battle against a national terrorist group whilst concurrently coming to terms with a global terrorist attack on March 11, 2004 in Madrid? If Gabilondo is correct that terrorism "has finally become a North American *and* global phenomenon, as violence *and* discourse" (74), where does the twin process of Americanization and globalization leave specific national-local politics and manifestations of violence? Do these politics have any role in shaping and influencing the metanarrative? Responding to the issues underwriting these questions Gabilondo argues that:

> It is probably "very good luck" for the Spanish state "to happen to have" a terrorist problem at home. Although this problem no longer allows the Spanish state to legitimize itself as a modern state with an exclusive right to violence, nevertheless, the global overdetermination of terrorism by North American/global ideology actually makes the Spanish state meaningful and legitimate to this new order, so that the Spanish state becomes a subset, a sub-state, of the latter. (2002, 74)

The key point to draw from Gabilondo is the extent to which 9/11 has reshaped and rearticulated national narratives of national terror in Spain. I complicate the relation further by considering the impact that national historical narratives have on the global metanarrative of terror. For instance, how does the narrative *of las dos Españas* inform the process in which global narratives of terror operate within the Spanish state? On the one hand, the 9/11 attacks in the USA radically constrained ETA's options in Spain. On the other hand, the Spanish government's attempt at dialogue with ETA indicated that national historical narratives ultimately shape and define the mass-mediated narratives of terror in Spain, arguably much more so than the global metanarrative of terror. The global metanarrative of terror cannot override national or domestic narratives, especially where those narratives are intrinsically linked to deep rooted historical debates and struggles.

Spain is one significant example where the burdens of its own history weigh down on the metanarrative of terror.

Conclusion

In *Politics Out of History*, Wendy Brown argues that in the post-Cold War world the past becomes "less easily reduced to a single set of meanings and effects, as the present is forced to orient itself amid so *much* history and so *many* histories, history emerges as both weightier and less deterministic than ever before" [original emphasis] (2001, 5). Understanding the constitutive narrative of *las dos Españas* and its functions in Spanish political discourse, therefore, is complicated by the fact that traditional, if ghostly, narratives and narrative traces emanating from the past still exist. Historical narratives are never superseded. Rather, the present is forced to orient itself amid so much history, and so many histories. In Spain, as social and political circumstances evolve, Spaniards must confront these lingering histories and memories.

The next chapter details the confrontation between history and memory as it relates to the long-suffering conflict between the Spanish state and the Basque separatist group ETA. The chapter investigates how a conflict that was once classified as a classical and domestic problem for the Spanish state, has, since 9/11, been exposed to the global metanarrative of terror. Moreover, since the conflict divides the two Spains it thus provides a discursive site in which both Spains can articulate their national narratives.

CHAPTER TWO

History, Terror and Myth
ETA, Spain, the State, and the Nation

> The stronger the drive to the unified nation, the integrated community, and/or the normal individual, the more powerful becomes the drive to convert differences into modes of otherness [. . .] The biggest impetus to fragmentation, violence and anarchy today does not emerge from political engagement with the paradox of difference. It emerges from doctrines and movements that suppress it. (Connolly 1995, xxi)

War, memory, terrorism, and nationalism are highly topical issues in the humanities and social sciences in the post-Cold war era, which is coterminous with the deepening of European integration in the European Union since 1992 and which includes the global ramifications of the events of September 11, 2001. This chapter locates the convergences of these critical trends and historical phenomena in contemporary Spain by paying particular attention to the re-emergence of regional nationalism and the conflict between ETA and the Spanish state. The study of nationalism, in particular, has emerged in recent years as one of the central concerns of political and social theorists. Nationalism studies are indebted to the publication in the early 1980s of Benedict Anderson's *Imagined Communities* (1983) and Ernest Gellner's *Nations and Nationalism* (1983), and also attracted renewed attention in the wake of post-Cold War conflicts in the Middle East, the Balkans and in places such as Rwanda. For most social science theorists, national identity is no longer considered as a static concept but rather as one that is constantly being redefined, that is, as a continually reconstructed category of identification.

For Benedict Anderson, the nation is an "imagined political community" because while members of even the smallest nation will never personally know the great majority of their compatriots, they all share the idea of a national community (1983, 6). Anderson identifies three basic characteristics of a nation. First, the nation is imagined as limited (geographically, within borders); second, it is conceived as sovereign (from God and from dynastic rule); and third, the nation is conceived as a community in itself. Yet, as Begoña Aretxaga correctly points out, "this constitutive sketch of the nation does not quite explain its extraordinary emotive capacities" (2005, 92). Thus, in order to comprehend the affective appeal of the nation, "one must examine the narratives and metaphors that make up the body of the nation, making it appear as a natural immemorial formation more than a specific historic and cultural product" (92). Different metaphors and narrative plots are therefore crucial in defining the parameters of the nation in order to generate emotional movement or empathy or involvement that imparts social and political meaning. However, if the nation is an unstable and ambivalent entity, for example, as can be found in the Spanish state (due to its multiple regional nationalisms), then it is not surprising that the "state-nation" conjunction attempts to resolve this ambivalence through various means. One of the means that the Spanish state has at its disposal to resolve this dilemma is the narrative construction of terror as an *a priori* threat to the unity of an imagined unified Spanish nation.

While Benedict Anderson suggests that national borders might be historical products of a particular kind of territorial imagination, Aretxaga points out that "borders are also the spaces where national imaginations are rendered unstable" (2005, 78). What happens, then, when state borders do not correspond with the outline of the imagined nation? Or as Aretxaga more profoundly asks, "What happens to national identity when an unimagined border forces a redefinition of the nation?" (78). This chapter looks at the tension between the state and the nation in contemporary Spain through the enduring political narratives of the Basque separatist group ETA and the Spanish national government. Although ETA declared a "definitive" cessation of its terrorist activities on October 20, 2011 (see Chapter Nine), my aim in this chapter is to explore the narrative conflict between ETA and the Spanish state and to suggest that these narrative battles continue to have an effect on contemporary Spanish politics.

There are many different ideologically and territorially based conceptions of "Spanish" identity in Spain. They combine to highlight the ambiguous and unstable nature of national identity in that country. As noted in Chapter One, one of the most significant narrative divisions is between the two Spains (*las dos Españas*), understood as a narrative battle between "conservatives" and "liberals" who fight "for the appropriation of the identity of the nation" (León 2003a, 2). Liberal Spain is more at ease with the concept of devolved powers to the regions; and modernity and Europeanism are the values that more clearly shape the Liberal concept of

Spanish identity. The narrative script of conservative Spain (often referred to as "Eternal Spain"—*La España Eterna*) is more in line with the traditional images associated with Spain (Catholicism, centralism, monarchism), which tend to establish Spain's difference within the European context (2). Conservative Spain promotes a centralized vision of the country and an essentialist concept of national identity that begrudgingly accepts regional differences. However simplistically, many historians have pointed to this ideological division as the reason for the breakout of the Spanish Civil War and the Spanish state's subsequent political conflicts. This divide, they claim, has haunted Spanish politics and society ever since.

Yet alongside the lingering phantom presence of the narrative of *las dos Españas* is another significant division and tension in Spanish identity debates and struggles: the division between the centre and the peripheries. Fernando León suggests that "perhaps foregrounding the politico-territorial controversy as the only driving force of Spanish history is somewhat exaggerated, but it can be rightly regarded as one of the deepest and most delicate problems which has prevented the emergence of an integrating national identity" (2003a, 3). Some writers, such as José Magone, even argue that the centre-periphery division is still the most salient one in electoral terms, while the left–right ideological division is more or less eroding due to social transformation and the impact of political marketing and the media (2004, 31).

The history of the formation of the Spanish state is a history of successive wars between medieval kingdoms, each with a separate identity and often with a separate and distinct language. In contemporary Spain, three of these regions (Catalonia, Galicia and the Basque Country) have maintained to various degrees their distinct language and customs and consider (or imagine) themselves to be nations in Benedict Anderson's sense. The Basque Country and Catalonia, in particular, were also the most oppressed regions under the Franco regime, with their language and cultural traditions under systematic attack by the regime's armed forces. Since the late 1980s, however, Spain has experienced a significant degree of federalization. The 1978 Spanish Constitution allowed for the creation of regional, self-governing Autonomous Communities, each with its own government and parliament. The historical regions of the Basque Country, Catalonia and Galicia were given preference by the central government, but John Hooper points out that after Franco's death it became obvious that to have granted home rule to only those regions, which had had statutes of autonomy under the Republic, "would have been seriously at odds with the mood of the times" (2006, 36). Other regions in Spain were thus also allowed to negotiate their own Statute of Autonomy even where there was no historic claim of a separate identity; this included Madrid, which was regarded as a natural part of Castile. Between 1978 and 1983 seventeen Autonomous Communities emerged and the process of devolution of powers to the regions has been continually consolidated and modified over the life of democratic Spain (see Chapters Four and Six).

The success of the Spanish transition to democracy, however, has not resolved all the nationalist problems in the Spanish state. Language policy in the three historic regions (Basque Country, Catalonia and Galicia), as well as in Valencia, has involved an incessant battle between the Autonomous Communities and the central government (and involved petitions to the EU in the case of Valencia). ETA's terrorist acts also remained a defining characteristic of the post-Franco era. This chapter engages with the idea that terrorism in Spain is a result of several unresolved questions in the formation of the Spanish state, and argues that those questions are linked to both the narrative of *las dos Españas* and the global metanarrative of terror. It is first necessary, however, to examine the emergence of ETA and Spain's transition to democracy in order to highlight how these unresolved questions of the nation (centre-periphery, centrist or federalist) have been constructed as a narrative device to legitimize the Spanish "state" while minimizing the potential disturbance of regional nationalism to the unity of the Spanish "nation." The chapter concludes by looking at how these narratives have evolved in the post-9/11 era and argues that the past may be the source of both legitimacy and illegitimacy in Spanish terror narratives.

The Basque Country: A difficult nation

During the 1980s and 1990s, many studies of globalization pointed to the radical weakening and transformation, if not disappearance, of the modern state. Globalization, however, is not only compatible with statehood, argues Aretxaga, "but has actually fuelled the desire for it" (2005, 256). Gabilondo, for his part, posits that the Basque Country in Spain is postnational in the sense that while its defenders remain thoroughly nationalist, they "also are fully aware that the state, as the upholder of the traditional site of nationalism, no longer is their political horizon or utopia" (2002, 59). How can we reconcile, then, a postnational Basque Country, with the fact that sovereignty and statehood is such an urgent desire in a globalized world in which states seem to be less and less independent? As Aretxaga (2005, 139) asks, why does this demand appeal to a new generation of youth socialized not only in Basque culture, but also in the transnational youth culture across the world? What puzzles Aretxaga is that the young activists who have taken leadership of the movement for Basque independence have no personal experience of the Franco dictatorship. Instead, they are the product of the democratic transition (179).

The two principle poles in the Basque "conflict" have been ETA and the central government in Madrid. These two opposing forces engaged in a physical and discursive battle and orchestrated a political confrontation that often polarized individuals: you are with the victims or with the terrorists; you support democracy or you attack democracy; and you are an *abertzale* (Basque patriot) or an *españolito/a* (supporter of the Spanish state). The problem lies in defining what a Basque identity is in relation to the historical tension between individual and collective rights. In the plurinational state of Spain what does it mean to be Basque? What should take priority: the individual rights of a citizen or the collective rights of an imagined Basque nation? Conceiving the Basque Country as a nation implies recognizing the collective rights and self-determination of the people that make up that nation. Many figures in the central Spanish government deny the Basque collective's right, and insist that only individual rights exist.

Critics of Basque nationalism often point out how artificial many aspects of the imagined Basque nation are. Sabino Arana, the founding father of Basque nationalism, invented not only a Basque flag, but also a name for the Basque nation (Euskadi). More importantly, critics also emphasize that at no time since the eleventh century (and then only briefly) have the Basques been governed by a Basque leader in a single political unit. Paddy Woodworth, rather wryly, responds to these criticisms by suggesting that they only highlight how constituent peoples construct nations, which are not "ahistorical absolutes handed down by God" (2001, 19). More facetiously, he adds, "most nations look more than a little ridiculous in the first phase of construction, when the raw mortar of rhetoric and myth is most apparent" (19).

According to the Basque nationalist narrative, as glossed by Woodworth (22–23), the Basques have occupied their own land since the dawn of humanity and were never conquered by the Romans, the Moors, the Visigoths, or the Franks. The basic structure of their society was egalitarian and democratic, and up to the nineteenth century Basque was the universal language of the region. More significantly, they recognize that while the Basques did not have a clearly defined unitary state, they did have a strong sense of themselves as a separate people. The Basques ran their own affairs, entering into alliances with Castilian Kings who swore to uphold the special privileges (*fueros*) that Basques enjoyed, which included their own tax system and exemption from customs and military service. This Golden Age ended in the nineteenth century when military defeat in the two Carlist Wars led to the abolition of the *fueros*. As part of the Spanish empire, the Spanish state promoted an influx of migrant workers into the Basque Country, especially from Galicia and Andalusia, thus diluting the ethnic purity of the Basque nation.

Critics of Basque nationalism also have a convincing counter-narrative. The Basques, they argue, are probably a primitive people who once inhabited a large part of the Iberian Peninsula. The general absence of Roman fortifications in the Basque Country is evidence of how little resistance the Basques offered the Roman Empire. Basque social structures, runs the counter-narrative, were often rigidly hierarchic, and elements of egalitarian democracy also existed in other rural Spanish communities. The lack of any significant vernacular literature before the nineteenth century indicates that the Basque language was a "primitive tongue of a marginalised peasantry" (23). In the Basque Country, Latin, and later Castilian, were the languages of administration and culture. Moreover, the counter-narrative argues that the *fueros* were a common feature of the relationship between the Spanish monarchy and many other regions, and that the Basque region was just as integrated into the machinations of the emerging Spanish state as other regions. The abolition of the *fueros*, "far from being a disaster, was a positive act of modernizing centralism and was actively supported by progressive liberals in Basque cities." As for the influx of immigrants, the counter-narrative argues that Basque nationalism represented "a backward looking and reactionary response of a regional lower middle class displaced by modernization" (23).

Marianne Heiberg argues that both of these conflicting historical narratives are "partially valid" (1989, ix), which in turn supports French historian Ernest Renan's dictum that "getting its history wrong is part of being a nation" (quoted in Hobsbawm 1992, 12). Despite such polemics, however, Basque nationalism has become a powerful force in the region and Basque nationalist parties have dominated the powerful autonomous government that runs three of the four Spanish provinces claimed by Basque nationalists.[1] Heiberg suggests that the real key to the success of Basque nationalism lies in the failure of Spanish nationalism. Madrid at the turn of the nineteenth century was "unable to endow the identity of 'Spaniard' with

---

[1] The Autonomous Community of the Basque Country is made up of three of the four provinces in Spain that Basque nationalists consider to be part of Euskal Herria (a name that refers to the four provinces in Spain as well as the three other provinces that are formally part of the French state). They are Vizcaya, Álava and Guipúzcoa. Navarra remains a separate Autonomous Community in the Spanish state.

advantages and dignity that outweighed 'Basque' or 'Catalan'"" (1989, 6). This failure was exacerbated by Spain's defeat in the Spanish-American War of 1898, which became embedded in Spanish collective memory as *El Desastre*, the loss of Spain's last remaining American and Asian colonies (Cuba, Puerto Rico, the Philippines and Guam). The Spanish defeat was seen as symbolic proof of the collapse of the nation. At a time when many other European powers were at their imperial peak, there was a sense of failure instead of pride in being Spanish (Álvarez Junco 2002, 24). *El Desastre* started the process of Europeanization, whereby nationalism was equated with a process of "regeneration." Nevertheless, Spaniards disagreed profoundly about core national values. Some argued for an insistence on allegiance to traditional values (conservatives), while others demanded reform and Europeanization (liberals). In this context, the crisis in Spanish identity consolidated the emerging peripheral nationalisms in the Basque Country and Catalonia. Thus, Álvarez Junco suggests, "The emergence of those threatening 'separatist' movements finally provided Spanish Nationalism with a cause to serve: the purely reactionary one of being the unifying ideology for all those opposed, not only to liberal or social revolution, but also to Catalan and Basque autonomy" (2002, 33). Hence, since the dawn of the twentieth century, the historic nations and their resulting nationalisms have been perceived as a problem by Spanish centralists.

Francoist excesses and the emergence of ETA

Immediately after the Spanish Civil War in the years between 1939 and 1945, the Basque Country was subject to a regime of state terror with no parallel in its history, including the elimination of all use of Euskera in Basque society (Conversi 1997, 80–81). While much of this repression had eased well before the early 1970s, young people were periodically arrested for speaking Euskera on the streets of the Basque Country in the final years of the Franco regime. Woodworth points out that although most of the Franco regime's prohibitions were enforced erratically, even in the early years of dictatorship, "there was a widespread sense that the Basque Country was occupied by a foreign, hostile power, turning the nationalist narrative of an occupied homeland into a kind of lived reality" (2001, 34–35).

By the early 1950s, the Basque Nationalist Party (PNV) was little more than a neo-traditionalist group awaiting the intervention of foreign powers to overthrow the Franco dictatorship. As other fascist parties in Europe had dissolved or were delegitimized by the end of the Second World War, few observers seriously believed that the Franco regime could survive in a post-war international system. The Basque diaspora (estimated at 150,000 exiles, including the regional Basque government during the Second Republic) waited for Allied forces to depose Franco and dismantle his regime. The Allies punished Spain for having been taken over by a right-wing dictator by instituting a UN-sanctioned trade boycott in December 1946 and excluding Spain from the Marshall Plan. But a military campaign to depose Franco never eventuated. The international cold shoulder given to Franco's Spain, however, did not last long. With the onset of the Cold War, strategic defence issues began to drive international and diplomatic policy responses to Spain given its proximity to Africa and its important location at the entrance to the Mediterranean (Gibbons 1999, 6). The failure of Western democracies, especially Britain and the USA, to isolate and exert pressure on the regime led many Basques to conclude that they could not depend on outside assistance (Conversi 1997, 83).

In 1952, tired of the older generation's inaction, a handful of Basque male students in the PNV formed *Ekin* (which means "To Act" in Euskera). The group was not simply eager to preserve Basque culture but aimed to "promote it as a means of expression for a modern community" (Conversi 1997, 84). *Ekin* first began to meet in secret in Bilbao and quickly found wider support in the rural heartland, a popularity linked to its early consideration of armed action as a possible means to defeat Francoism and to revitalize a nation on the verge of losing its cultural identity. For these young intellectual men, notes Woodworth, "the PNV appeared unable or unwilling to channel Basque nationalism into effective opposition to Franco's dictatorship" (2001, 33). Tensions between some of the *Ekin* youth leaders and the PNV leadership eventually led to a split in 1958, and the creation of a new group called *Euskadi Ta Asktasuna* (Basque Freedom and Homeland, ETA), on the anniversary of Sabino Arana's foundation of the PNV (31 July). ETA's doctrine was immediately more radical than that of the PNV, rejecting autonomy and instead calling for the full independence of all seven provinces that the group claimed as Basque. Significantly, ETA shifted away from the PNV's identitarian focus on Basque race and ethnicity, by emphasizing the Basque language Euskera as the key vector of Basque nationality. During the course of the 1960s, ETA's doctrine about Basqueness was further refined by socioeconomic factors drawn from the study of Third World armed liberation movements. The acronym ETA was typically encircled by the slogan *Iraultza ala Hil*, "Revolution or Death," and the group defined itself as the "Basque Revolutionary Movement for National Liberation," eventually accepting as Basque anyone "who lived and sold their labour in the Basque Country," a definition that Woodworth points out, excluded the Basque nationalist bourgeoisie (2001, 37). Armed resistance developed into an attractive tactical option given that the Francoist state continued its repression of the Basque Country right up until Franco's death in 1975, although the repression was less severe than in the immediate aftermath of the Civil War.

In its first two years ETA began bombing Francoist statues and emblems. In July 1961, the group attempted to derail a train carrying Francoist veterans to a Civil War commemoration. Although the attack failed, reportedly because ETA took too many precautions to avoid risking human life, the consequences were severe and hundreds of activists were arrested. Yet, the failed attack, argues Woodworth, "gained ETA a reputation in both nationalist and anti-Francoist circles" (2001, 36). The thwarted train attack demonstrated ETA's revolutionary theory of the action-repression-action spiral in practice. This theory posited that violent action provokes an indiscriminate state response, which in turn generates popular support for further action (36). The action-repression-action spiral is a theory based on the principle that selected violent attacks would provoke the whole Basque population. These events would spiral until the masses spontaneously rose up against the Spanish government in a revolutionary army of national liberation. After the attack, ETA's leadership took refuge in France to avoid the repression, and that transborder tactic became a hallmark of ETA. Since ETA was the only group using armed action against the dictatorship, it quickly moved to the forefront of the anti-Franco struggle. Indeed, in the Basque Country, ETA faced little competition in occupying the symbolic centre of Basque opposition to Spanish centralism (Díez-Medrano 1995, 180). As Woodworth remarks, "Even those democrats who disagreed in principle often felt some private admiration for young men daring enough to challenge the fearsome repressive machine which the old man had at his disposal" (2001, 38).

ETA's armed actions became more serious in August 1968 when the group killed Melitón Manzanas, a hated police commissioner. This was ETA's second killing and first planned assassination. The Franco regime responded on cue, imposing a state of emergency and arresting more than two thousand Basque residents (Edles 1998, 128). The siege lasted for months and for the first time the Basque Nationalist Party, through one its publications, announced that "it was not opposed to the use of violence" (Kurlansky 2001, 243). Finally, sixteen *etarras* were arrested and charged. The subsequent trial in Burgos in December 1970 was the pinnacle of ETA's "legitimacy" in the anti-Franco narrative script and became a test case of competing strength, according to Woodworth, "between an increasingly senile Francoism and the entire democratic opposition" (2001, 39). By 1970, then, ETA had returned Basques to their self-image of the 1930s and

1940s. Once again, the heroic Basques were standing up to Fascism. European ambassadors were recalled for consultation; the Vatican pleaded for clemency; and general strikes plagued the Basque Country and other areas of Spain. European journalists condemned the human rights violations of the Franco regime. Six of the accused were given death sentences. But three days after receiving appeals from nine governments, Franco commuted them to thirty years jail, reassured, according to Woodworth, "by large stage-managed demonstrations in favour of the status quo" (2001, 39). Although the Burgos trials and subsequent jail sentences significantly diminished ETA's membership, the trials remain one of ETA's most important propaganda triumphs. As historian Raymond Carr notes, the events in Burgos became "a trial of the regime as much as of the terrorists themselves" (1982, 733–34). Since most of ETA's targets during the 1960s and 1970s came from the ranks of Francoist security forces, the narrative script of young, brave Basques fighting fascism was easy to fabricate and circulate. ETA's credibility as an anti-fascist group was further consolidated on December 20, 1973 with the assassination of "The Ogre," Admiral Carrero Blanco, Franco's confidante and planned successor who was widely perceived as the "father" of state terrorism in Spain. According to Carr, it was "one of the most brilliantly planned [assassinations] in the history of terrorism" (1982, 734). Paradoxically, with this assassination ETA is widely credited with sealing the fate of the Francoist regime. ETA had shown that violence could be a very important weapon and spur to regime-change. "The lesson," according to Woodworth, "would not be unlearned easily, even when the political conditions of the state had changed utterly" (2001, 41).

Within a couple of years of Carrero Blanco's assassination, ETA split. One group, the political-military faction of ETA, or ETA(p-m), accepted that the basic conditions of democracy had been created. Its leaders embarked on policies that by the early 1980s would bring most of its members home from underground, exile, or prison, and into normal politics. The other group, the military faction or ETA(m), insisted that ETA was involved in a justified war of independence against Spanish occupation. ETA(m) dramatically escalated its attacks and its list of legitimate targets grew longer and longer. ETA's success since the split was helped significantly by the group's renarrativization of Basque mythology. Over time, according to Zulaika and Douglass, "ETA [. . .] constructed martyrs and legends, an entire liturgy of anniversaries and gatherings of the fallen, as well as a rich iconography of tortured bodies, pictures of dead friends, and tombstones" (1996, 24).

Democracy at any cost / "Nothing had changed"

The Franco regime, argues Aretxaga, in its "very ordinariness, its over-whelming presence [and] eclipsed reality [. . .] made both the Francoist state and life under Francoism, a state of terror, one so intimate, so familiar, so institutionalised as reality, that the state of terror became the normal state of being" (2005, 129). Writing about her personal experience growing up in San Sebastian, Aretxaga recounts how she began to realize that "the terrorists of whom the press and the television spoke might not be such monsters as they were made out to be, and that the Generalissimo might not be such a benevolent figure as the *Noticiero Español*, the official newsreel of the state, presented him" (2005, 129). Indeed, the nearly forty years of Francoist dictatorship had been characterized, according to Aretxaga, "by a timeless time filled with the silence of massive violence, a silence that structured the terror of the regime as a permanent absent presence. Silence was a crucial part in the normalization of a state terror" (129).

With the tumultuous transition to democracy after Franco's death in 1975, Spain faced a new set of questions and problems that were not always easy to resolve. The Spanish state at this time, attempted to erase many of the worst excesses of the Francoist state machinery from its political narratives. Yet, the lingering presence of ETA and sporadic violence from other left and right wing groups, were, according to the former Socialist president of the Spanish government (1982–1996), Felipe González writing in *El País*, "el único fantasma del pasado que no hemos podido superar" (the only spectre that we have been unable to overcome) (2001).

"The spectres of the past," argues Joan Ramon Resina, "can radicalize the present" (2000, 3). The slowness of some aspects of Spain's transition to democracy, such as the reform of the state's armed forces, favoured the continued radicalization of ETA and Basque nationalists, and fed into the idea that "nothing had changed." Although King Juan Carlos appointed Adolfo Suárez Prime Minister in July 1976, with the brief to modernize and democratize the Spanish state, the process was always subject to compromise in the attempt to avoid any confrontation between the two Spains. Suárez called elections in June 1977, the first multi-party democratic elections since 1936. The Spanish electorate voted firmly for the centre, sidelining both the Communists and the extreme right, and cementing the systemic process of reform from within, rather than by the radical change that many constituencies in Spain, such as peripheral nationalists, called for. As a result, many of the old institutions, and the men who ran them, remained in place, making the conflict in the Basque Country much more difficult to resolve.

After the first two years of slow steps towards liberalization, the Unión de Centro Democrático (UCD, Union of the Democratic Centre) government was under pressure to counter the rise in terrorist violence. By July 1978, the transitional UCD government, fearing an army uprising, introduced new anti-terrorist legislation that suspended detainees' rights, including the right to see a lawyer. This was supplemented in August 1978 with a "special measure" allowing the approved detention of persons, incommunicado, for up to ten days (Clark 1990, 41). The law effectively turned the Basque Country into a police state. According to Gibbons, abuses of the law by the police were widely recognized to have taken place in the Basque Country, and those abuses were broadcast by ETA to attract sympathy for the cause and justify its ongoing campaign of bombings (1999, 23). In 1979, King Juan Carlos promulgated a third measure introducing criminal penalties for "apologia for terrorism," or printing or saying anything that could be construed to defend terrorist acts or groups (Clark 1990, 41). In 1980, all three measures were streamlined into the Organic Law on Citizen Security, which was in effect for four years. The justification for such laws was that given the difficulty of obtaining evidence and witnesses, the "police have to resort to any available means in order to conduct the investigation" (Vercher 1992, 230), pre-empting legislative changes in the USA and other western democracies by almost twenty years. Such laws prompted Zulaika and Douglass to declare that "once again, only savage 'terrorism' can justify the preservation of the old regime's most dubious practices such as torture and evasion of the law" (1996, 176).

The fallout from the laws was far-reaching and arrests multiplied. The overwhelming presence of the despised Civil Guard and police in the Basque Country, "deepened the feeling of occupation and kept alive the anti-repressive consciousness generated under Franco, a consciousness that was being capitalized on politically by ETA(m) and used to legitimate their military offensive" (Aretxaga 2005, 155). The years between 1978 and 1982 were the bloodiest in ETA's history, and the laws only galvanized the action-repression-action spiral that ETA had always advocated. Against this backdrop, sections of the army that, under Franco, had been accustomed to running the country did not easily tolerate any demonstrations of radicalism which they regarded as symptoms of a failing post-Franco order. On February 23, 1981, an attempted coup d'état (popularly known as *El Tejerazo*), led by Colonel Antonio Tejero of the Civil Guard threatened the future of democracy:

In one of the most extraordinary pieces of live television in European history, bursts of sub-machine gun fire raked the ceiling while Tejero, brandishing a pistol like a demented John Cleese, ordered the deputies to 'Sit down, fuck it!' There were courageous exceptions, including Suárez, but most of the parliamentary deputies took cover under their seats. (Woodworth 2001, 64)

The Spanish public was kept in suspense for more than twelve hours, as they waited helplessly to see what the King, the commander-in-chief of the armed forces, would do. The film *El Calentito* (2005) by Chus Gutiérrez, recreates this tense moment as experienced in a bar frequented by Madrid's *movida* youth. Antonia, a middle-aged transsexual who is able to run the bar thanks to the sexual favours she provides to members of the Guardia Civil, understands the significance of what the coup means and considers fleeing to London. Finally, in a televised address, the King repudiates the coup and demands support for the Constitution. Most Spaniards, like the characters in the film, were relieved. Shortly thereafter, ETA's political wing renounced the use of violence in fear of provoking another military coup.

With this context in mind, it is understandable why much hope was placed in the new 1978 Constitution, which was heralded in many quarters as the "official close" of state-sanctioned violence. People voted "yes" in the constitutional referendum because they could no longer "live in the past." Carlos Hugo de Borbón states that the 1978 Constitution was "the best path with which to construct a democracy that evades the dialogue of fists and pistols" (quoted in Edles 1998, 108). Yet, despite the positive symbolic promise of the new Constitution, the Basque Country was the only region in Spain that did not approve it. Again, this was to have unforeseen repercussions in the enduring Basque conflict.

In order for the new democratic consensus to work and to avoid any replay of the Civil War, the 1978 Constitution was purposefully ambiguous. The sentence that proclaimed "the unity of the Spanish Nation" was qualified by the recognition of minority "nationalities," which were guaranteed the right to form autonomous governments with extensive regional powers. As Golob puts it, "individual Basque citizens theoretically enjoy universal rights to civil and political liberties—*but not to their collective psychic geography*" [my emphasis], since the Spanish state has placed considerable limitations on the extent to which the Basque Country is free to construct a nation-state (2002a 34–35). More ominously, the Constitution granted the army the power and responsibility to defend the territorial integrity of Spain. Woodworth argues that "at first sight that might seem innocuous, even axiomatic. What else do armed forces do, after all?" (2001, 4). But to Basque nationalists it had the smell of giving the army the role of a "government in the shadows" (4). To complicate matters further, Navarre became a separate region under the new Constitution, to the dismay of many Basques. For the Basques who wanted autonomy, the autonomous regions were "a parody of their dream," and many young Basques blamed the Basque Nationalist Party for these developments (Kurlansky 2001, 276). Yet, between 1975 and 1985, the Basque Country gained increasing regional autonomy and state-like institutions, such as a government and parliament, a judicial and educational apparatus, its own police force, and even its own revenue system. But Basque radicals continued to argue that the Constitution was not endorsed by the majority of their people. In their view, then, "ETA's violent campaign was a legiti-mate, even necessary, form of resistance to the undemocratic imposition of an alien state structure" (Woodworth 2001, 4). The early 1980s, therefore, saw a clash between the narrative of the Spanish state and those of the Basque Country, not least because of divergent collective memories. Peter Burke argues that "history is not just written by the victors but is also forgotten by them' (1989, 97). Resina, however, suggests that losers cannot afford to forget; they need to brood over the past because their memory is compulsive (2000, 88). The Basque Country was the largest part of Spain that did not necessarily want to forget the past and accept the prevailing "sacred" democratic narrative script.

Evidence of the narrative clash was almost immediate. In the Spanish state's first democratic elections since the 1930s, ETA(m) argued that the elections could not be truly democratic as long as political prisoners remained in jail and the state apparatus was under the control of Franco's successors (Aretxaga 2005, 154). For ETA(m), a rupture with Francoism was a precondition for a legitimate democracy. However, ETA(pm) and other nationalist groups such as Euskadiko Ezkerrra (EE, Basque Country Left), considered the elections a means to achieve true democratic change. In March 1979 general elections were called to form the first Spanish parlia-ment in the new Spanish democracy. ETA(m) formed the coalition, Herri Batasuna (HB, Unity of the People), to run the electoral campaign with the aim, "of showing their political strength, but without the intention of participating in the new parliament, which they did not recognise" (Aretxaga 2005, 155). Solidly behind ETA, Herri Batasuna, which refused to neither recognize Spanish democracy nor participate in its institutions, attracted many young voters. The strategy was a success. In the first autonomous elections in the Basque Country, HB proved to be the third strongest political force behind the PNV and PSOE. According to Aretxaga "their strong showing in the election revealed the existence of a powerful minority that did not believe in the legality of the newly elected institution" (2005, 155). And in stark contrast to most of the Spanish political establishment, HB refused to criticize ETA for its terrorist attacks (Encarnación 2007, 957).

Paloma Aguilar has stated that "as memory evolves, so events which take place after these remembered events can modify their recollection" (1999, 19). That evolution may explain, in part, why the memory of repression persists in the Basque Country. In her *Symbol and Ritual in the New Spain* (1998) Laura Edles highlights the consensual nature of the Spanish transition to democracy, but also emphasizes how Basque leaders became estranged from the consensus process. A further complication to the prevailing democratic narrative script was the meaning of democracy itself. For Basque nationalists, the traditional meaning of democracy was Basque local self-rule (the *fueros*). As Edles puts it, "the *Fueros* is the genuine (sacred) 'democracy,' symbolically opposed to the (evil) false centralist 'democracy' of the Constitution/transition" (134). She adds: "That the *Fueros* 'are' the Basque Constitution desacralizes the 'Spanish' Constitution for Basques" (137).

In competing legal and illegal ways, ETA and many Basque nationalists therefore contested the new social contract forged in the pacting of the mid-to-late 1970s, because pacting attempted to detach post-Franco Spain from the excesses of the Franco dictatorship. Many Basques did not recognize themselves in this constitutive story of a new, albeit democratic, Spanish nation. But, as Aretxaga points out, despite its inherent contradictions, "the Spanish social democratic government was not Franco's dictatorship. Not to realise this was to miss completely the fact that a struggle against the new state required new directions and new methods" (2005, 157). Yet ETA(m) was using in the 1980s and the 1990s the same political analysis and tactics that it had used in 1977.

ETA's escalation of terrorism in the early 1980s is rather baffling. As Woodworth (2001, 50) points out, these were the years when every jailed member of ETA was released under a series of amnesty arrangements. These were also the years in which the Basques voted in favour of a Statute of Autonomy that gave them more self-government than they had ever previously enjoyed. Indeed, the Basques were granted a degree of regional power almost unprecedented in Europe (50). A likely explanation for this scenario was that unlike the Spanish government, which centred its narratives along the idea of change, the discourse of radical nationalism was articulated in terms of the opposite idea: the continuation of the Francoist state with a democratic disguise (Aretxaga 2005, 159). For Aretxaga, although this discourse might seem incomprehensible to an outsider, it is "convincing for those who have experienced the continuation of repressive practices (detentions, torture, assassinations, disappearances and restrictions of civil liberties) as a part of everyday life" (159). Support for radical nationalism was, according to Aretxaga, "effectively underpinned by the Spanish government's repressive policy toward radical nationalism" (2005, 155). Basque radicals were convinced that any compromise on full independence would mean the death of Euskera in one generation. As I argue in the next chapter, the presence and activities of the *Grupos Antiterroristas de Liberación* (GAL) reconfirmed in the 1980s the impression that the Basque Country was still occupied by a foreign and oppressive government (Woodworth 2001, 51).

Contrary to the picture disseminated by official propaganda, however, the transition itself was a period of extreme violence. According to Lidia Falcón:

> The so-called amnesties were not, in legal terms, any such thing since those granted in the first years of the transition did not pardon all crimes, but rather obeyed a continuous selection procedure which maintained the classification of criminals, pardoning first some 'crimes' and later others. [. . .] At the same time, police repression was violently exercised against protesters demanding implementation of the most basic legal reforms during the transition's early years. [. . .] The demonstrators were attacked with water cannons, beaten and detained, as they had been during the dictatorship. (2002, 16)

But in the 1980s, the newly sacred democratic script was becoming well embedded throughout the rest of Spanish society. Edles (1998) argues that Spain's transition to democracy can be understood using the categories of the "sacred" and the "profane." The "sacred" is the emotionally charged symbol of the good; the "profane" is its symbolic opposite, the emotionally charged symbol of the bad (21). That is, democracy in Spain was the new (sacred) religion, the symbolic opposite of (profane) authoritarianism or dictatorship (52). For Edles, the profane is the legacy of the Civil War and is represented by irrationality, intolerance, confrontation, violence and extremism. The sacred, on the other hand, is democracy itself, represented by the affirmative values of reason, rationality, tolerance, pluralism and moderation. Moderation was understood as a modern, rational attitude: the sacred symbolic opposed to old (profane) irrationality and extremism (55). The new democratic government, as well as the opposition, "came to define democracy as their most important goal, and regime and opposition elites— and the masses—came to define violence as an inappropriate means to achieve it" (15). This relegated ETA violence in the realm of the profane and a threat to the new democratic order. Thus, according to Funes:

Non-Basque Spaniards who had supported or sympathized with the ETA during the Franco period and the subsequent transition to democracy now began to rethink their stance. Their opposition increased dramatically as ETA's actions became more and more violent and indiscriminately targeted civilians. The idealistic image of itself as a group of committed freedom fighters struggling against a dictator that the ETA had promoted began to erode. As a result, by the end of the 1980s, a new consensus was beginning to take shape. (1998, 494)

The key event that led to much of the collapse of ETA's remaining support occurred in July 1997. ETA kidnapped Miguel Ángel Blanco, a PP local councillor in the Basque town of Ermua. ETA issued an ultimatum: if the government did not return all ETA prisoners to the Basque Country within forty-eight hours, Blanco would be shot. In Woodworth's words, "It was a gratuitously cruel demand, because even if the government had found it democratically acceptable to concede, the logistics and time-scale of such an operation were virtually impossible" (2001, 346). The public response, particularly in the Basque Country was unprecedented. In Bilbao alone 100,000 people demonstrated against ETA carrying out its threat. But an hour after the deadline expired, Blanco's body was found with his hands tied and two bullets in the back of his head. He died some hours later (2001, 346). In the week following the shooting, millions of Spaniards demonstrated in cities across Spain. In the Basque Country Herri Batasuna members faced, for the first time, social isolation and even physical attacks. Thus, by the late 1990s, the organization had forfeited almost all its ideological resonance and appeal.

Narratives of violence

Each new action is greeted with a sense of "Can you believe what they have done now?" It is in this regard that a successful terrorist action may be likened to "scoring a goal" and the reactions of the enraged authorities to that of the bull charging the matador's cape. (Zulaika and Douglass 1996, 136)

Gerald Cromer's *Narratives of Violence* (2001) argues that the propaganda of nationalist and separatist groups differs from that of ideological groups in form and in content. The former is based on narratives that present the nationalist struggle as a repetition of the past (35). Thus, national terrorists tell projective narratives in an attempt to convince themselves that they

are the real patriots, and to persuade their fellow-countrymen and women
to follow their lead. Terrorist propaganda hails past acts of bravery and
resistance in order to encourage similar actions in the present. It therefore
consists of a series of projective narratives that are at once descriptive and
prescriptive (35). Basque radicals thus explain their resort to violence as a
justifiable reaction against particular actions of the government and the
structural violence of the system as a whole.

Projective narratives of violence are complicated by the fact that they
do not denote a particular kind of violence, but instead constitute an overdetermined discursive and performative site. This is nowhere more
evident in the Basque Country than in the phenomenon of *kale borroka*
(street fighting). *Kale borroka* is a style of violence employed by Basque
youth characterized by aggressive rioting against the Basque police, burning of public property such as municipal buses and garbage containers,
attacks on public buildings and ATM machines with home-made petrol
bombs, and violent intimidation. As Aretxaga points out, these acts,
although not easily classifiable as terrorism, provoke unparalleled levels of
social anxiety because of their capacity to attract hundreds of young people, and "partly because they are perceived as the future recruits of a
hardened and more politically intransigent ETA" (2005, 139–40). *Kale
borroka*, argues Aretxaga, is shaped by a political culture over-determined
by the complex terms of "terrorism" and the "state" (2005, 141). At issue,
she argues, is how the state is "imagined and experienced as a powerful
object of threat and desire" (141). This new form of youth violence
emerged in conjunction with two political and technological developments: the disclosure of the involvement of the Spanish government,
socialist party, and security forces in the assassination of Basque separatists
under the cover of a paramilitary group called GAL (see Chapter Three);
and the emergence of a Basque police force and their use of new technologies of control, including street video surveillance (143). Such
technologies were accompanied by technologies of disguise and in the
police use of hoods to hide their identities. In turn, Basque nationalist
youth resorted to alternative technologies to create "autonomous spaces of
discourse and action," such as pirate radios and internet networks "from
which to combat what they perceived as suffocating state control" (2005,
144). Basque youth also took to wearing disguises and hoods when rioting. These technologies of control and autonomy transformed political
culture into "a ghostly space in which the state and youth violence
were/are at once all pervasive and impossible to locate in a single structure, organization or site" (2005, 144). Projective narratives of violence
flourished on both sides and circulated through different social channels,

creating a social reality of fear where the boundary between the real and the fantasy was impossible to locate (144).

In Aretxaga's field work in the Basque Country, she spoke with Jabi, one of the leaders of the youth movement involved in *kale borroka* who called this *la lógica del tensionamiento* (the logic of tensing):

> The question for us is that if we are going to have an adequate peace at the end of the war, then what we have to do is to make sure that there is war and not to deactivate it. So we redirect that false debate about violence and we begin to put things in their place. This is when we enter into the strategy of *tensionamiento* (tensing), which means that in order for there to be distension (untensing) there needs first to be tension. (Jabi, quoted in Aretxaga 2005, 244–45)

Terrorism therefore has an extremely useful agenda-setting function. Low-level terrorism, as the phenomenon of *kale barroka* attests, can put the issue of political change on the public agenda. The government can reject but not ignore terrorists' demands. By challenging the legitimacy of the state, terrorists hope to provoke the state into overreacting. From the perspective of terrorists, this may contribute to a further weakening of the legitimacy of the state, which in turn may lay the foundation for a change of allegiances and loyalties between groups and society (Engene 2004, 27).

The overreacting of the state is manifested in the Basque Country by the presence of the Basque police, the *ertzaintza*. The *ertzaintza*, according to Aretxaga, "played a key role in reorganizing the scene of violence in the imaginary of radical nationalists" (2005, 182). Until the introduction of the Basque police, radical nationalists conceptualized the scene of violence in the Basque Country as one of a liberation struggle that pitched Basques— as an ethnic minority—against the oppressive forces of the Spanish state. With the *ertzaintza* assuming tasks formerly associated with the Spanish police, however, the scene of violence was complicated. The confrontation became one between Basques: radical nationalists versus the Basque government. This confrontation, argues Aretxaga, thus "came to signify a split in the imagined national community and furthermore a split within Basque identity itself" (182). In Aretxaga's analysis, the divisions were compounded by the fact that the Basque "state" was enforcing Spanish law, and could thus be seen as at once Spanish and Basque (209). Aretxaga argues that the derogatory insult of *cipayo* (the name used some hundred and fifty years ago for the soldiers of Indian origin serving in the British colonial army), which Basque radicals use for members of the *ertzaintza*, effectively divests the *ertzaintza* of Basque identity through the accusation of betrayal

(251). With that resemanticization, the *ertzaintza* becomes a legitimate target of nationalist violence and the boundaries of national identity are clearly re-established. Projective narratives of violence, therefore, serve to preserve Basque national mythologies by condemning the condemners and disavowing the dominant political narratives of the state.

The logic of compromise: On desire, denial, and death

> In this maze of rumours it is not truth that counts, for it cannot be extracted from the narratives. (Aretxaga 2005, 236)

When observing the Basque "conflict" or the Basque "question," it is difficult to distinguish either between myth and history, or history created by myth. The layers of symbolization affecting the conflict complicate the debate. For example, the enormous symbolic and affective resonance that Pablo Picasso's *Guernica* has, not only in the Basque Country, but throughout Spain, is incalculable. The fight between Madrid's Reina Sofia Museum and Bilbao's Guggenheim Museum to display the painting is evidence of a struggle to claim ownership of historical memories. What would the messages have been had the painting be given to the Basque Country? Would it have made the painting's tortuous imagery even more unbearable? Located in the Basque Country, the painting would no longer be about humanity and violence in the scheme of things, but about humanity and violence in a specific time and place. It would be impossible to ignore the Basque context when viewing and reading Picasso's painting.

A country's "political past," suggests Engene, is important because "it may be repoliticized for new purposes in the political present" (2004, 38). The Basque problem has provided a means for Spanish governments to demonstrate firmness and resolve in order to win votes in the rest of Spain. Although the ETA conflict was a low intensity conflict (even if there was intense suffering for those directly affected), it was easy to appeal to its impact in order to defend certain policies of power. The suffering of the Basque Country was used to obtain electoral advantage by ensuring that people only talked about the Basque conflict, effectively relegating other pressing national issues to the margins of public discourse. Consequently, the label "terrorist" acquired social and cultural specificity in Spain. It was therefore difficult for the mainstream Spanish media to distinguish between violent and democratic nationalism. Thus, democratic nationalists had to renounce their nationalist claims (whether legitimate or not) while ETA was using violent tactics. Many democratic Basque nationalists argued that this was a strategy adopted by the Spanish government to prevent all nationalist claims whatsoever. Even today, Basque nationalism continues to be mass-mediated as being, in essence, the same as terrorism, making many people in the Basque Country dismiss the identity-marker Basque as undesirable. Such responses point to the decentring of the Other in relation to terrorism. The perpetual, narrative-driven process of decentring becomes at once internalized and repetitive, with no apparent end.

The process also makes the issue of regional nationalism complicated and ambiguous. Nationalism, according to Žižek, "functions as a species or a supplement to racism, as a delimitation from the 'internal' foreign body" [original emphasis]. He adds: "On that account, 'non-racist nationalism' is formally impossible today, since nationalism itself, in its very notion, is posited as a species of racism (the 'other' against who we assert our national identity always threatens us 'from within')" (2005, 79). It is therefore impossible, according to Žižek, to demarcate clearly between good nationalism and bad aggressive nationalism (79). Basque nationalism cannot be separated from the violence of ETA; the word nationalist itself has become dirty, almost an insult in the Spanish political context (the Spaniards are democrats, whereas the Basques are nationalists). It is understandable, then, as Narotzky and Smith posit that "the mere fact of autonomous thinking, of having ideas, has become synonymous with political dissent, and therefore is received by others as a dangerous activity" (2002, 203). Resina argues similarly when he suggests that the state's brand of culture has been constituted to eliminate any competing claims to collective expression: "Whatever was not universal in the state's sense became ideological, partial and—the suggestion was ever present—fanatic" (2000, 10–11). One reason for this is that the mass-mediated narratives distance the terrorist as the personification of evil. But, as Aretxaga points out, this distancing,

> encouraged by a stereotyped image of the terrorist in the mass media might work in the United States and perhaps also in the rest of the Spanish state, but not in the Basque Country, for the simple reason that the "terrorists" turn out to be one's neighbours, acquaintances, or family members— people who are too close and whose lives we know, and who we cannot disregard so easily because they form part of the intimate social framework. (2005, 166)

For Aretxaga this position is counter-productive because the more the social reality in which ETA's violence takes place is denied, the more violent and destructive it seems (166). This happens with the perpetuation of the myth that since 9/11 national security requires the sacrifice of rights and liberties. It also requires the misuse of language. In Spain, the misuse of language relates to the oft-repeated slogans by the right that Spain is being broken up or Balkanized, or that dialogue with ETA meant supporting the terrorists and negating the victims. By displacing violence away from the state and onto the Basque nation, the state, as Jacques Derrida argues in his *Acts of Religion*, lives in forgetfulness of the violence of law from which it was born (2001, 283). Consequently, the state's "amnesiac denegation" leads to the hypocritical politics of compromise,

> that promotes acceptance of the adversary's coercion both in order to avoid the worst and while saying, with the sigh of the parliamentarian, that this is certainly not ideal, that, no doubt, things would have been better otherwise but that, precisely, one could not do otherwise. (283)

A telling representation of the logic of compromise in the context of the Basque conflict in Spain, is the film *El Lobo* (2004), directed by Miguel Courtois. The film is based on a true story, and focuses on Txema, an ETA infiltrator working with the Spanish secret service, who, in the early 1970s, brings down a quarter of the organization, including its upper echelons. At the end of the operation Txema considers himself to be invincible. In an interesting exchange with the secret service officer, Ricardo, who masterminded the operation, Txema reveals that ETA must be finished off or else they will tear the Basque Country apart and impede democracy. He argues that he has the means at his disposal to reconstitute ETA into a benign political organization that renounces violence permanently. Surprisingly, Ricardo, the secret service officer, responds, "And then what do we do? Open up a shop? This country is about to change. Without terrorism, the Left would demand too much. We need it to soften the transition. [. . .] They do their job, I do mine. Like you, José María. Now we're anti-terrorism experts. We're indispensable to any government."

As the film illustrates, no matter what the particular circumstances, the state is not simply affected by terrorist attacks, but rendered meaningful in dialogical relation to those attacks. Terrorism strikes at the very core of what the state is about; it challenges, according to Engene, "the state's right to be the sole dispenser and regulator of violence" (2004, 22). Yet the state can live with this challenge, if not thrive on it. Derrida's concept of the violence of compromise is apt here, because it reminds us of the logic of compromise that functioned during Spain's transition to democracy (2001). That is, the state compromises on terrorism by allowing ETA to continue to function, its aim being to effect loftier objectives: the establishment of a democratic structure within the limits of what "Eternal Spain" deems acceptable. The state is thus in denial of its original complicity in promoting violence.

The state, by having allowed Basque terrorism to function, argues Aretxaga, "has contributed to the creation of a fantasy scenario in the radical Basque imaginary that perceives the Basque Country as part of the Spanish state by virtue of a colonial relation, regardless of how independent its autonomous institutions are" (2005, 211). National identity, therefore, is delineated along a polarized line—Basque/Spanish—that does not permit mediation. The state acts like a colonial power that must keep the "colonies" in check. Clearly, both parties have advantages in this situation. The state, according to Aretxaga,

> blames terrorism for all its deficiencies and channels the latent discontent among its citizens, as a result of economic inequalities and growing social insecurity, toward the enemy. ETA finds a political rationale to continue, legitimizing its actions as a response to the violence of the state and the vicious cycle can keep going ad infinitum. (173)

Aretxaga thus posits that within this relationship "there is a hint of imaginary intimacy, a mutual obsession and fascination that dominates and defines the joint identity of these two politico-mythological actors" (173). In that situation there is no mediation. One position mirrors the other, and language ceases to generate meaning or dialogue, being caught in a circular exchange of the same tautological accusations: "You are violent, I am democratic; no, I'm democratic and you are violent" (175). In sum, the state and terrorism form part of the same political imaginary and their actors have a phantasmic but mutually intimate co-relationship, with each side depending on the other for its own definition and legitimacy (174). As the next chapter will show, the relationship is more intimate than at first apparent.

Since September 11, 2001, the above schema was further complicated by the ensuing War on Terror. Exposed to the global metanarrative of terror, the Basque terror question ceased to be simply a domestic problem for the Spanish state. In this discursive context, the Spanish state was strengthened by the global reorganization that placed terror narratives at the centre of global political discourse. ETA, however, required transnational support in order to sustain itself as a legitimate agent. The September 11 attacks in the USA, according to Gabilondo, denied to ETA not only a new theoretical discourse that would allow it to continue, but also the possibility of any discourse, given that the narrative of terrorism constructs terrorism as no longer local or existing within the West (64). ETA, and other local terrorist groups, were subsumed into the global metanarrative of terror.

Conclusion: On terror and evil

In contemporary Spanish political rhetoric evil and terrorism are virtually interchangeable. In light of Hegel's dictum that "the true source of Evil is the very neutral gaze that perceives Evil all around" (1977, 401–2), it is worth thinking about where the correlation between evil and terrorism came from. Whose interests does such a correlation serve? In the Spanish setting, the equation Terrorism = Evil is narratively mediated and inevitably overloaded. The subject who over-identifies with the equation is perceived as the fanatic. As Gabilondo points out, the ex-President of the Basque Nationalist Party, Xabier Arzallus, was frequently referred to in the Spanish press as "Taliban Arzallus," suggesting a link between Basque nationalists and the retrograde Taliban (2002, 64). Another example comes from former Spanish Prime Minister Aznar who in 2001 stated that no distinction could be made between the terror attacks on the World Trade Centre and the car bombs placed by ETA (64). Such pronouncements lead to the almost comic situation in Spain where, on the one hand, the centre-right Popular Party over-identifies its subject-position as the only party that morally and ethically opposes terrorism in absolute terms, while on the other hand, the centre-left Socialist Party scrambles to be perceived by the public as tough on terrorism.

Narratives of terror in Spain are further complicated by the positions adopted by the relatives of the victims of terrorism, and by many politicians and journalists, that ETA as a terrorist organization did have any ideology or motive. Accordingly, ETA violence was regarded as senseless, if not a result of madness. Many Spaniards could not understand the motives and logic behind ETA's attacks, and condemned and denounced those attacks as blind strikes against democracy and society as a whole. The refusal to credit ETA with a political character led to a de facto depoliticization and criminalization of the whole radical Basque movement. The political party Herri Batasuna was thus banned in 2003 (officially because it refused to condemn ETA's attacks) along with various youth groups and publications with links to the *abertzale* left. Batasuna's leader Arnaldo Otegi, was arrested in 2009 and spent six-and-a-half years in prison for attempting to "reconstruct" the political party. Since Spain's transition to democracy, therefore, terrorism has been narratively mediated by, and on, all sides of politics as an apolitical phenomenon or force that transcends political boundaries. At the same time, Spanish leaders have treated terrorism as the most pressing political issue in order to gain electoral leverage. It was only after the onset of the global economic crisis and the definitive end of ETA terrorism in 2011 that narratives of crisis began to supersede narratives of terror in Spanish political discourse (see Chapter Nine). The next chapter looks at the inverse of the Basque conflict by exploring the role of state terrorism on narratives of terror in the Spanish state. State terror in the form of the GAL scandal undermined the myth of a peaceful transition to democracy and complicated further the Spanish state's official narratives of terror.

CHAPTER THREE

Terror and the State
The GAL, Fantasy, and the (Un)imaginable

> Terrorism is the sizzle in many a plot of intrigue, as any moviegoer or reader
> of the best-seller list knows. (Zulaika & Douglass 1996, 47)

At the end of December 1994 the public confession of two policemen trig-
gered a political crisis in Spain by implicating the democratic state in the
use of paramilitary terror. Not since the attempted coup d'état of 1981,
which brought the phantom of military rule to the surface of Spain's new
democracy, had a national scandal so deeply shaken the core of Spanish
democratic identity. The paramilitary death squad was known by the
collective name *Grupos Antiterroristas de Liberación* (GAL, Antiterrorist
Liberation Groups), and between 1983 and 1987 it would claim twenty-
seven mortal victims, nine of whom had no connection whatsoever with
ETA. Many more were injured in GAL attacks, including very young children, representing about a quarter of the casualties caused by ETA over the
same period, and a much smaller fraction of the eight hundred or so people
killed by ETA since 1968 (Woodworth 2001, 11). Because the GAL used
ETA's own tactics—assassinations, kidnappings and bombings—this
scandal became known as a "dirty war" and demonstrated how the official
narratives celebrating Spain's transition to democracy were tenuous and
subject to confusion and displacement. Taking into account the emotive
capacity of terror attacks and the imaginative capacities of people, I build
on Strathern and Stewart's argument that imagination is involved in cases
"where people envisage themselves as the performers of violence as well as
on the part of victims and witnesses" (9). In this chapter, then, I consider
both ETA violence and the GAL as functioning in the realm of the "unimaginable." That is, they are transgressive acts of violence that either lie outside
of our imaginations, or acts of violence that disturb the dominant state
and/or national narratives: ETA because it no longer fit with the prevailing
narrative script of the transition; the GAL because it transgressed the official state narratives of the time that were attempting to erase violence and

confrontation from the new Spanish state's founding narratives. As a result, the relation between the state and terrorism belonged to the same political imaginary, and their actors were imbricated in an intimate phantasmic relationship with each side depending on the other for its own definition and legitimacy (Aretxaga 2005, 281).

In his article "Confronting Terrorisms" (2007), Gregory Miller suggests that since the September 11, 2001, attacks in the USA, scholarly responses have been divided over whether states should use harsh policies to punish terrorists and thus deter future acts, or instead focus on root causes and reduce the incentives for terrorists (331). The first view suggests that when states respond aggressively, they develop a tough reputation and deter future terrorism. The second view suggests that harsh government policies breed more terrorism, resulting in cycles of violence. As noted in Chapter Two, the Basque separatist group ETA often provoked repressive measures specifically in order to increase the group's popularity. Proponents of the second view, therefore, suggest that "when states respond in a conciliatory manner, they remove whatever legitimate claims the terrorists might have had, thus reducing domestic support" (332).

Although these debates have become commonplace in many Western countries since 2001, similar debates had been occurring in Spain since the early 1980s. In light of those debates, this chapter does not seek to reverse the thrust of the villainy in terrorism argument ("the real terrorist is the state"), but rather to point to the relationship between terrorism and counterterrorism in the Spanish state. It does so in order to argue that the political narratives stemming from the GAL scandal, far from undermining the legitimacy of the democratic state, functioned, (to paraphrase Žižek), as a condition of the state's stability and a means of reinforcing the social order (2005, 55). Put another way, the state's need to reduplicate itself across the violent divide between legal and illegal violence—via the police and via GAL—points to the importance of terrorism in legitimizing the inherent state. As Gabilondo argues:

> It is the culminating point at which the state acknowledges its powerlessness vis-à-vis terrorism while creating a surrogate terrorist self that mirrors the state and thus legitimizes it, specularly, as the only upholder of violence—legal and illegal. This is the narcissistic moment when the state drowns in the reflection of its own violence. (2002, 65)

The GAL scandal did not lead to the disintegration of democratic principles and narratives in the Spanish state. Rather it served to reinforce the post-Franco Spanish order. Instead of engendering a crisis of democracy or a questioning of the efficacy of the democratic transition, the mass-mediated response to the GAL became a protest against the Socialist government's handling of counterterrorism rather than a debate about paramilitary transgressions hindering democratic values. The latter debate, however, is pivotal. It points to the role of violence as a legitimating function of the state. Moreover, the GAL scandal was yet another terror event that became intertwined with the narrative of *las dos Españas*. The GAL scandal can and must be re-read as a sign of what the myth of the peaceful transition had to repress in order to become the dominant narrative of the new democratic Spain. The lingering debates that the official narratives of the transition attempted to erase had come back to haunt the present politics. In Aretxaga's words, it was as if "the shock of a ghastly 'real' had erupted through the cracks of democratic discourse, disturbing it with a growing anxiety about the (bad) nature of the state" (2005, 215).

Terror and the "unimaginable"

Zulaika and Douglass's anthropological conception of the sacred and the taboo (via Freud and Levi-Strauss) is useful to consider the state's transgression into employing death squads. The "unspeakable act of terrorism," they argue, "is the quintessential taboo in modern political discourse" (1996, 149). The taboo and the sacred are in dialectical and dialogical relation to each other: "the stronger imposition of a taboo by the counterterrorist, the greater the sacredness obtained by the realm of violence" (226). Counterterrorism cannot bear the desacralization of terrorism because that would ultimately mean the categories of "good" and "evil," "us" and "them," and "civilized" and "uncivilized" would fall apart. Zulaika and Douglass therefore ask: What are the restrictions imposed by terrorism discourse on its framers? (1996, 181). The answer is that personally, politically and morally, "terrorism is the utterly *untouchable*" [my emphasis] (181). That is, the fight against terrorists demands that they be "contained" and "isolated" (179). One approach that the state utilizes to contain terrorism, as seen in Chapter Two, is to narratively neutralize and depoliticize the terrorists' discourse, while simultaneously making terrorism the most urgent challenge in and to the state. Another means that the state has at its disposal in order to fight terrorism is to enact transgressions of the law that lie in what Jacques Derrida calls the realm of the mystical (2001, 269).

In his *Acts of Religion* (2001), Derrida argues that what the state fears is not so much crime or robbery (regardless of their scale), as long as the crimes transgress the law with an eye toward particular, usually material, benefits (268). This is why the violence of organized crime is not a threat to the existence of the state. The state, rather, is afraid of founding violence, that is, violence "able to justify, to legitimate [. . .], or transform the relations of law [. . .], and so to present itself as having a right to right and to law" (268). Founding violence includes all revolutionary situations:

> all revolutionary discourses, on the left or on the right [. . .] justify the recourse to violence by alleging the founding, in progress or to come, of a new law, of a new state. As this law to come will in return legitimate, retrospectively, the violence that may offend the sense of justice, its future anterior already justifies it. The foundation of all states occurs in a situation that one can thus call revolutionary. It inaugurates a new law; it always does so in violence. (269)

These moments, claims Derrida, are terrifying because of the sufferings, the crimes, and the tortures that inevitably accompany them, and also because such violence is "uninterpretable" or "undecipherable," hence its mystical qualities (269). ETA violence, then, threatened the Spanish state because its violence was founding violence. ETA had the ability to project a revolutionary discourse and undermine the state's official narratives. The state had to respond to that violence, even if that meant transgressing the institutions and the rule of law of the sacred democratic order.

With the transition to democracy widely considered to be complete after the election of the Socialists in 1982, it was also assumed throughout Spain that ETA violence would stop. The common narrative script of ETA violence at the time assumed that the group's goal was to attack the undemocratic Spanish state, or those governments that were clearly the successors of the Franco regime. In 1982, with the election of the PSOE, it was assumed that there was no longer any reason for ETA to continue attacking the Spanish state. Spain was finally free from tyranny and had entered into the sacred realm of "real" democracy. The Socialist government would thus give the Basques room to manoeuvre for more autonomy within the constraints of the new parliamentary democracy. As argued in Chapter Two, the prevailing national script in the post-Franco era erased violence from Spain's official narratives. Where once ETA violence could be imagined by the state as a sign of its own democratic deficit, ETA violence now became unimaginable. The unimaginable refers to transgressive acts of violence that either lie outside of our imaginations, or acts of violence that disturb the dominant state and/or prevailing national narratives.

"If terrorism is emblematic of the times in which we live," suggest

Zulaika and Douglass, then "it is partly because of the transformative powers of our imaginations" (1996, 186). The power of narratives of terror does not lie only in events of terrorist actions. As Strathern and Stewart posit, that power is also dependent "on the great multiplications of reactions to these acts and the fears that these acts arouse in people's imaginations" (2006, 9). We can, therefore, also define as the unimaginable any shocking and potentially violent response to an event (Strathern & Stewart 2006, 9). With every ETA attack the GAL responded with "an eye for an eye"; and ETA had an ideal recruiting agent in GAL and its activities. ETA's propaganda machine could now argue that despite the transition to democracy, the state operated no differently than it had under Franco. The story and anti-story of the death squads, then, are keys to understanding two related points about the terror narrative in Spain: the phantasmatic relationship between terror and the state; and the legitimating function of state sanctioned violence.

Fantasy and the GAL (the story)

> The rule of law is defended in the courts, and in the salons, but also in the sewers (Former Spanish Prime Minister Felipe González quoted in Woodworth 2001, 217).

Viva González!

The process in which an authoritarian state transforms itself peacefully into a liberal-democratic one is fraught with paradoxes. Writing about the Eastern European transition to liberalism, for example, Žižek states:

> To put it bluntly, those who triggered the process of democratization and fought the greatest battles are not those who today enjoy its fruits, not because of a simple usurpation and deception on the part of the present winners, but because of a deeper structural logic. Once the process of democratization reached its peak, it buried its catalysts [. . .] What we had was a genuine 'primitive accumulation' of democracy, a chaotic story of punkers, students with their sit-ins, committees for human rights, and so on, which literally became invisible the moment the new system established itself—and with it, its own myth of origin was likewise extinguished. (2006, 15)

A similar process happened in Spain. The idealism of many radicalized youth during Franco's dictatorship quickly dissipated with his death, and most young radicals simply assimilated into the new democratic system. As highlighted in Chapter Two, the Spanish electorate sidelined both the extreme left and right in the first democratic elections after Franco's death, and the process continued throughout the 1980s and 1990s. Evidence of the illegitimacy of extreme ideologies is amply demonstrated in the changes that the PSOE went through in the late 1970s and early 1980s. After the party's legalization in the mid-1970s, the PSOE moved to the centre by dropping its old class-based rhetoric for a social-democratic program of economic and social modernization. The move was accompanied by the adoption of nationalist rhetoric that included referring to the Spanish "nation" and not to the Spanish "state" (Smith & Mar-Molinero 1996, 26). Many members of the Socialist party, and its media supporters, such as the newspaper *El País*, reinforced the link between modernization and a "new beginning" by equating "national reconciliation" with "democracy" (Edles 1998, 56). All of these rhetorical choices were bolstered by the promise of Spain re-entering Europe and acquiring European values. In their early campaign slogans, the PSOE made explicit the connection between Europe and modernization: "The Key to Europe is in your hands. Vote PSOE." Although González was perceived as an inexperienced politician, he was also without experience in the (profane) politics of the Franco era, and thus was presented as the literal embodiment of the new (sacred) generation and a new beginning for Spain (Edles 1998, 76).

The ideological reorientation of the PSOE was successful, and in 1982 the party won national government for the first time since the 1930s, led by the youthful and charismatic González. Although the PSOE victory was expected, the scale of it astounded everyone: nearly 50 percent of the Spanish electorate opted for the Socialists. As Paddy Woodworth notes:

> It was a landslide victory, and a landmark: the long-haired generation of the Sixties had come in from the streets and taken over the national parliament. This was the youngest government Spain had ever had, and one of the youngest in Europe. Not one of its members could be tarred with the ugly brush of the dictatorship. This was to be a real, new start. (2001, 6)

The PSOE is credited for consolidating Spanish democracy, integrating Spain into the European Union, and promoting rapid economic growth. More importantly, the PSOE was also responsible for reworking Spanish nationalism in a post-Franco era. As the ruling party, it appeared to respect the country's cultural and linguistic pluralism by ushering in the

Autonomous Communities. The PSOE celebrated the quincentennial of Columbus's "discovery" of the Americas in 1992 by framing that historical and imperial discourse in terms of technological and scientific advance. The party also presented Spain as a bridge between Europe and Latin America, and between Europe and the Islamic world (Smith & Mar-Molinero 1996, 26). As these reorientations indicate, the PSOE was successful in imagining and constructing a new nationalist mythology that would placate much of the pluralist population in the 1980s and early 1990s.

Yet although most parts of Spain quickly transitioned into a respectable two party democracy, one section of the Spanish state remained in the margins of the revolution: ETA. To the surprise of the Spanish left, ETA not only continued its attacks, but intensified them. In the words of Žižek, "In working through the symptom we are precisely bringing about the past, producing the symbolic reality of the past" (1989, 57). If ETA was a symptom of the Franco regime, that symptom reminded the Spanish state that the unimaginable was always already present. The PSOE believed, wrongly, that with a socialist party in government, the ETA problem would be solved and that ETA would cease its activities. At the very least, the socialists expected some breathing room from the Basque radicals until they settled into government. As Encarnación points out, "championing human rights and advocating self-governance for Spain's ethnic minorities are signature issues for the PSOE" (2007, 951). Moreover, many of the party's leaders themselves were victims of Franco's repression, and as the leading opposition party at the inception of democracy, the PSOE, along with other parties from the left, harshly criticized the Suárez administration for its heavy-handedness in handling ETA. For Basque nationalists, however, the newly invented nationalizing mythologies promulgated by the PSOE were still illegitimate. Basques were deeply sceptical of Spanish democracy, and saw no clear break with the old regime.

The election of González and the PSOE in 1982, then, led to tougher antiterrorist policies in order to appease right-wing critics who believed the PSOE to be soft on terrorism (Clark 1990, 52). One of the immediate consequences of this shift in policy was registered in the mass-media. The PSOE quickly introduced laws allowing for the forced closure of media outlets deemed to be apologists for terrorism. The laws targeted the Basque newspaper *Egin* and the magazine *Punto y Hora*, and journalists, editors and even interviewees from both publications were routinely arrested and charged with "publishing articles that insulted the Spanish government and the king" (Clark 1990, 53). Also targeted were the leaders of Herri Batasuna who were frequently in court in this period for remarks made in press conferences, now read as apologia to terrorism. The PSOE reversed the amnesty trend, and the record of González's first two years in office was scarred by countless reports of alleged torture in Spanish prisons. According to Aretxaga, in response to Basque violence the PSOE government combined an intensification of repression with the offer of a political exit strategy for ETA members: personal pardons, or "the reinsertion" as it was generally known (2005, 156). The Socialist government was thus caught between reform and continuity. Each dramatic advance in democracy, from the legalization of the Communist Party, and the negotiation of the Constitution and the establishment of the Autonomous Communities, was shadowed by the threat of a military coup and the State's reactive recourse to its own modes of violence. By 1983, the GAL, sponsored by the Socialist government, would launch its dirty war in French territory to deal with the terrorist problem.

The "Dirty War"

The organizational principle of a dirty war, according to Woodworth, is the inverse of the idea in any normal military strategy, or indeed in any enterprise involving a hierarchy: "Unlike conventional military commanders, the organisers of a dirty war protect themselves by knowing as little as possible about the details of the operations on the ground. This gives them 'deniability' should any embarrassing facts come to light" (2001, 46). In an interview with Paddy Woodworth, senior writer for *El País*, Javier Pradera, hypothesized the GAL affair as follows:

> [. . .] someone in the state apparatus, we don't know who, accepts the offers from these groups who say: 'Give us money and cover and we will clean up things for you. If you give us a free hand, we will finish off ETA in a very short space of time. We don't want to do it in an amateur way, like it was done until now, and under the fear that we would be reprimanded for doing it. We want to do it with the security of having the political support of a left-wing and democratic party'. Well knowing them [the PSOE leadership] as I knew them at the time, I think they could have fallen into that trap. (quoted in Woodworth 2001, 409)

As the following excerpt from an editorial of the Madrid newspaper *Diario 16* demonstrates, the mass-mediated narratives of the time did not necessarily regard the use of state violence as taboo:

> The activists of ETA, who are not men, who are beasts. To what degree do

beasts deserve human rights? . . . Beasts are enclosed behind the heaviest bars that there are in the village; first they are hunted by all kinds of tricks. And if in the venture someone is killed, bad luck, or good luck. . . . No human rights come into play when a tiger must be hunted. The tiger is searched after, is hounded, is captured, and if necessary killed. (*Diario 16*, March 23, 1981, quoted in Zulaika and Douglass 1996, 157)

While some commentators in the news media speculated that the GAL might be financed by wealthy Basque businessmen, given that ETA's activities were hindering the economic development in the Basque Country, ETA supporters had no doubt that they "were now being subjected to a full-scale clandestine offensive by the Spanish security forces" (Woodworth 2001, 97).

The masterminding of a dirty war was facilitated by the presence of ultra-right paramilitary groups that had operated in Spain since the early 1970s, and these groups were willing to do the government's dirty work. Militant opposition to the Franco dictatorship in the early 1970s had provoked a resurgence of the Spanish ultra-right, and paramilitary groups became commonplace in the Basque Country in the years before, and after, the death of General Franco. Clandestine groups known as the *incontrolados* emerged and operated outside of the Francoist legal system, but were either tolerated or sponsored by the state apparatus (Woodworth 2001, 46). It was common for these groups to attack Basques on the streets, in bars, on public transport and at demonstrations (Clark 1990, 39). According to the historian Paul Preston, "the first signs that there was a fascist right in Spain ready to use violence outside the usual state channels and institutions of repression had been seen in the universities in 1963" (1990, 167). As a response to the growth of leftist student groups the *Defensa Universitaria* emerged, its members including mainly Falangists, together with a few Carlists and extreme right-wing Catholics. They acted, according to Preston, "both as police spies, informing on leftist militants, and as terror squads, breaking up anti-regime meetings, beating up individuals, and intimidating female leftists" (167). By 1970, the position of hard-line Francoism had worsened and *Defensa Universitaria* was reorganized as *Los Guerrilleros de Cristo Rey* (the Guerrillas of Christ the King), and strengthened by the addition of paid thugs, a process probably masterminded by Admiral Carrero Blanco's more or less private intelligence service, the *Servicio de Documentación de la Presidencia del Gobierno*. It was common knowledge in the Basque Country, according to Aretxaga, that these groups were linked to the security forces, in particular the Civil Guard (2005, 218). These loose organizations were not in any sense political parties, but rather freelance "patriots" organizing themselves wherever they perceived Francoism to be in danger. They operated in an ad hoc fashion under many names, which they changed according to their location and targets. In 1975, the *Batallón Vasco-Español* (BVE, Basque Spanish Battalion) was formed by military officers, coordinated by units of the Spanish military and staffed by the mercenaries who were responsible for Spain's first dirty war. The BVE killed five ETA members and injured over two dozen others without any connection to terrorism (Encarnación 2007, 961). Encarnación, in fact, argues that the creation of the BVE in 1975 "coincided with the beginning of the transition to democracy because the military probably reasoned that battling ETA under democracy would be a lot more difficult than under the Franco regime" (961).

But neither of these groups was as dangerous and as far-reaching as the *Grupos Antiterroristas de Liberación* (GAL), which was sponsored by members of the Socialist Party and allegedly endorsed by Prime Minister Felipe González after negotiations with the French government failed. The Spanish government attempted to persuade the French government that Spanish democracy was genuine and that the Basques had no legitimate reason to resort to violence. When the French failed to respond, the Spanish government launched a policy of direct intervention against ETA on French soil (Clark 1990, 61). The GAL had a dual agenda: to eliminate ETA members; and to persuade the French to act more forcefully against Basque refugees. The BVE was the prototype for the GAL, the overall goal of the Spanish government being, according to Aretxaga, "to create a state of disorganization and psychological pressure and, through intimidation, to lessen ETA(m)'s political control" (2005, 156).

Since the attacks took place almost exclusively in France, the Spanish government and the security apparatus often condemned the GAL as murderous and criminal, qualifying that approach by adding that since they were operating in France there was nothing the Spanish government could do about the group's activities. Other politicians, such as the former Francoist Interior Minister Manuel Fraga, refused to condemn the GAL, stating that it was "the logical result of the action of ETA. He who lives by the sword dies by the sword" (quoted in Woodworth 2001, 96). Although the Dirty War was effective in damaging ETA's infrastructure, it did not destroy ETA. The group emerged from its experiences with the GAL as a stronger, more efficient force with more political credibility. However, the GAL was successful in the sense that it made the French government cooperate on antiterrorist measures, thus ending the so-called French sanctuary. In Spain there was widespread ambiguity in public reactions to the GAL phenomenon. Although many citizens took the pragmatic view that ETA deserved a taste of its own medicine, for others the increasingly credible allegations of police complicity with the GAL began to corrode the PSOE's reputation as a democratic party. For Basque radicals, moreover, the GAL scandal consolidated the perception that the transition to democracy was a fascist façade, and it radicalized even more Basque youth.

The first major press investigations into the operations of GAL appeared in Spain in the spring of 1984. They were based on revelations from GAL mercenaries, and for the most part appeared in the newspaper *Diario 16*. The interviewees colourfully described the GAL as "an exterminating angel" (irony, given that is the name of a film by Luis Buñuel) and asserted that the GAL does not kill innocent people (Woodworth 2001, 189). By the early 1990s it was clear that at least some of the money used to hire GAL assassins came from secret accounts maintained by the Spanish Interior Ministry. Once the story of state involvement in terror was broken in the media in the early 1990s, the scandal eventually contributed to the end of the fourteen-year reign of Felipe González and the Socialist Party in the general elections of 1996. The investigation, which continued for more than fifteen years, eventually led to the confessions of very senior Socialists. However, the identity of the shadowy *Señor X*, the GAL mastermind, was never uncovered. The name derives from the investigating judge, Baltasar Garzón, who infamously alluded to such a person and the idea of a *Señor X*, the mysterious and sinister mastermind purported to be behind the GAL, caught on in the Spanish media. In the GAL media narrative *Señor X* was, if not the star protagonist, then certainly an ingenious plot device. The name has appeared, according to Woodworth, in countless political speeches, headlines and cartoons (2001, 221). Although *Señor X* was closely associated with Felipe González, Garzón always insisted that the X is a symbol referring to someone or something unknown, and nothing more.

The identity of *Señor X*, indeed whether or not such a person exists, still remains a mystery. The official state investigations into the GAL absolved Prime Minister Felipe González of any wrongdoing, but they did establish links between his administration and the GAL, and several high-ranking people from his administration were held to account. These included two policemen involved in the affair, José Amedo and Michel Domínguez. When Amedo and Domínguez were first sentenced harshly for organizing some of the GAL attacks, the state, at the time, was absolved of responsibility. Woodworth suggests that most people in Spain were probably relieved by this outcome: "Insofar as an honourable effort had been made to investigate the GAL, democratic justice had done its job, without shaking the state, or the ruling party, to its foundations" (2001, 241). But the story was not to end there. Amedo and Domínguez cooperated with the judiciary to bring José Barrionuevo, the Secretary of State for Security, Rafael Vera, Minister of the Interior, and Julián Sancristobal, the Civil Governor of the province of Vizcaya, to justice. In 1998 they were sentenced to ten years in prison. Lesser conspirators also received lengthy prison terms for their part in the criminal GAL venture. In the words of a leading Popular Party jurist, "the pestilence of the sewers had reached the best salon in the palace" (quoted in Woodworth 2001, 256).

The anti-story

I couldn't care less about the rule of law if someone wants to kill me. Because the rule of law never protected me against ETA. It never protected anyone else either. When I die, I am going to regret only one thing, not having been able to kill the *etarras*, not having liquidated all of them. That would have solved problems for a lot of people. (José Amado quoted in Woodworth 2001, 200)

As Woodworth (2001) and Encarnación (2007) point out, scholarly attention to Spain's dirty war has been scant. For Encarnación, "this may well be the result of how ill-fitting the disturbing story of the GAL is within the prevailing narratives of Spain's Cinderella-like transformation from a paradigm of authoritarian rule under Franco to a model new democracy" (951–52). This is also true within Spain, where literature on the GAL affair (whether popular or academic) is scant. The mainstream film by Miguel Courtois, GAL (2006), has gone some way in rectifying this situation, but the film pays close attention to the media investigation of the scandal by the daily newspaper *Diario 16*, and does not attempt to synthesize the larger questions raised by the GAL, such as the downfall of the Socialist Party and the nature of Spanish democracy itself. This is in sharp contrast to the plethora of literature published monthly in Spain about ETA and its role in the potential Balkanization of Spain.

According to Encarnación in "Democracy and Dirty Wars in Spain" (2007), the mainstream media narrative to explain the emergence of the GAL is straightforward: the PSOE desired to show that it was not "soft on terrorism" and "to demonstrate to the military and the right-wing opposition that the PSOE possessed the will and the know-how to battle ETA" (2007, 952). Encarnación, however, argues that the emergence of the GAL was "a product of the institutional culture of the Spanish military inherited from the Franco regime and [was] shaped largely by that regime's history of counterterrorism practices" (952). The emergence of government-sponsored death squads, he argues, "is best understood as a continuation rather than a departure of the state's counterterrorism strategies" (952). He suggests that it is unlikely that the PSOE would have embraced the strategies of violence against ETA were it not for the existence of such proclivities within the military (960). These continuities expose the myth, which pervades much of the literature on Spain's democratization, that the end of the Franco regime in 1977 meant "a clean break with the past" (964). There is probably some truth to the claim that the PSOE wanted to prove its credentials in government by appearing "tough on terrorism," even if that meant transgressing the rule of law. Encarnación is also probably correct in suggesting that there were continuities in the Spanish military from the Francoist era to the democratic era, and that the Socialist government did not have full control of the traditionally autonomous Spanish military.

I am not interested here in detailing the investigation process that led to the uncovering of the GAL scandal and its state supporters, because it has been done well elsewhere, particularly in Paddy Woodworth's *Dirty War, Clean Hands* (2001). What does compel my attention are two different narratives of projection related to the GAL scandal: the PSOE's narratives of justification of the dirty war; and the PP's narrative of *pasando página* (turning the page, moving on), which sought to deflect the potential damage to the credibility of the Spanish state and its armed forces caused by the GAL. This analysis highlights how narratives of the GAL scandal in Spain were intertwined with the narrative of *las dos Españas*. My analysis then leads to a discussion of the legitimizing role that the GAL scandal played for the Spanish state and how that role contributed to reinforcing the post-Franco order of things, once again undermining the myth of a peaceful transition.

Narratives of justification and continuity

The GAL investigation by the media and the judiciary took some fifteen years. During the 1990s, the media battle became fierce, especially between the newspapers *El País* and *El Mundo*. *El País* saw itself as the Spanish newspaper of record, a claim that *El Mundo* regarded as meaning tacit support for the Socialist government. *El Mundo*, on the other hand, considered itself committed to investigative journalism, while its critics argued that it was a sensationalist instrument at the service of right-wing interests, particularly those of the PP. But as Woodworth points out, "despite the inevitable media distortions and partisan editorial interests, it could be argued that such ferocious competition drove much sensitive information into the public domain" (2001, 323). One remarkably consistent factor, however, was the paradoxical narrative that the Socialist leadership promoted about itself and its relation to the GAL. The PSOE wanted to stress that it was not responsible for the GAL. Yet it also promoted the idea that the GAL's activities were heroic and deserved the gratitude of the people. In an interview, the former Prime Minister Felipe González pointed out that the fight against terrorism was an unequal struggle, precisely because democrats were obliged by their own convictions to use legal methods, while the terrorists could use whatever violent methods they chose (Woodworth 2001, 264). Another standard narrative of justification was that incidents of terrorism in Spain are like those in other countries where terrorism has attacked democracy: "but the whole world applauds Clinton and Bush, where there is a terrorist attack, people say 'Let's go after them wherever they are hiding.' Applause all round. 'There is a president capable of fighting terrorism'" (González quoted in Woodworth 2001, 342).

The Socialists' narrative of justification had some credibility when the former Prime Minister González said that "people do not want to understand that we inherited a State apparatus, in its entirety, from the dictatorship" (quoted in Woodworth 2001, 407). The ghosts of Spain's transition to democracy could always potentially erupt into public view, reminding Spaniards of the unimaginable. The state sponsored death squads were also proof that the transition from authoritarianism to democracy was not as smooth as previously thought. The difficulties in controlling the military might have been a powerful argument to present to the Spanish electorate. But the Socialists resorted to left-wing rhetoric that evoked the politics of the 1930s rather than the 1990s. Instead of representing a modern, centre-left party, the PSOE came to symbolize the rhetorical excess of the narrative of *las dos Españas*, which no longer had the same appeal in a Spain that belonged to NATO and the EU. By the late 1980s, the PSOE had increasingly resorted to branding the democratic right as inheritors of Francoism, stressing the need to support the left against the right, even comparing the opposition leader José María Aznar to Franco and Hitler (Hooper 2006, 63). At a PSOE summer camp, González said that Barrionuevo and Vera were "found guilty because they belonged to a left-wing government," hinting that the whole scandal was some kind of conspiracy orchestrated by the undemocratic right (2001, 398). In street protests, supporters chanted slogans from what seemed to be a time warp: "*Vosotros, fascistas, sois los terroristas*" (You fascists are the real terrorists). This was an old anti-Franco slogan, which according to Woodworth, the PSOE had not used against the parliamentary right since the transition: "'They are putting us in prison like they did before,' they roared, forgetting that the condemned men had enjoyed all the guarantees of due process which had been systematically denied to the victims of fascism—and to the victims of the GAL" (2001, 394).

Many socialists were aggrieved that the dirty war, which they believed began before they took office and ended during their mandate, should be attributed to the PSOE: "We have decided not to avenge the past out of respect for peace, progress and the future. We do not want to put in question the transition to democracy, which would deny the Spanish people a part of their collective history of which they feel proud" (González quoted in Woodworth 2001, 394). According to Woodworth, this extraordinary statement implies that the transition would somehow be negated if the PSOE told its full story (394). The PSOE's hint of something murky lying in the shadows and depths of the Spanish transition to democracy had very different lessons for the Spanish left and right. The Socialist rhetoric that the right are fascists in democratic disguise no longer washed with much of the Spanish public. The PP, as the leading opposition party, naturally sought to make political capital out of revelations that linked closely the González government to crimes of kidnapping, torture and murder. But when the Popular Party assumed power in 1996, the "seductive logic of statesmanship" and "reasons of state," came into play, and Aznar repeated the ambiguous phrase "pasar página" whenever the GAL issue arose (2001, 314).

A CESID (*Centro Superior de Información de la Defensa*, Spanish Intelligence Agency) document leaked to the Spanish media, and considered to be the "Founding Document of the GAL," confirmed that the PP took its policy of turning over the page seriously. The document underscored "the leading role played by the Spanish military intelligence in creating the GAL and in enticing the PSOE into endorsing the use of extra-judicial killings in its struggle against ETA" (Encarnación 2007, 964). The PP understandably did not want to delve deeper into the scandal because the CESID papers cast Spanish military intelligence and the Guardia Civil in a bad light. In Woodworth's words:

> The Partido Popular, and its electorate, had no problem in pursuing Socialist functionaries, and even a few senior police officers, for operating death squads. But it went against every conservative fibre at the Partido Popular's core to raise questions which were likely to bring the Spanish army and the Guardia Civil into serious disrepute. (2001, 314)

Instead, Aznar insisted that the need to modernize Spain was more important than investigating the GAL scandal (339). Not surprisingly, Aznar's government chose not to release a single CESID paper to the investigating judges. In an editorial *El Mundo* editor Ramírez told Aznar that his decision was "the first great disappointment of your mandate." He highlighted the paradox that, in insisting on the secrecy of documents that had (mostly) already been published, the government had effectively authenticated them (Woodworth 2001, 319). The PP government under Aznar subsequently pardoned most of the high public officials who had been found guilty in relation to the GAL scandal.

Meanwhile, a significant side-show was playing out in the Spanish courts and media during this time. Relatives of thousands of torture victims and disappearances under the Chilean and Argentinian dictatorships had approached Spanish investigating magistrates to see whether these crimes could be tried under Spanish jurisdiction. Judges such as Baltasar Garzón thought they could be, both under International law against torture, war crimes and genocide, and on the grounds that some of the victims had been Spanish citizens (Woodworth 2001, 349). Interestingly, many people in the PP, the PP appointed chief prosecutor at the Audiencia Nacional, Eduardo Fungairiño, and the Attorney General Jesús Cardenal, disagreed. In December 1997 a report on the subject by the chief prosecutor sparked a parliamentary row that revealed how deep and complex the fractures in Spanish society had become:

> [The chief prosecutor] argued that the Argentinian military, in seizing power illegally, had 'only sought the temporary substitution of the established constitutional order through an institutional intervention which aimed [. . .] to remedy the inadequacies of that constitutional order and maintain the public peace'. (Woodworth 2001, 349)

The chief prosecutor, then, mounted a legal defence of military dictatorship as a guarantor of public order. According to Woodworth, a similar statement from such an authority would have provoked a furore in any democracy. In Spain, where the PP and the PSOE had diametrically opposed views on Franco's military rebellion against the Republic, Fungairiño's statement reopened raw wounds (349). Understandably, the PSOE, supported by the United Left, led the charge against Fungairiño and Cardenal. But unexpectedly, the Basque Nationalist Party voted with the government to block the PSOE protest: "The party argued that it could not accept any lessons on democracy and dirty wars from abroad from the Socialists, as long as that party was defending a leader accused of masterminding death squads in the Basque Country" (349).

Such developments demonstrate how the GAL scandal was narratively appropriated as the latest battleground in the war between *las dos Españas*. There were, however, some innovations to the long-running narrative script. Although the PP became the chief defender of due process and the rule of law, its perceived defence of military dictatorships also resurfaced the murky and unimaginable Francoist past of the Spanish right. The PP's error in seeming to defend the Argentinian and Chilean dictatorships sowed doubts in many Spaniards of the PP's democratic credentials. It is understandable that some Spaniards perceived some truth in the PSOE's overblown rhetoric that the PP were really fascists in democratic disguise. But the biggest errors, at least discursively, were committed by the PSOE, which failed to project a convincing and sound narrative about its misadventures in using paramilitary death squads. Instead of seeking to debate Spain's transition to democracy and the role of the military in democratic Spain, the Socialists resorted to playing the victim in Spanish politics, projecting the narrative that the left was being ejected from power unfairly by the right in an electoral replay of the Spanish Civil War. This narrative frame failed to convince the Spanish public and the PSOE was sent to the electoral wilderness for eight years. For its part, the PP's policy of turning the page appeared simply to preserve the status quo and the post-Franco order of things. Perhaps the PP should have considered Tzvetan Todorov's suggestion that before turning a page, you need to read it (2003, 6). Leaving the discursive murk hidden only ensured that it would resurface in another guise eight years later with the March 11, 2004, terrorist attacks in Madrid.

Conclusion: On the state, power and the imagination

The GAL scandal had all the characteristics of a good story. The story was about state officials who become terrorists for the purpose of eliminating Basque terrorism. To that end they invented a terrorist organization called the GAL. Zulaika and Douglass suggest that the use of state terror under the auspices of the GAL exemplifies the "epistemic murk" by which narratives of terrorist savagery "become indispensable for maintaining terrorism discourse and policy" (Zulaika and Douglass 1996, 160). Since the Basque terrorist during Spain's transition to democracy was widely regarded as a frontal assault on Spanish norms, the state apparatus positioned terrorism beyond the ordinary realm of humanity. According to Zulaika and Douglass, such positioning translates immediately into the premise that:

we cannot afford to be too humane when confronting terroristic inhumanity, that perhaps we should not be overly concerned with law while combating evil itself; that we, too, perhaps must practice a little terrorism, but of the right kind, in order to contain the malignancy. Confronted by the unmitigated evil of "terrorism," shouldn't we accordingly be prepared to break, or at least bend, any rule ourselves in order to behead the repellent monster? (1996, 155–56)

Or put another way, Hardt and Negri argue that "today the enemy, just like the war itself, comes to be at once banalized (reduced to an object of routine police repression) and absolutized (as the Enemy, an absolute threat to the ethical order)" (2000, 13). The fact, therefore, that terrorism is imagined as the cause of unimaginable mass destruction and casualties, and as a threat to democracy, peace, human rights, ways of life, civilization and the international system itself, helps justify the state's fight against the unimaginable by also entering into that unimaginable realm. In doing so, the state appears to be at once in control and out of control.

In its desire to overcome the terrorist's power, then, the Spanish state relied on fantasy. In order to defeat terrorism, the state became the imagined terrorist. It is not too far-fetched to suggest that the Spanish state was able to mimic or parody the ideological excesses of Basque terrorism, blurring the boundaries between fiction and reality and also "endowing encounters between the state and terrorism with a phantom quality" (Aretxaga 2005, 263). The PSOE's implication in the fantasy of terrorism confirmed the worst fears and anxieties of many Basques about the haunting power of the Spanish state. By fetishizing terrorist techniques, the Spanish state was transformed into the all-powerful and highly threatening enemy. Just as ETA deploys a war mentality against the state, so the state becomes trapped in a war mentality against Basque terrorism (173).

The issue of whether non-state actors or the state itself resort to violence to further their political ends raises the key question of legitimation. According to Richard Jackson, "perhaps the most important feature of counterterrorism discourse in the EU after September 11 is that it is founded on a series of misinterpretations and misunderstandings of terrorism and its characteristics" (2007, 242). The dominant discursive conception of terrorism, he argues, appears to be ideologically and politically biased in that it ignores the arguably much greater problem of state terrorism:

If terrorism is understood to mean violence directed towards or threatened against civilians designed to instil terror or intimidate a population for political reasons, then it can be argued that state terrorism is arguably a much greater security issue than dissident or nonstate terrorism. Significantly, it can be argued that a great deal of the contemporary substate terrorism is a direct response to prior state repression and terrorism. (242)

This paradox is also noted by Belinda Davis, who reminds us that, as an act, terrorism has traditionally been most commonly associated with the state, given the degree to which we perceive states to be "the legitimate bearers of a monopoly of power, including over the means of physical violence" (2003, 38). This paradox, she argues, "is consistent with the definitions offered by Laqueur and some others: that so-called terror has historically contained a potent element of legitimacy" (38).

In order to explore this point, it is useful to consider Žižek's discussion in *The Metastases of Enjoyment* (2005) of Rob Reiner's film, *A Few Good Men* (1992), a court-martial drama about two US marines accused of murdering a fellow soldier. Žižek demonstrates clearly that what holds together a community most deeply is not so much identification with the Law that regulates the community's normal everyday practices, but rather "identifi-cation with a specific form of transgression of the Law, of the Law's suspension" [original emphasis] (55):

> The military prosecutor claims that the two Marines' act was a deliberate murder, whereas the defence succeeds in proving that the defendants simply followed the so-called 'Code Red,' which authorises the clandestine night-time beating of a fellow-soldier who, in the opinion of his peers or the superior officer, has broken the ethical code of the Marines. [. . .] The function of this 'Code Red' is extremely interesting: it condones an act of transgression—illegal punishment of a fellow-soldier—yet at the same time it reaffirms the cohesion of the group—it calls for an act of supreme identification with group values. (2005, 54–55)

Like the Marines in *A Few Good Men*, the GAL operatives used clandestine methods that were part of an unwritten code to fight ETA's unimaginable violence. According to Žižek, explicit, public rules do not suffice for the control of public order, so they have to be supplemented by a clandestine unwritten code (55). That code, he argues, must remain under cover of night, unacknowledged, unutterable: in public, everybody pretends either to know nothing about it, or to actively deny its existence (56). The narra-tives of state terror are also simultaneously public and secret, wrapped in fictional plots and images. The unwritten code of clandestine violence violates the explicit rules of community life. Yet, at the same time, that code exerts pressure on the individual to comply with the state's mandate of group identification (56). The GAL scandal thus illustrated, as Žižek suggests, that the state can transgress public rules in order to fight transgressions it defines as operating in the realm of the unimaginable.

In producing terror, then, the state actually produces itself, at least discursively, in the imaginations of the people experiencing the full brunt of state power. Terror here lies not simply in great acts of violence, but as Davis suggests, in "the potential for future, usually unpredictable violence, and therefore it is also about fear and rhetoric" (2003, 39). It does not matter that the GAL only killed twenty-seven people. More importantly, with the very unpredictability of the GAL, the state had the ability to control the Basques through fear, and this fear served as the source of state legitimacy. This points to what Žižek calls "the performative power of political discourse" (2005, 21). Accordingly, it is arguable that the performative and theatrical nature of the GAL's dirty war was a remnant or trace of the former Franco dictatorship's own performative power, now sublimated through GAL to preserve the state's discursive power in the imagination(s) of the Basque terrorists. The GAL, as a counterterrorism discourse and/or strategy, functioned ideologically to maintain the state's dominant position by delegitimizing all forms of nonstate, counterhegemonic violence.

The GAL scandal was thus a vexing phenomenon. Although this example of state terror was new, it was linked to the old practices of state violence. If the relationship between terror and the state was an intimate experience by which the state set the stage for a political fantasy, to what extent did this fantasy convince the Spanish electorate of the state's efficacy? If many Spaniards could rationalize the presence of the GAL in terms of an eye for an eye, could they also accept the state's role as murderer, when memories of state violence and the profane politics of the Franco era remained fresh? It is one thing to turn a blind eye to an unaffiliated group made up of mercenaries who kill *etarras*; it is another thing altogether to accept that that group is being organized and financed by one's own democratically elected representatives. The unimaginable here is not in the fact that the state employed paramilitary death squads. Rather, the scandal of the GAL lay in the realm of the unimaginable because it challenged the unstated national myth laid down during Spain's transition to democracy: that the violence of the state belonged to Spain's murky past, and that past ended with the consolidation of democracy.

As Tzvetan Todorov reminds us: "the recollection of violence past feeds violence in the present: it is a mechanism for revenge" (2003, 170). Police counterterrorist operations in Spain became much more discriminate and selective after 1988. No episode of illegal violence in the state response to ETA has been reported since that time (Alonso & Reinares 2005, 275). Once the GAL scandal was brought to public attention and properly investigated, subsequent governments have been more careful to act within the law. As the next chapter highlights, under the Popular Party government (1996–2004) the strategy was twofold: to toughen the laws on terrorist (and associated) activity; and to develop a rhetoric of radical political polarization by which all dissenting voices are discursively criminalized (Martí et al. 2007, 129). Yet while the Spanish state was not to return to the use of clandestine violence to defeat terror, the idea of revenge and justice continues in the mass-mediated narratives to the present day. As Vázquez Montalbán puts it, *"contra Franco vivíamos mejor"* (we lived better under Franco) (quoted in Gil Calvo 2008, 118), indicating that fighting against an internal and invincible enemy characterized by absolute injustice justified everything. The logic undergirds ETA's use of armed struggle, and it was also one deployed by the Spanish government to fight ETA in the form of the GAL.

The next chapter moves away from the Basque conflict and sets out the political narratives propagated by the Aznar government between 1996 and 2004. When Aznar was elected in 1996, he promised to make Spanish politics boring. As Hooper points out, "For most of his first term, he was as good as his word. But his next spell in office was to be a very different affair. He and his ministers were to lurch from one drama to the next until they met their fate in a nightmare of carnage and reproach" (2006, 73). The chapter explores how the Aznar years explicitly brought back the narrative of *las dos Españas* in Spanish political discourse. The re-polarization of Spanish politics during the Aznar years would have enormous implications on counterterrorism policy, the March 11 terrorist attacks in Madrid and the attempted peace negotiations with ETA in 2006–2007.

CHAPTER FOUR

The Aznar Years (1996–2004)
History, Politics and Narratives of the Spanish "Nation"

> If you wear a T-shirt with a Galician flag, no problem; but if you wear one with a Spanish flag, then people think you're some kind of fascist. (Cristina Boo, former student at Santiago University, quoted in Galán 2006, 2)

Spain, like most Western states, has developed into a stable two party democracy and many of its citizens' concerns are the same as in other similar countries: the welfare state, unemployment, immigration, education and healthcare. Throughout the 1990s, Spain, again like cognate Western states, increasingly experienced a collapse in the ideological vote in national and regional elections. The decline of the traditional divisions around religion and ideology has led to all-embracing main parties. Most voters can be found in the centre and both the PSOE and the PP compete for their votes. Any sign of radicalization towards the left or the right may harm their respective chances in elections. Yet, even before the September 11 terrorist attacks in the USA, Spanish political discourse in the post-Franco era was also dominated by the two controversial issues of terrorism and regional nationalism. These issues tend to be politicized by political elites and consequently receive vast amounts of media coverage. Terrorism and regional nationalism (the centre-periphery divide) are politicized issues that often engender vitriolic political debate on the front pages of Spain's major newspapers. But, the fact that most Spaniards locate themselves at the centre of the political spectrum does not explain the polarization of political discourse over the Aznar years (1996–2004). Nor does the centrist voting behaviour of the Spanish electorate, and the purported collapse of the traditional divisions between left and right under globalization, explain the extreme political rhetoric circulating in the mass-media that emanates from the two major parties.

This chapter argues that the narrative of *las dos Españas*, which was more or less neutralized by the Spanish transition to democracy's myths of compromise and forgetting, resurfaced during the Aznar years and culminated in what became known as *crispación* during Zapatero's first term in office (see Chapter Six). Where once the narrative divisions in Spain were played down to avoid confrontation, since 1996 these divisions have been politically manipulated in order to galvanize certain sections of the community into action, which normally takes the form of non-violent demonstrations across Spanish cities. Although this polarization of the Spanish people and state since 1996 is not as extreme as that of Spain in the 1930s, and certainly not as violent, it has altered the Spanish political landscape, both in terms of rhetoric and discursive imagery. This chapter thus seeks to evaluate the narrative debates related to terrorism/political violence and regionalism/nationalism during the Aznar years. The chapter does not offer an exhaustive account of these narratives, because they are many, complex and multi-layered depending on the constituencies involved. Instead, the remit of this chapter is to highlight some key trends in the political polarization during the Aznar years in order to foreground how that polarization informed and haunted the aftermath of the March 11, 2004 attacks in Madrid and the peace process between ETA and the Spanish government (2006–2007).

Examining the narrative battles between the two major Spanish political parties from 1996 to 2004 helps understand the relevant historical context of these events and how the beliefs that bound the principal political players became fetishes, tied to outdated interpretations of the narrative of *las dos Españas*. This chapter is thus interested in questioning what happens when the ideologies tied to the narratives of *las dos Españas* exist as traces of their former selves. That is, I am concerned with reading the narrative of *las dos Españas* not in terms of ideological conviction but rather as a tool for political manipulation and electoral gain.

In order to discuss these issues, this chapter is split into two sections. The first section challenges the concept of the two Spains and posits that there are in fact multiple Spains. Nonetheless, the section sets out the potency of the narrative of *las dos Españas* and the scholarly debate circulating around Spanish nationalism. I posit that both the Spanish left and right utilize their respective narratives of the Spanish nation in an attempt not only to appeal to the Spanish electorate but also to synthesize their modern electoral platform with their constituent ideological histories. The second section provides an overview of the Popular Party, and then focuses on two specific narratives projected by the Aznar administration that had significant ramifications for two key political events in Spain: the March 11, 2004 attacks; and the peace process with ETA in 2006–2007. The first

Aznarian narrative I call the narrative of no conflict, which refers to Aznar's counterterrorism strategy and the PP's official line. In that strategy terrorism was regarded as a judicial and police matter only, which implied that no underlying conflict needed to be addressed. This narrative reasoning would lead to profound differences between the PP and the PSOE and the eventual political stalemate in the so-called peace process with ETA. I call the second Aznarian narrative the narrative of Spanish glory, which relates to Aznar's reorientation of Spain's foreign policy away from the European Union and into a transatlantic alliance with the USA. With that narrative, Aznar projected the idea that Spain was rightfully reclaiming its status in the international system and that Aznar was marching Spain back into the annals of history. This narrative became the single most contentious issue of Aznar's second term, and tied his image inextricably to that of US President George W. Bush, given the PP government's support for and participation in the invasion of Iraq in 2003. Most commentators agree that Spain's role in the Iraq war was not only highly problematic given the depth of opposition in Spain, but also a motivating factor in the terrorist attacks in Madrid on March 11, 2004, arguably leading to the PP's downfall. The Aznarian narratives were not simply controversial, however. They also challenged some of the founding myths of Spain's transition to democracy. The spectre of Aznarian narratives still haunts Spanish politics today.

Narratives of the nation

En la España moderna, nadie ha dicho nación, durante un siglo y medio, sin decirlo contra alguien (In modern Spain, nobody has used the word nation in a century and a half, without using it against somebody). (Albiac 2008, 25)

In *The Reinvention of Spain* (2007), Sebastian Balfour and Alejandro Quiroga point out that "for generations of Spanish intellectuals, writers and politicians, Spain has been a problem. Some even doubt its existence as a nation" (1). In the recent publishing event *Las historias de España* (2013) José Álvarez Junco and Gregorio de la Fuente trace what they refers to as "historia de la historia de España" (the history of Spanish history) (xv). It is, in essence, an essay on the evolution of "visions" of Spain throughout the centuries, including in its panorama such eminent names in Spanish history as José Ortega y Gasset and Marcelino Menéndez y Pelayo. Reading through their tome, it is remarkable the extent to which Spanish intellectuals had a propensity to declare the trajectory of Spanish history as "exceptional," leading to the long-standing dictum that "España es diferente" (Spain is different). In the collection *Is Spain Different?* (2015) edited by Nigel Townson, the contributors utilize a comparative approach to question the extent to which Spanish history has been exceptional or different to similar European states. While there are some notable divergences, the contributors also point out that, in many respects, Spanish history has not been particularly exceptional.

Scholarly discussion about "Spanish" national identity and nationalism, however, has been surprisingly limited. Indeed, according to some popular historians, for example, Fernando García de Cortázar, Spanish nationalism "has disappeared today as a political, institutional and social reality, or even as a part of the state's public policy" (Núñez 2001, 719). Instead, until the mid-1990s, academics tended to focus on the peripheral national identities, such as Basque, Catalan and Galician, and not on the Spanish per se (707). Balfour and Quiroga point out that the discussion of national and identity in Spain "has tended to be inward-looking, a battleground between Spanish nationalisms and regional nationalisms" (2007, 11). According to Flynn, "As I was told in 1991 by a Spanish acquaintance, 'we had a certain idea about what politics and Spain were supposed to be shoved down our throats for so many years, so why should we care about any of it now?'" (2001, 708). Another theorist, Juan Linz, asserted in 1993 that "there doesn't exist one book about Spanish nationalism and I must confess that I am not able to think of anyone in Spain or abroad who, at present, may have assumed this project" (1993, 82–83). In 2001, Núñez succinctly summed up the state of the field: "At present one of the least researched areas in Spanish politics is the ideological, political, and social presence of Spanish nationalism [as opposed to peripheral nationalisms]" (2001, 719).

For Núñez, scholars both inside and outside of Spain have neglected the Spanish national core, that is, Spanish nationalism and national identity, because of what might be called "the bad reputation of Spanish nationalism at the end of Francoism and because of the desire to embrace a new democratic 'nation' of autonomies after the dictatorship" (1993, 138). He argues that the obvious lack of regard by many politicians and Spaniards for Spain's formal national symbols (for example, the flag, national anthem, and so on) in the 1980s and early 1990s is another likely reason why scholars have downplayed Spanish nationalism in the years after the dictatorship. Spain's national symbols, decided upon during the transition, are too closely associated with Franco and the right to be valued by the majority of the population, especially those on the left (175). In effect, Spanish nationalist discourse disappeared from the public sphere, including from the statements and speeches of most political parties and leaders. For Núñez, this disappearance "was related to the delegitimization of Spanish nationalism, particularly among liberal and left-wing milieux, and expressed itself in a sometimes chaotic fashion in the difficulties felt by most democratic parties during the first phase of the Transition period with public use of the term 'Spain'" (2001, 724).

Since the mid-1990s, however, the issue of what constitutes Spain and Spanish nationalism has emerged as an important topic for many scholars, even if the list of publications is not as extensive as studies of Basque and Catalan nationalism (Balfour 1996; Bastida 1998; Tusell 1999; Fusi 2000; Núñez 2001; Muro & Quiroga 2005; Taibo 2007; Balfour & Quiroga 2007; Humlebæk 2014). After the Aznar years, Spanish nationalism has also become a significant issue in the mass-media and is a regular topic for TV and radio debates. As well as theorizing the traditional two Spains, academics, intellectuals and journalists have tried to synthesize the social changes since Spain's transition to democracy. Attempts to define the Spanish nation on the part of leading Spanish thinkers consist mainly of familiar tropes that are almost always defined in negative terms. These include the "decadence" of the Spanish nation, the internal "enemy," the national "crisis," and, almost always, modern "degeneracy" (Juliá 2004, 18).

Spanish sociologist and political commentator, Enrique Gil Calvo, sees three dominant ideological groupings in Spain, instead of the traditional left and right split, and has sought to explain why and how these groupings are at loggerheads (2008). The first grouping is *el europeo* (the European), which refers to Spaniards who identify as progressive or on the left and strongly support the European Union. These Spaniards agree with Ortega y Gasset's dictum that "Spain is the problem, Europe is the solution," and regard Spain's economic miracle over the last few decades as the direct result of EU financial assistance (2008, 17–18). The second group is *el antiespañol* (*nacionalista*) (the anti-Spanish [nationalist]), which designates Spaniards who resist Spanish as an identity marker and consider themselves to have an exclusive and exceptional identity (this grouping mainly refers to Basques, Catalans and Galicians). And the final group is *el Americano* (*estadounidense*) (the American [United Statesean]), and comprises Spaniards who behave as if they were a US nouveau riche, despite their affinity with the Spanish flag. These Spaniards are usually situated on the right of the political spectrum, are conservative and middle-class. They are the direct inheritors of the old Francoism, and considered themselves defeated by the Spanish transition to democracy and were, until the mid-1990s, on the defensive. Thanks to the victory of the Popular Party in 1996, and the economic boom that followed, these Spaniards have recovered their dominant economic and social status (19). The problem lies, according to Gil

Calvo, in the fact that none of the three Spains is willing to recognize the legitimacy of the others (22).

Gil Calvo further suggests that the Spanish nation is imagined by Spaniards as a body that is ill. Borrowing again from Ortega y Gasset's declaration that Spain is "constitutivamente enferma" (constitutively ill) (Álvarez Junco & de la Fuente 2013, 378). Gil Calvo suggests that sickness of one of the body's parts renders the rest of the body immobile. The breaking up of Spain is, in effect, the excision of a part of the body that will leave the other body parts incomplete and even undesirable. The Spanish nation (body) is thus always in need of therapeutic measures in order to save the health of the ill-stricken whole. The problem is that the politicians (the healers) are in an eternal struggle with each other to treat the ailing body and to choose the right remedies. The PP, the PSOE and the regional nationalists project different narratives to save the body from ever-increasing and ever-threatening diseases in the form of rival political ideologies. For example, during Zapatero's first term in office (2004–2008) the PP peddled the narrative that Spain was in the middle of a grave, national crisis that threatened the state's very existence (see Chapter Six). The worst manifestations of this crisis were the Balkanization of Spain, the end of the political consensus established between the right and the left during Spain's transition to democracy, and Basque terrorism (ETA). For the PSOE, on the other hand, there was no crisis in Spain. Instead, Spain was more or less healthy and the only problems that the country was facing were political conflicts caused by the PP's strategy of *crispación* (a vitriolic form of political polarization) and its incessant strategy of blocking the government's reforms, which the PSOE believed were essential to facilitate better territorial integration (Gil Calvo 2008, 154). The PSOE regarded the PP as unilateral and as promoting a politics of resentment. For the PSOE, Aznar was like Franco, a patriarch who attempted to reconstruct a patrimonial Spain by excluding socialists and nationalists from government institutions. And finally, to complicate matters, the regional nationalists were almost as pessimistic on the future of Spain as the PP. They continued to denounce Spanish centralism, which they decried as hindering their political institutions and capacities for self-government. They read their national identities as fragile and under threat by both globalization and the imperialism of the Castilian language (154).

There are then, in agreement with Gil Calvo, three different narratives of the Spanish nation that are at political odds in contemporary Spanish politics. As he points out, the more than five million immigrants who have entered Spain since the early 1990s could also be considered another social grouping. His argument is that there are no longer two Spains as there were in 1936, but multiple Spains. And these Spains are further complicated by the existence of the seventeen Autonomous Communities, each with its own regional identity (20).

The complex logic of multiple Spains notwithstanding, the Spanish mass-media continues to refer to the two Spains. It is possible that much of the mainstream media does not want to define regional nationalists as special groupings, for that would guarantee them a discursive political character on a par with the two major political parties. Indeed, that is still discursively unacceptable in Spain, especially for the right. The political character of immigrants is also more or less ignored in the Spanish media, except before elections, but even then, attention is scant. That said, although I acknowledge the problematical nature of the two Spains theory to explain the Spanish nation, what interests me is the persistence of the left and right divide in Spanish nationalist narratives. Spaniards cannot be neatly situated in either one or the other political camp, but the main schisms and differences between the PP and the PSOE on the question of territorial integrity, and the devolution of powers, are significant in that they feed into the logic of discourses of (counter)terrorism. It is important to consider, then, both the traditional right-wing and left-wing nationally narrative as glossed by Xosé-Manoel Núñez (2001).

Right-wing national narrative

The Spanish right defines Spain as a single, though multicultural, nation. In their view, "further symbolic recognition of Spain's cultural plurality would be an excessive concession" (Núñez 2001, 731). Spanish right-wing intellectuals highlight that the Spanish regions have always been a part of a greater national community whose best incarnation is the present State of the Autonomous Communities (730). According to this teleological conception of history, argues Núñez, "Spain is a true outcome of historical experience, and its objective 'body' has adopted different forms over time" (731). In contrast, right-wing observers and politicians accuse the stateless nationalisms of appealing to "historical fantasy and a non-scientific literary imagination," the rhetoric of stateless nationalisms thus being merely the inventions of second rank intellectuals (731). The PP advocates full uniformity of power competencies for all Autonomous Communities, meaning that every Autonomous Community should more or less have the same rights and concessions. The PP discourse denies, however, that the nationalities have the capacity to be sovereign, and rejects the idea of "divided sovereignty" proposed by minority nationalist parties (734).

Spanish right-wing intellectuals publish a plethora of reactive literature, (books and essays that critically respond to left-wing literature) which often become veritable best-sellers. Yet, much of this literature, according to Núñez, "is not concerned with theorizing on the Spanish nation, and even less with explicitly vindicating Spanish nationalism" (730). Instead, such publications "strongly criticize Basque radical nationalism, pointing out its anti-democratic and violent aspects" (730). Right-wing nationalism, and particularly the PP's policies in the Basque Country and Catalonia, have made good use of confrontations with the peripheral nationalists and have exploited the language conflict. During the 1980s and 1990s a number of books and leaflets, as well as articles in journals and newspapers, insisted on the discriminatory cultural and linguistic policies implemented by Catalan and Basque nationalists, and warned that Castilian would be persecuted in these regions. For example, there was an orchestrated right-wing offensive against the 1983 Catalonian Linguistic Normalization Law, which re-affirmed Catalan and Castilian as co-official languages in that region (Brassloff 2006, 115). And on 12 September 1993, the conservative daily newspaper *ABC* published a condemnation of the Catalan leader Jordi Pujol and his government with the headline, "Igual que Franco pero al revés: persecución del castellano en Cataluña" (The same as Franco but in reverse: the persecution of Castilian in Catalonia). The article and the newspaper's editorial argued that the level of Catalan teaching being imposed in Catalan schools was comparable with the suppression of Catalan in schools during the Franco regime (Mar-Molinero 2000, 163). This was the first step, such critics claimed, in the Balkanization and destruction of the Spanish nation. At nostalgic stake in most right-wing commentary is the alleged traditional and natural supremacy of Castilian, which reveals that for many members of the Spanish right, "Castilian remains a defining cultural marker of Spanish national identity [and] a common tie uniting Spaniards of any regional origin" (Núñez 2001, 729).

Left-wing national narrative

Despite the Spanish left's difficult history in the twentieth century, it managed to recover a form of Spanish nationalist discourse in the 1980s that can be traced back to the traditions of Spanish regenerationism and liberal republicanism during the early part of the twentieth century (Núñez 2001, 735). According to Núñez, "the new patriotic discourse set in motion by Spanish Socialists since 1982 incorporates appeals to modernity, interregional solidarity and a strong desire for full integration into the European common project symbolized by the European Union, as a way of reinforcing democracy" (736). This discourse, Núñez adds, combines belief in the existence of a Spanish political nation with the recognition of diverse cultural nations (the Basques, Catalans, and Galicians). According to this definition, Spain is a nation of nations, whose existence is legitimized in history. In this narrative, cultural pluralism and political sharing of power with regional administrations is accepted, although Spain is the only entity allowed to have full sovereignty (736). In other words, the Spanish left promotes a form of Spanish patriotism, which avoids the label nationalism, as a necessary way of maintaining the social cohesion of Spain as a political community (738). Some leftist leaders and intellectuals claim that the idea of Spain as a sole cultural and political nation should be emphasized. The aim is to maintain the social balance among Spain's territories and allow the state the capacity to transform society. A strong central state thus serves as a social reform instrument. In this narrative, minority nationalists lack national solidarity, as they seek to avoid contributing financially to the development of Spain's poorest regions (738).

Where is the centre?

We have, therefore, three distinct narratives of the Spanish nation, circulating on either side of the left/right divide. While tenuous, and applied arbitrarily at times, it is, nonetheless, a potent mass-mediated division. Both left and right teleological narratives of the Spanish nation effectively marginalize any regional nationalist claims of difference or sovereignty. The Spanish right, while accepting the plural nature of the Spanish state, denies regional claims for more autonomy by arguing that throughout history Castilian has always been a unifying force on the state, and that the regions suffer from a democratic deficit, as evidenced by nationalist violence and discriminatory language policies. The Spanish left, while more accepting of the idea of Spain being a nation of nations, also considers a strong central government system as imperative for the healthy functioning of the Spanish state. The left's difference with the Spanish right lies more in its use of language and imagery, explicitly rejecting the overt nationalism of the Franco era and instead cloaking its ideology in a more benign patriotism that delegitimizes all forms of nationalism as backward and regressive, including the nationalism of Basques, Catalans and Galicians. The narratorial reluctance to use the term national, or even Spanish, according to Núñez, and the denial of the labels nationalist and nationalism, allowed progressive-oriented intellectuals from the mid-1980s to oppose minority

nationalist claims (724). This strategy consisted of repudiating and criti-
cizing all forms of nationalism as potentially totalitarian, ethnocentric and
exclusive.

The problem, however, posed by the Spanish left and right both positing
the need for a strong centre, is the location and figuration of that centre.
According to Stapell, Madrid has simply been assumed by both Spanish
regionalists and theorists "to represent some kind of vague, yet monolithic,
national identity against which peripheral regions define themselves"
(2007, 177). Stapell suggests that the formation of Spanish national identity, or the perceived imposition of a national identity by some regions, is
not specifically related to Madrid as the centre: "It depends instead on the
domination of institutions that yield power and, subsequently, the ability
to articulate an overlaying national identity on all regions, including the
capital itself" (180). Stapell is correct to suggest that the centre is the state
apparatus rather than Madrid. But his argument denies the fact that Madrid
is narratively mediated (in much of the Spanish media, as well as in the
political rhetoric of regional nationalist parties) as the symbolic and
literal/physical centre of a purportedly quintessential Spain.

This would help explain why the Autonomous Community of Madrid,
under the leadership of Esperanza Aguirre (PP) between 2003 and 2012,
tended to adopt the worst rhetorical excesses of Basque nationalism, which
Aguirre herself considered to be Spain's biggest problem. Aguirre was (and
is) one of the PP's strongest powerbrokers, and is often compared to
Margaret Thatcher. She promoted, according to historian and political
commentator José Luis Calleja, a narrative that Madrid is the quintessential, authentic Spain. The Zapatero administration did not understand this
Madrid, and worse still, treated it with contempt (2008, 87). This is,
according to Calleja, "el victimismo de Madrid" (the victimism of Madrid),
an idea that Aguirre consistently promoted when claiming that Madrileños
are not just distinct to other Spaniards, but superior as well. Under her leadership, she claimed that Madrid was the city that defended the idea of Spain;
that is, a nationalist and united Spain in a perpetual struggle against
regional nationalisms and Socialists who wanted to break Spain up (89). Her
narrative strategy, argues Calleja, was extremely successful in the new
millennium at the ballot box (87). Substitute, Madrid with Euskadi (the
Basque Country), Calleja suggests, and it could be any Basque nationalist
speaking (88). Echoing the techniques of Basque nationalists, the Spanish
flag was a consistent Aguirre backdrop and she embraced the idea of "la
patria verdadera" (the true Spain) (89). She promoted the idea to Madrileños
that the central government in the hands of Socialists is unnatural and the
cause of permanent tension. By mimicking the Basque nationalists and

their sacralization of Basque folklore, Aguirre also championed the folklore that Madrileños care about. The PP, then, is superior to the Socialists because it believes in the Zarzuela and Santo Isidro (94). Calleja thus suggests that Aguirre's brand of nationalism was projected by Aguirre and her supporters as quaint, whereas Basque or Catalan nationalism was narrativized as a threat.

The important issue in the nationalism debates is not whether there are two or more Spains, or to pinpoint where the centre is, but rather how to explain the historical process by which regional nationalisms were discursively marginalized over the Aznar years and how legitimate and illegitimate nationalism/patriotism was narratively constructed by both the left and the right in official discourse. This marginalization is not only a political strategy. It also feeds into the logic of terror narratives as projected by the two major parties. This point is discussed further in the next section.

The rise and rise of the Popular Party (PP)

In 1993, after eleven years in office, the Spanish public seemed disenchanted with the Socialist Party. As Woodworth says, "If, in the fateful phrase of Socialist politician, Alfonso Guerra, Spain was now 'unrecognisable to her own mother,' many people were disturbed by the image their country had adopted" (2001, 246). The PSOE had enjoyed a monopoly of political power at many levels in Spanish society for an unhealthily long time. The Socialist Party's continued electoral success was widely attributed to the persistent unattractiveness of the Spanish right-wing parties as a credible alternative. Also, thanks to the tendency by the PSOE in the elections of 1986, 1989, 1993 and 1995 to discredit the Spanish right as the direct descendant of the former authoritarian regime, and the fact that Manuel Fraga, the PP leader, was also an uncharismatic leader who appeared to belong to the past, the PP was rejected by the majority of the population (Magone 2004, 91). But as Woodworth points out, in the early 1990s, that changed with the appearance of a new opposition leader, José María Aznar:

> The distinctly uncharismatic but doggedly determined leadership of José María Aznar had begun to bear fruit for the Partido Popular. He highlighted its makeover as a modern European party of the centre-Right, and understated the Francoist associations of its older members. Nostalgia for the old regime among its ranks became so discreet as to be almost invisible. Since the centre had collapsed in 1982, the conservatives had seemed too right-wing for modern Spain, but Aznar gradually persuaded the

public that he offered a viable democratic alternative to González. (Woodworth 2001, 246)

From the early 1990s, the PP adopted a more pragmatic attitude towards Spanish politics. By the 1993 national elections, the party had moved toward the centre. Although the party still attracted the right-wing electorate, it also managed to attract a substantial number of moderate voters. For the first time since González's resounding win in 1982, the two main parties were only separated by four percentage points. Part of the PP's success lay in the relentless series of political scandals that were preoccupying the PSOE, not least the GAL scandal, which the PP was using to discredit the Socialists. Although scandals also plagued the PP during this time, in Woodworth's words "most of the muck raked was sticking to the PSOE" (2001, 247). But despite the scandals, the PSOE narrowly won the 1993 election. It seemed that the Spanish electorate was still uneasy about electing a centre-right political party, even eighteen years after the end of Francoism.

Aznar's resentment at losing what seemed to be an unlosable election, resulted, according to Woodworth, in "a new style of recklessly destructive opposition" (2001, 248). The PP leadership believed that the party lost the 1993 general elections because it was not sufficiently tough enough on the PSOE, despite its armoury of media supporters (Calleja 2008, 259). On an almost daily basis, the PP began to attack the PSOE administration and its policies, from counterterrorism, to political scandals and foreign relations. The PP successfully created a climate of mass-mediated hostility and venomous rhetoric to the extent that, according to Calleja, it was difficult to find anybody willing to publicly defend the PSOE by 1995 (260). The severity of the PP's polarization led Calleja to suggest that the PP has two personalities: it is a reasonable and moderate party modelled on the European democratic Christian tradition when in government; but it is also an ultra-extreme party when in opposition (263). Given that the majority of Spaniards identify on the centre-left of the political spectrum, the PP has to hyperactively discredit the Socialists on every level in order to win government.

By 1996, the accumulation of scandals hurting the PSOE prompted the Convergència i Unió (CiU, Convergence and Union), the Catalan Nationalist Party, to withdraw its support for the Socialists, spurring early elections. The PP won government for the first time, although without an absolute majority, effectively toppling the González PSOE government. Ironically, the PP had to seek the support of two regional nationalist parties, the PNV in the Basque Country and the CiU in Catalonia, in order to govern. Since the PP began its history as a leading advocate of a strong and centralized government system for Spain, Felipe González remarked that "there never was a defeat as sweet as this" (Gibbons 1999, 39). Ironically, the PP's victory forced Aznar to further moderate the party's positions in relation to the State of Autonomies and other regional issues. For many scholars and commentators, the democratic election of a right-of-centre conservative political party in Spain was the final step in the consolidation of Spain's transition to democracy. Many had feared that Spain would become a one-party state after the Socialists had won five successive elections.

The PP's big achievement in reorienting its ideological character cannot be underestimated. It was brought about by a major transformation of party organization strategy, particularly in the way campaigns were fought and the media were used, which clearly took the losing Socialist Party by surprise (Magone 2004, 92) By the mid-1990s the PP was transformed into a credible catch-all party, perceived by the electorate to have left behind the rigid conservative ideology of the former generation. It was a party able to attract young new voters, which agreed with the short assessment of Aznar that ¡España va bien! (Spain is doing well) (93). Four years later, the PP won the March 2000 national elections in a landslide and gained a much coveted absolute majority, meaning that it was no longer required to negotiate with Basque and Catalan nationalists to govern. The 2000 national elections saw the two major parties further tone down their ideological rhetoric, and both the PSOE and PP took pains to portray themselves as centrist parties (Roller 2001, 212). The 2000 election was a turning point for the PP, in that the results reflected a general view amongst the electorate that the PP was no longer the inheritor of the Francoist legacy but was now a modern conservative party (222). The victory, according to Elisa Roller, dispelled sociological stereotyping of Spanish voters as situated primarily on the left of the political spectrum, and reflected the new social and political reality of Spain, its electorate and its political parties. This was based, Roller argues, "on a decline in the traditional ideological polarisation of the Spanish electorate and the adoption of new, more pragmatic, values in voter choice" (209).

But in spite of all the transformations of the PP since its foundation in 1977, it continues to symbolize the conservative undercurrent of Spain (Magone 2004, 90). The PP instinctively advocates a unitary conception of Spain that goes back to the origins of the formation of the Spanish national state. The notion of an España una y católica (a united Catholic Spain) still characterizes the PP's political culture, although no longer in a rigid authoritarian way. Whereas for many Spaniards the return to the right in power symbolized a return to order, for many others it also brought to the fore prevailing fears about the right in their memories of the past (Narotzky & Smith 2002, 193). Thus, while Spanish sociologist Victor Perez-Díaz suggested that "electing a conservative government is a way of exorcizing the spectre of Francoism," (quoted in Sancton 1996) the spokesperson for the CiU, Miguel Roca, was sceptical of Aznar's insistence that Francoism is dead, since for the first time, there was no far-right party running in a Spanish election. 'Where are they?" he asked, "evidently hiding in Aznar's party" (Sancton 1996).

According to Martí, Domingo and Ibarra, the Aznar years can be divided into two periods: the first legislature (1996–2000), when the PP needed the support of regional nationalists; and the PP's second legislature (2000–2004), when the PP had an absolute majority (2007, 130). The first legislature saw the PP act with some caution and restraint, perhaps due to a need to form political alliances with moderate nationalist groups in Catalonia and the Basque Country, particularly on the issue of counterterrorism. The second legislature witnessed an ideological polarization that would escalate dramatically over the course of the government's four years in office. According to Martí, Domingo and Ibarra, the PP toughened the law on acts of terrorism—and overall acted within the law. But it also adopted an entirely new rhetoric by which suspected subversive or associated activities or opinions became criminalized (131). This dramatic change in discourse was part of the PP's new political and electoral strategy (131).

The PP's brand of polarizing discourse was manifested in what is often referred to as constitutional patriotism; that is, since overt Spanish nationalism remained taboo the 1978 Spanish Constitution was instead made into a sacred document. As Sebastian Balfour and Alejandro Quiroga point out in *The Reinvention of Spain* (2007) it was the Socialists who adopted the concept of constitutional patriotism into its political platform in an attempt to foster solidarity in the electorate (90–91). But the PP at the turn of the century not only embraced the concept of constitutional patriotism but tried to monopolize it (93). Woodworth questions the logic of this type of nationalism:

> It would seem self-evident that a constitution that was drawn up under the shadow of dictatorship, with the army rattling sabres from the wings, might be in need of reform a quarter of a century later, when democracy had put down much deeper roots. Aznar insisted, however, that any move to seriously overhaul this document would endanger both the unity of the state, and the democratic system, itself. (2004, 14)

Constitutional patriotism, arguably a hallmark of the Aznar years, eventually became a mainstream official ideology supported by both the left and the right and their media sponsors. Constitutional patriotism effectively implied that any move by regional nationalists, or any group that campaigned for any type of reform outside the limits placed by the 1978 Constitution, was considered to be acting outside legitimate political discourse. The following chapters examine what this meant in practice over the Aznar and Zapatero years. But to finish this chapter, I want to discusss two related narratives deployed by the Aznar administration that had a profound effect on Spanish politics, and arguably on the recent trajectory of Spanish history: the narrative of no conflict and the narrative of Spanish glory.

The narrative of no conflict

Chapter Two provided a narrative account of what is known as the Basque conflict. This conflict was set out admirably in Julio Medem's documentary *La pelota vasca, la piel contra la piedra* (The Basque Ball: Skin against Stone) (2003). At the premiere of the film, however, conflict immediately arose after Medem proposed what many sectors in Spain regarded as an illegitimate argument: in the Basque Country there was an unresolved conflict that allowed one to understand, but not justify, the existence of terrorism, and that the only way to stop the violence is to resolve the underlying conflict. Although critics did not suggest that Medem was complicit in ETA's actions, they did question the argument that two equal and opposing forces, ETA and the Spanish state, were at loggerheads. Rather, they argued, the Spanish state was embroiled in a legal and democratic struggle against a group of terrorists, and the terrorists thus had full responsibility for fuelling the conflict, not the Spanish state. This argument led to an intractable narrative dilemma. Where the Basques saw conflict, the Spaniards saw terrorism. When the Basques spoke of dialogue, the Spaniards spoke of surrender. Moreover, according to many Spaniards, particularly on the right, there could be no peace process, because for there to be peace there must first be a war.

ETA was once perceived as a political leftover of Francoism, but Aznar and the PP projected the idea that there was no conflict between the Spanish state and the Basque Country. Upon entering office, in a direct jab at his predecessor González, Aznar pledged to fight terrorism "within the law and with the full extent of the law," a reference to the Socialist's misadventures in the use of paramilitary death squads (Encarnación 2007, 971). Aznar's pledge rejected state terrorism and indicated that maximum support would be given to security and judicial institutions in combating terrorism. It also had a further implication, which was to be crucial in defining Aznar's distinctive approach to the problem. As Woodworth put it, "the pledge suggested that ETA's terrorism was only a problem for the police and the judiciary; that is, there was no political dimension to be addressed, and no underlying conflict requiring resolution" (2004b, 175).

A common refrain by politicians and journalists on the right during those years was that dialogue with ETA was impossible because the group does not listen to reason. Instead, the only recourse is to apply the law and to convince ETA that violent acts will not help achieve the group's goals. But, as Aretxaga points out, "This is, of course, the position of the Spanish government, which counteracts violence with growing repressive legislation. Yet in the Basque Country, the law has an ambiguous character, inscribed as it has been in a long history of police abuse. A politics of violent confrontation feeds into the logic of occupation of radical nationalism, reproducing a spiral of endless violence" (2005, 247). The denial of an underlying conflict, coupled with increasing counterterrorism legislation to combat ETA, were the contradictory policy hallmarks of the Aznar era. The policies allowed Aznar to pursue constitutional patriotism with zeal, and to deflect discursively all responsibility for terrorism onto Basque society, where it remains today.

Aznar and the PP were able to electorally exploit the Basque and terror issue because of the many social changes, some promoted by the PP itself, in Spain. The ending of ETA's ceasefire in December 1999 and the perception of many Spaniards that Castilian was being persecuted in Catalonia, fed into the idea promoted by the PP that nationalist parties advocated an exclusive type of nationalism. The PP channelled the idea into patriotic fervour. The mass demonstrations across Spanish cities in the aftermath of the assassination of PP councillor Miguel Ángel Blanco, in 1997, were evidence for the PP that a tough antiterrorist policy would be a magnet for votes. Woodworth suggests that the demonstrations confirmed the government's view that a comfortable majority of the Spanish people would support a police offensive against ETA and resist any political negotiation (2004b, 176). The PP, suggested Woodworth, "saw that although the 'bash the Basques' strategy might fail in the region itself, it was enormously popular in most of Spain" (2004a, 12). At a concert in commemoration of a Socialist councillor killed by ETA, a young Madrid audience booed when a performer sang in Catalan. Although such incidents were rare, Woodworth suggests that they were symptomatic of a profound change: "the state was being set for a revival of overt Spanish nationalism, which had dared not speak its name for years because of its association with Francoism" (11).

Aznar's personal history was also a significant factor in the unprecedented anti-ETA fervour of the 1990s. In 1995, an attempted attack by ETA on his life with a remote control car bomb led Aznar to consider terrorism as Spain's greatest threat. After the attempted assassination Aznar came to view negotiations with ETA as undemocratic and as an affront to those who had suffered its consequences. Aznar viewed a close alliance with the USA as the best way of combating terrorism, especially after September 11, 2001, and he was committed to the notion that the world community had to find a much more radical way to fight terrorism.

The PP's official stance that there was no underlying conflict in the Basque Country led to the introduction of a series of measures that toughened criminal procedures for suspected and convicted terrorists. In order for this strategy to work, Aznar's phrase "within the law but with all of the law" became elastic (Woodworth 2004b, 176). When it was in its interests, the PP government simply changed the law. The PP's most notable anti-terrorist strategy was the 1999 anti-terrorist pact it signed with the PSOE, an attempt to forge an intra-party consensus on counterterrorism policy. The pact, according to Encarnación, "served to provide checks and balances on government actions against terrorist organizations, by requiring that the governing party not take any counterterrorism action without consulting with the opposition party" (2007, 971). The pact led to a new law in 2003 that outlawed Batasuna, and a series of groups closely associated with ETA, effectively criminalizing a broad network of loosely connected social, cultural, and media associations, merely on the basis of their suspected connection or complicity with ETA (Martí et al. 2007, 132–33). The Socialists supported the law, but, as Woodworth points out, in the political climate of the Aznar years, "anyone who opposed the law was likely to be branded as an ETA sympathiser" (2004a, 13).

Although the PP's tough approach was criticized by the Basque regional government, the laws enjoyed wide support across Spain. Democrats of all colours argued that a political party with ties to a terrorist group and that does not condemn terrorist attacks should not expect the protection of the law and the state privileges given to political parties. Such privileges only serve to strengthen the radical terrorist networks and lead to more attacks. This is a sensible and logical argument, but it also feeds the polarization of the Basque radical imagination that Basque civil rights are being denied by an oppressive state. Worse still, it has contributed to the widespread idea among Basque moderates that the PP was using the struggle against ETA as a "battering ram against Basque nationalism in general" (Woodworth 2004a, 11). The banning of Batasuna meant that radical Basque national-ists were deprived of political representation; as a result the moderate PNV became radicalized. This became quickly evident when the PNV leader produced a blueprint known as the Ibarretxe Plan that called for Basque self-determination (see Chapter Six).

Although the PP administration officially denied the existence of a Basque conflict, it sought to politicize the Basque issue as much as possi-ble. It was apparent, as Martí et al. also argue, that "an almost symbiotic relationship seemed to develop between ETA and the PP, thus also breathing new life into the more radical strands of Basque nationalism" (2007, 131). This is further demonstrated by the Irish journalist Paddy Woodworth who reported that one of Aznar's senior ideologues admitted privately to him (n.d.) that ETA's attacks actually served the PP's inter-ests, because if the violence ended, the party could no longer refuse to negotiate with the PNV. Such negotiations, the PP leadership thought, would undermine the unity of Spain (2004a, 12). Projecting the narrative of no conflict allowed the state to endure a degree of terrorist activity in exchange for not ceding any more ground to Basque nationalism. The strategy allowed the PP to implement in practice its narrative of what it imagined the Spanish nation to be: a multicultural, yet unified, state with a dominant Castilian identity.

If Aznar and the PP had limited its political rhetoric to a "bash the Basques" policy it might have found itself a political winner. After all, the politicization of terror for electoral purposes signified the return of a reac-tionary culture rooted in the Francoist authoritarian tradition, which had resonance for a significant sector of society (Martí et al. 2007, 132). The Aznar years also promoted narratives that challenged some of the founding myths of Spain's transition to democracy. The narratives disturbed many Spaniards who began to question whether the Spanish right was remodel-ling Spain in the image of the former Franco regime, albeit in a democratic guise.

The narrative of "Spanish glory"

Verdicts by commentators from diverse sources and across the Spanish political spectrum, suggests Paddy Woodworth, "attest to the extraordi-nary weight given to what has been called the 'Aznar factor'" (2004a, 8). Heywood describes Aznar as "confrontational," and as having "an aggres-sive style of doing politics" (1995, 392). More flatteringly, *Time* magazine described Aznar as a "macho [man] with killer political instincts" (Graff 2004). This was a radical departure from the post-Franco political style of compromise and led Aznar into controversy on a number of occasions. For example, when the oil tanker *Prestige* caused an environmental disaster off the coast of Galicia, the Aznar administration's response was publicly perceived as tardy and non-transparent. And a mass public general strike in June 2002, called when Aznar attempted to push through labour market reform without the backing of the PSOE and the unions, further revealed Aznar's misreading of public sentiment. But it was his non-negotiable pro-war stance in 2002, when he backed the US led invasion of Iraq, and his handling of the aftermath of the March 11 attacks in Madrid, that best illustrated his stubborn authoritarian style.

Aznar had definite ideas about Spain's place in both Europe and the world. He believed that Spain should not confine itself to a subordinate position in the EU; rather, it should look beyond the EU to world leadership. According to his memoir, *Eight Years as Prime Minister* (2005), Aznar is convinced that Spain is one of the great nations of Europe and the world, but "like all great nations, it has great responsibilities and an important leadership role [. . .] Spaniards have to start looking at the past without an inferiority complex" (2005, 78). Javier Pradera, writing in *El País*, suggests that Aznar's memoir "is haunted by the dream of restoring to Spain the place she had held until the 18th century and then lost at the Congress of Vienna, after which she was no more than a satellite of foreign powers, especially of France" (2005, 2). In his memoir Aznar also admits to a desire to solemnly formalize Spain's return "to where it ought to be." One of Aznar's ambitions included gaining membership for Spain in the exclusive G8 club (Woodworth 2004a, 7).

Valentí Puig, a conservative writer and supporter of Aznar's foreign policy vision, provided a clearer rationale for Aznar's foreign policies by arguing that Aznar's realignment was rooted soundly in Spanish national interests (2004, 69). Puig argues that a closer relationship with Washington encouraged the USA to assist the Spanish government's fight against ETA, as well as to smooth relations with the Moroccan government. Even before September 11, Aznar had argued that in order for Spain to grow economically and politically, Spain's engagement with the rest of the world needed to be bolder and wider. Hence, Aznar sought to confront the traditional Spanish fear of commitments abroad. Aznar's vision was wider, perhaps, than most Spaniards understood. The vision was a creation of a Hispanosphere that could form an alliance with the emerging Anglosphere in a broad political, economic and security alliance based on shared values and free markets (70). The term Hispanosphere is, according to Puig, the

Hispanic complement of what James Bennett described in the Winter 2003/04 issue of *The National Interest* as the Anglosphere, which brings together the oceanic civilization of the English speaking world (71). Alongside neo-liberalism, the projection of the Hispanosphere encompasses the values of the open society and reformism rather than revolution, a preference for society over the state, free market versus a planned economy, citizenship as opposed to ethnicity, and civil authority versus military power (73). Hence, under Aznar, the so-called values of the Anglophone world and the values espoused by the Popular Party in Spain met and conjoined.

This international context needs to be considered when assessing Aznar's embroilment in the Iraq War in 2003, for it provides a fuller and more complex picture of the Popular Party era under Aznar. The international arena is also one key to understanding the ideological metanarrative of the War on Terror and its implications on Spanish political debates. The September 11 attacks in the USA in 2001 allowed Aznar the opportunity to internationalize his antiterrorist policy and, at the same time, to boost Spain's international profile. Part of this goal stemmed from a deep set desire on the part of the Spanish right to revive Spain's sixteenth and seventeenth century global and imperial role.

Aznar convinced US President George W. Bush, that the USA should support Spain in the struggle against terrorism, and that it was thus necessary to coordinate international action against all types of terror, from national groups like ETA to international networks of Islamists. After the 9/11 attacks, Bush, Jr., heeded Aznar's advice (Ekaizer 2004). Both Aznar and Bush had made counterterrorism the backbone of their domestic policy. Thanks to US support, ETA and Batasuna were elevated to the status of international terrorist organizations (Woodworth 2004a, 13). Aznar saw an opportunity in the USA's increasing international isolation over the Iraq issue for Spain to regain its historic international position and partially recuperate the glory it lost in the Spanish-American War of 1898. Since that war, which saw Spain lose its remaining four overseas colonies, Spain had been on the margins of international conflict. Strengthened by an absolute majority in 2000, and the fact that he was resigning his leadership in 2004, Aznar felt he was free to follow his convictions and leave his mark on Spanish history.

It is likely that Aznar considered this shift in policy as his most significant political legacy. According to Woodworth, Aznar believed the new policy would liberate Madrid from subservience to Paris (Woodworth 2004a, 19). In retrospect, it is difficult to comprehend why Aznar was willing to damage Spain's relationship with France, the key country that

Spain relied on in the fight against ETA. But the polls indicated that the Spanish people were not necessarily following Aznar. Although in the USA the Iraq War helped George W. Bush win more votes, in Spain, the war was hurting the PP. Aznar had seriously underestimated the depth of public opinion on the issue. On Saturday February 15, 2003, fifty-six demonstrations erupted across Spain. There were an estimated two million demonstrators in Madrid and Barcelona alone. Although most demonstrators were from the left, a significant number of PP sympathisers also marched. Even the Spanish film industry's Goya awards became an anti-war vehicle, and with their statements on Spain's involvement in Iraq, the actor Javier Bardem and the director Fernando León de Aranoa became icons of the anti-war movement. More importantly, the mobilization against the war helped consolidate Zapatero's leadership, which had been questioned by some PSOE veterans. The PSOE was steadily rising in the polls and had a ten point lead over the PP just two days before the commencement of the war (García-Abadillo 2005, 217). Most of the PP supported Aznar, but in the end, although Spain supported the war, Spain did not participate directly in the invasion of Iraq, instead sending a floating hospital, the Galicia. After the initial invasion Aznar sent 1300 Spanish troops in March 2003 as part of the coalition peacekeeping force. But the government's insistence that Spain was not directly participating in the invasion fell on deaf ears when the first missiles began to fall on Baghdad. In the first four days of the war, PP offices were vandalized across Spain, including in Madrid, Mérida, Palma de Mallorca and Pontevedra (215).

According to Bustelo, the Spanish electorate was not convinced of the soundness of Spain's participation in the Iraq war because no pedagogic effort was made to explain why it was necessary or imperative. The arguments raised were scarce and based on personal credibility, and delivered in a paternalistic tone that could be summarized, according to Bustelo, as follows: "it is logical that Spaniards reject war, but I can assure you that I know why it is necessary; the government knows what is best for Spain, and to take it out of the sidelines of history" (2005, 9). The PP government, then, underestimated the extent to which its reorientation of government policy did not coincide with the modern post-Franco narratives of the Spanish state. The transition to democracy in the late 1970s was successful because of the various pacts of compromise, and the unofficial policy of forgetting the ghosts of the past. The PP did not recognize how deeply the narratives of compromise still operate in Spanish political society. Nor did the PP recognize that violence had ceased to be regarded by most Spaniards as a noble trait of Spanish identity. But although the PSOE increased its vote in the regional elections across Spain, the PP managed to stem a landslide loss. The PP leadership interpreted the results of the elections as indicating that the Iraq issue had been forgotten by the people, once and for all, and it lay dead and buried. Neither Aznar nor the PP expected the terrorist attacks in March 11, 2004. Three days later, on March 14, 2004, the Spanish people finally had an opportunity to express their frustration with the government not only over the Madrid attacks but also over the war issue.

Conclusion

The success of the Spanish right in creating a stable and electable democratic party was a key event in Spain's transition to democracy. Much of that success can be attributed to Aznar. But it cannot be denied that Aznar left Spain more deeply divided than at any time since the Franco dictatorship (Woodworth 2004a, 8). The Aznar years saw a return of the division of the two Spains in terms of the left and right's narratives of Spanish nationalism and terrorism. Although the PP left office with ETA at one of its weakest historical points, it left Basque society more deeply divided, and democratic Basque nationalism more radicalized, than ever before. Much of this political division, however, was constructed in partisan rhetoric. Aznar was willing to shed his party's ideological convictions when it suited him politically, especially in his first legislature when he required the support of Basque and Catalan nationalists to govern. The Aznar years hence saw the emergence of the narrative of *las dos Españas* as a political tool for the electoral mobilization of middle Spain. In order to achieve that mobilization, regional nationalists were narratively marginalized as exclusive nationalists with a democratic deficit. Due to the left's commitment to a united Spain and a strong central state, the PP's narratives largely remained unchallenged. This was also true in the Spanish government's fight against ETA terrorism. The vitriolic anti-ETA climate promoted by Aznar left little room for the Spanish left to contest the PP's more questionable policies lest they be branded ETA sympathisers. After 9/11, the emerging global metanarrative of terror also gave Aznar a fruitful context in which to promote his domestic terror agenda.

But the trajectory for Spain that Aznar was taking was broken suddenly with the March 11 attacks. That event opened a running political battle between the PP and the PSOE that further polarized Spanish politics and society. The next chapter details the three days between March 11, 2004 and March 14, 2004, that arguably changed the course of Spanish history.

Instead of playing down partisan divisions in the face of one of modern Spain's greatest crises, the narrative divisions between the PP and the PSOE, and between the two Spains, were exacerbated. The result was that many of the unofficial pacts agreed upon during Spain's transition to democracy were also shattered. It is apt here to recall Jacqueline Rose's suggestion that "the modern state can be read as a symptom, as a social construction that contains an ungraspable excess and which relies on fantasy for an authority it cannot fully justify" (1996, 8). The PP government's handling of the March 11 attacks typified that kind of ungraspable excess. It was also clear that many of the PP's narrative responses to the bombings relied excessively on fantasy, to the extent that most Spaniards could not distinguish between what was really real or fiction, and the PP could not convince most Spaniards of its own narrative realness.

CHAPTER FIVE

Blame Games and Narrative Battles

The March 11, 2004 "Terror" Attacks and the March 14 General Elections

> Some significant percentage of the Spanish electorate was mobilized after the massacre to shift the course of the campaign, throw out the old government and replace it with one whose policies are more to Al Qaeda's liking. What is the Spanish word for appeasement? (Brooks 2004, 27)

This chapter revolves around one particular year—2004. That year could possibly join 1492 (the year Columbus encountered the Americas) and 1898 (the year Spain lost the Spanish-American War and its remaining American and Asian colonies in what Spanish elites referred to as "El Desastre") as one of the most significant years in the history of the Spanish state. After eight years of Popular Party rule which steered the Spanish state away from pacifist Europe and into a Hobbesian alliance with the USA (by participating in the US-led invasion of Iraq in 2003),[1] one tragic event radically altered the course of contemporary Spanish history.

On March 11, 2004, ten bombs exploded in and around Madrid's Atocha station, killing 191 people and wounding another 1,500. The March 11 attacks were executed by thirteen Islamic terrorists 911 days after 9/11 whose *modus operandi* was imitated (four trains, four planes) (Gil Calvo 2005, 9). The attack occurred three days before the March 14 national election, and it was generally believed that José María Aznar would lead the Popular Party into its third term in office. The PP promptly blamed the attack on

---

[1] I am here referring to US political commentator Robert Kagan's thesis in *Paradise and Power* (2003) that the USA is still embroiled in a Hobbesian world, whilst the EU has entered into a Kantian "perpetual peace" as a result of US military protection. For Kagan, this explains Europe's diverging views on military action and multilateralism.

the Basque Separatist group ETA. Although within hours the evidence indicated that it was an Islamic group that had most likely perpetrated the attack in the context of the wider global War on Terror, the government continued to tell the story that ETA was responsible:

> 11 March 2004 has taken its place in the history of infamy [. . .] There are no negotiations possible or desirable with these assassins that have so often sown death through all of Spain. We will defeat them. We will succeed in finishing off the terrorist band, with the strength of the rule of law and with the unity of all Spaniards. (Former Prime Minister José María Aznar quoted in Tremlett 2004, 1)

Three days later, in a climate of civil division and suspicion, the people unexpectedly ejected the government from power and elected the Socialists under the leadership of José Luis Rodríguez Zapatero. The PSOE, in turn, immediately withdrew Spanish troops from Iraq and in the process was perceived by conservative political commentators around the world, to have sabotaged its relations with the world's sole superpower the United States.

As Narciso Michavila correctly points out, terror attacks during elections in Spain are nothing new (2005, 3). The scale of the attack on March 11, 2004, however, was unprecedented. For Michavila, the electoral implications of these attacks were very different than if ETA had been their author (3). An ETA attack would have benefited the governing party, given its clear accomplishments in the fight against ETA terrorism. However, an attack by Islamists would put responsibility for the deaths on the shoulders of the PP, due to its support of the USA in the war in Iraq, which Spanish public opinion clearly opposed. Confusion regarding who had carried out the attacks led to a climate of confrontation between the government, which insisted almost to the very end that the main suspect is ETA, and the most critical of the news media, which suspected from the start that it was the work of Islamists.

The March 11 attacks instigated a narrative battle between the two major political parties. The PP promoted the narrative that ETA was responsible for the attacks while the opposition PSOE projected a counter-narrative that accused the government of misinformation and blamed the attacks on Islamists. This chapter thus examines the clash between the global metanarrative of terror on the one hand, and the narrative of *las dos Españas* on the other, a battle that was played out during those three fateful days in Spain. The chapter argues that the narrative battle was won by the opposition PSOE because its narrative promoted continuity with the historical pacts of compromise negotiated during Spain's transition to democracy. The PP narrative, on the other hand, failed because it attempted to undermine those pacts, and because it raised the ire of many Spaniards due to the perception that the PP narrative was authoritarian and manipulative. In order to understand this perception it is first necessary to explore the relationship between emotions and crises.

On crises and emotions

In *Governing After Crisis* Boin, McConnell, and Hart suggest that life is punctuated from time to time "by critical episodes marked by a sense of threat and uncertainty that shatters people's understanding of the world around them" (2008, 3). The March 11 attacks were such a crisis in Spanish politics. Crises, the authors argue, "are episodic breakdowns of familiar symbolic frameworks that legitimate the pre-existing socio-political order" (3). Of particular interest for this chapter is the fact that crises often test the resilience of a society and expose the shortcomings of its leaders and public institutions (Drennan & McConnell 2007). When a crisis occurs in a society, political leaders must deal with the immediate threat, and also "come to terms with the vulnerabilities and the public disaffection that the crisis may evoke" (Boin, McConnell & Hart 2008, 4). As a consequence, governments often fail to cope. When the crisis in question is widely held to have been unforeseeable and uncontrollable, the potential damage to a government is relatively limited. But with the March 11 attacks in Madrid, however, there was a widespread perception that the threat could have been foreseen and possibly avoided altogether (for example, by not participating in the Iraq War). Coupled with the fact that the official response to the attacks was considered by many Spaniards as manipulative, the potential damage to the government that the March 11 attacks presented was incalculable.

When confronted with crises, public leaders face three distinct challenges. First, the actual emergency response; second, an immediate and comprehensive public information and communication response; and third, managing the fallout of the crisis in the weeks and months after the crisis (Boin, McConnell & Hart 2008, 8). In this chapter I am particularly interested in the second challenge—the public information and communication response—where, as we shall see, the Aznar administration failed seriously. Governments need to tell people what is going on, what might happen next and what it means to them. Failure to do so in a timely and authoritative fashion can, according to Boin, McConnell, and Hart, open up "a Pandora's box of journalistic and web-based speculation, rumour, suspicion and allegations that can easily inflame public opinion and sour the political climate, even as emergency operations are still under way" (8). This is what happened in Spain during the three days between the March 11 attacks and the March 14 general election.

Crises also have a way of becoming politicized rather quickly. According to Boin, McConnell, and Hart:

> political, bureaucratic, economic and other special interests do not automatically pull together and give up their self-interest just because a crisis has occurred. They engage in a struggle to produce a dominant interpretation of the implications of the crisis. The sheer intensity of these struggles tends to produce unpredictable twists and turns in the crisis-induced fates of politicians, policies and institutions alike. (2008, 9)

The days between March 11 and 14, 2004, therefore, saw the Aznar administration attempt to project a dominant narrative to explain the terrorist attacks in Madrid, whereas the opposition and some media projected a counter-narrative to discredit the government. Ultimately, the opposition's narrative was more successful in convincing the Spanish electorate of its legitimacy. But how can we understand the process in which one narrative was more successful than the other? One approach would be to consider the role that emotions play during moments of crisis. Sociologist Ian Burkitt argues that "it is impossible to fully understand the attempts of governments to govern a population and direct conduct, along with the resistance and opposition to this, without acknowledging the central place of emotions in these power relations" (2005, 693). For Burkitt, emotions are powerful collective forces that are involved in the reconstruction of social groups as well as the maintenance of the status quo. Because of this, "governments will always be tempted to stir powerful emotions in their strategies for directing conduct: inciting, inducing and seducing a people" (693). The March 11 attacks in Madrid clearly illustrate the way governments use emotion to direct conduct, yet they also show how this has unpredictable and unintended consequences for all involved (680).

For Durkheim, collective emotional forces were both irrational and too powerful. They were social currents, like currents of opinion, "which acted as coercive forces upon individual behaviour and consciousness, shaping conduct and thought" (681). But Burkitt aims to go beyond Durkheim's position that emotions are irrational forces too complex to analyse. Burkitt points out that recent scholarship posits that emotions can be understood as "intelligent responses to perceptions of value and, as such, part of the system of ethical reasoning" (682). According to Burkitt, this does not preclude the possibility that emotions can operate in unpredictable and disorderly ways. Rather, emotions can be understood as "discursive feelings and responses to others with whom we are socially related" (692). Burkitt also argues that you cannot separate people's emotional responses and judgements from the power relations in which they are located.

This is important. The analysis of any process of narrativization must come to terms with the fact that the stories we create as subjects to make sense of the world are emotional. By ignoring emotion we are limiting the depth of our understanding of the potency of narratives in shaping and shifting collective and individual consciousnesses. Emotions should be understood as operating in the vast network of power relations. According to Foucault, power is "a total structure of actions brought to bear upon possible actions: it incites, it induces, it seduces" (1982, 220). As Burkitt argues, incitement, inducement and seduction all involve emotion:

> In order to incite, people must be provoked or stirred in some way, with anger being the usual response to provocation. To induce, people must be persuaded or motivated in a way that calls out a certain type of conduct. [. . .] Finally, the act of seduction must produce a desire or ongoing for a person, object, goal or ideal. (2005, 683)

Indeed, accepting emotion as a legitimate part of political analysis is controversial. As Burkitt points out, "emotions by their very nature are ambivalent, making them hard to predict and difficult for governments, or any other political group, to manipulate them" (2005, 684). Of course this does not mean that governments do not try to manipulate emotions. Burkitt's point, rather, is that the unstable and unpredictable nature of emotions means that governments are not always successful. By considering emotions in this chapter, I am not suggesting that Spaniards were emotionally deceived into changing their vote on March 14, 2004. Michavila's study of the elections suggests that people who acknowledge that the attacks affected their vote had the greatest ability to reflect on their actions (2005, 16). Instead, this chapter attempts to demonstrate that the Spanish experience is evidence that individual and collective emotions do not always correspond with the will of the government elites, partly because of the persistence of historical narratives that most Spanish people continue to live by. Far from being manipulated by the government, the March 11 crisis indicated that many Spaniards responded positively to the opposition's counter-narrative because that narrative was more emotionally resonant. The opposition narrative played upon prevailing fears in the electorate of a war-mongering and manipulative government, recalling some of the worst excesses of the discredited Franco regime.

The March 11 terror attacks: Constructing the narrative

We have a dangerous tendency of attributing greater significance to actions that concern us more directly. (Todorov 2003, 161)

In the March 2004 elections, two new faces were leading the two main political parties: Mariano Rajoy was Aznar's chosen successor of the PP, and José Luis Rodríguez Zapatero was the new face of the PSOE. The PP ran a campaign emphasizing its record in government: a market-oriented economic program, a strong national stance against territorial and constitutional reorganizations and concessions, and a much stepped-up campaign against domestic terrorism. Each of these themes, suggested Valentina A. Bali, "had evolved under Aznar's two terms in power" (2007, 673). Against the national and patriotic themes invoked by the incumbent PP party, the Socialists were left to conduct a more defensive campaign, which focused in a less coordinated fashion on issues such as welfare, housing, political transparency, and the PPs' unpopular support for the war in Iraq (673). The political polls were virtually unanimous: the PP was on the verge of a third electoral victory. But three days before the election the attacks in Madrid halted what was one of Spain's most civilized election campaigns. In the words of Casimiro García-Abadillo, "A partir de ese día ya nada sería igual" (From that day on nothing would ever be the same) (2005, 19).

In *Politics Out of History*, Wendy Brown argues that "when constitutive cultural and political narratives are disturbed and undermined, insecurity, anxiety and hopelessness washes across the political landscape" (2001, 5). This is the scenario in which the conservative PP government found itself in the three days between the March 11 attack and the March 14 national election in 2004. Any political party (especially when in campaign mode) communicates to the electorate a narrative that it hopes will convince the people to elect it into office. The effectiveness of this narrative is naturally challenged during times of national crisis. Yet it is conventional wisdom that people usually give their governments certain leeway during times of crisis or social terror. The March 11 attacks need not have spelled political disaster for Aznar and the PP, and it could be argued that the attacks could have presented the incumbent government with an opportunity to solidify its electoral position. Aznar said that "La gestión de esos tres días fue la que tenía que ser (the handling of those three days was as it was supposed to be)" but not everyone in the PP agreed with that statement (quoted in Cernuda 2008, 111). So why did the PP's ETA narrative of blame backfire?

This section provides a brief chronology of the three days in question in order to attempt an answer to this question. There are inherent problems in constructing such a narrative. If it is true that "terrorism is an event, a news story, a social drama, a narrative," as Zulaika and Douglass posit, then "the initial problem that the writer must confront, as is the case with any storyteller or historian, is selection of the narrative form in which to plot the events and the arguments" (1996, 65). Like any historical narrative, it is virtually impossible to guarantee one hundred percent accuracy. The March 11 attacks in Madrid became a mass-mediated debate and were politicized by all stakeholders in Spanish society. It is therefore extremely difficult, and potentially controversial, to construct a narrative about three of the most highly charged days in modern Spanish history, without facing the inevitable charges of subjectivity and partisan interests. This leaves social scientists in a difficult position. There is no neutral ground to begin the analysis or frame an objective debate. Given these limitations, my attempt here is to present as best as possible two important elements of the debate. First, I provide a chronological outline of the key events during these two days that are undisputed (such as press conferences, meetings), taken from sources such as Casimiro García-Abadillo's book *11-M La Venganza* (2005) which is considered an authoritative account by many Spanish journalists and José A. Olmeda's "A Reversal of Fortune" published in *Governing after Crisis* (2008). Second, I attempt to outline the main narrative lines adopted by the PP government and the PSOE opposition. These narratives are constructed from news sources, press statements and media commentaries. The purpose of these sections is not to glorify one political party or ideology at the expense of another. Rather, my aim is to examine which political narratives were more convincing to the Spanish electorate, and to determine to what extent these narratives disturbed the pacts of compromise agreed upon during Spain's transition to democracy.

March 11, 2004

At 7.35 a.m. ten bombs exploded on four trains in and around Madrid's Atocha station. Immediately after the attacks most political pundits and Spanish citizens believed that ETA was responsible, despite a partial cease-fire declaration and ETA's increasing weakness. The *lehendakari* (President of the Basque regional government), Juan José Ibarretxe, and the President of the PNV were the first major leaders to respond to the attacks, and both unequivocally blamed ETA. Those first moments set the tone for the rest of the day. Almost nobody doubted that ETA was responsible, despite declarations made by Arnaldo Otegi, the leader of the illegal Basque political party Batasuna, that placed responsibility for the attacks on the "resistencia árabe" (Arab resistance) in response to Spain's role in the Iraq War. In the government's view, ETA had realized the barbarity and severity of its attacks, and was now trying to deflect the blame on to other groups. Ángel Acebes, the Minister for the Interior, told a reporter in a press conference that ETA had been "cheap and treacherous by denying its involvement" (Olmeda 2008, 69).

At 11 a.m. an emergency meeting was held at the Ministry for the Interior to organize the necessary logistics for dealing with the human catastrophe. Instead of convening with his official crisis management group, Aznar summoned an informal crisis cabinet of his most trusted advisors that failed to include the minister of defence and the director of the National Centre for Intelligence (Olmeda 2008, 68). Aznar reportedly placed the blame on ETA at the outset and much of the meeting was dedicated to organizing large-scale protest demonstrations across Spain. The banner, according to Aznar would be non-negotiable with the other political parties, and would read "Con las víctimas, por la Constitución y para la derrota del terrorismo" (With the victims, for the Constitution and for the defeat of terrorism) (García-Abadillo 2005, 43).

The PP inferred explicitly in the media that ETA perpetrated the attacks; virtually all Spanish media ran with the official theory and used ETA in their headlines. The National Centre for Intelligence released a report stating that "it is believed to be nearly certain that the terrorist organization ETA is the perpetrator of these attacks" (Olmeda 2008, 69). The Minister for the Interior Ángel Acebes became the government's public face during these three days, and he used this document to posit that ETA was indeed responsible, reminding the public of ETA's four previous attempts to execute a similar type of massacre. Aznar, in his first appearance in front of the cameras at 14.30 p.m. also implied that ETA was responsible, but conspicuously, he did not refer to ETA directly:

> Todos sabemos que este asesinato masivo no es la primera vez que se intenta. Las fuerzas y cuerpos de seguridad han impedido varias veces que viviéramos esta tragedia. [. . .] Nunca permitiremos que una minoría de fanáticos nos imponga nuestras decisiones sobre nuestro futuro. (We all know that this is not the first time that a mass killing has been attempted. The security forces have impeded such a tragedy various times. [. . .] We

will never permit a minority of fanatics to impose on our decisions and our future). (García-Abadillo 2005, 47–48)

The PP leadership also undertook some questionable actions that day that led to charges that the PP manipulated the communications industries, although most of these actions only became widely known well after those fateful three days. The PP's communication office instructed the Spanish Embassy in New York to seek a UN resolution that not only condemned the attacks, but also attributed blame to ETA. Senior level PP staff also began calling the foreign media informing them that officially ETA was responsible for the attacks. Meanwhile, Aznar was calling all the editors of Madrid's and Barcelona's newspapers to personally tell them that ETA was responsible. Reports leaked to the news media that the explosives used in the attacks were the same type of explosives that ETA usually used further reinforced the PP narrative.

As the PSOE, according to Olmeda, "did not offer an alternative narrative on the day of the attacks, the PP official narrative prevailed" (Olmeda 2008, 70). The PSOE reportedly had misgivings about the authorship of the attack as early as the morning of the March 11 attacks. But it was decided by the PSOE leadership that although they would not mention ETA in their media appearances they would not blame the attacks on Islamist groups. Zapatero believed it was reckless to put the Prime Minister's words in doubt and supported Aznar's calls for a demonstration (García-Abadillo 2005, 45). But the PSOE leaders felt that the government should have negotiated the demonstration with the other political parties and suspected that Aznar wanted to capitalize on the public's indignation for electoral gain.

New evidence, new narratives

On early March 11, a white van was found with seven detonators and a cassette with Arabic writing on it. The contents of the cassette tape were translated by 18.00 p.m. The cassette contained recitations of passages from the Koran that describe the battle between Islam and its enemies. This evidence seemed to put in doubt the official story promoted by the government. The cassette tape, however, was not strong enough evidence to reorient the entire investigation. According to the police, similar cassettes could be bought at almost any mosque across Spain (Olmeda 2008, 70). By late afternoon on March 11, rumours of the van with clues that did not necessarily point to ETA began to circulate in the media. Coupled with Aznar's poor excuses as to why he did not mention ETA by name, many journalists became suspicious of the government's official version of events. By the evening of March 11, 2004, the government still insisted that ETA was responsible, but it also admitted that a van with detonators and Koranic verses had been found. Acebes, in a press conference at 20.20 p.m., said that he had instructed the security forces to follow every lead, but that the main line of investigation continues to be ETA (Olmeda 2008, 65). That evening, King Juan Carlos's television message did not mention ETA by name.

At 21.30 p.m. on March 11, the Reuters news agency reported that the London based newspaper *Al-Quds al-Arabi* had received an email from the Abu Hafs al-Masri Brigades claiming responsibility for the attacks. The group was allegedly responsible for attacks in Istanbul several months before. The Spanish security forces did not find the declaration credible. The declaration was reported, however, in the world's largest news media organizations and websites. That evening, Zapatero phoned the director of *El Mundo* informing him that he was convinced that Al-Qaeda perpetrated the attacks and that in his opinion the government knew it (Olmeda 2008, 67). By 22.00 p.m. the radio station *Cadena Ser* was reporting that three distinct sources had confirmed that a suicide bomber had caused the first explosion at Atocha station. This new "evidence" enabled the opposition, according to Olmeda, "to develop a counter-narrative in accordance with its electoral platform" (71).

March 12, 2004

On March 12, the counter-narrative theory about the attacks that emerged on the evening of March 11 developed quickly, particularly in the media owned by the PRISA Group, which supported the Socialist Party (*El País, Cadena Ser*). The counter-narrative was spurred by yet more evidence pointing to Islamic terrorists, such as the discovery of a backpack with a nondetonated bomb, and a mobile phone with a prepaid card. According to Olmeda:

> the framing contest was being waged in different media. The PSOE's media supporters openly questioned the government line. Meanwhile, the PP media supporters and also public television did not seem to realise that their frame was being disputed. We can only speculate why they did not address the emerging counterframe. (2008, 73)

By March 12, virtually all political parties disputed the PP government line. Ibarretxe, who the day before had been the first to accuse ETA for perpetrating the attacks, called on the government to clarify who was responsible for the attacks (García-Abadillo 2005, 90). The *Congreso de los Diputados* (Spanish parliament) rewrote their condemnation of the attacks, erasing all mention of ETA. The group finally released a statement in the Basque newspaper *Gara* and on Basque radio television EITB at 18.00 p.m., which announced: "La organización ETA quiere hacer saber que no tiene ninguna responsabilidad en los atentados ocurridos ayer en Madrid" (ETA would like to declare that it had no responsibility for yesterday's attacks in Madrid) (90). ETA's statement went further by attempting to demarcate the PP's role in the attacks:

> El Gobierno del PP ha hecho una firme apuesta a favor de sacar fuera de las fronteras de España y Francia el conflicto que vive Euskal Herria e inter-nacionalizarlo. Entre los beneficios que Aznar esperaba obtener a cambio de su subordinación y colaboración leal con el Gobierno de Bush también está terminar de una vez por todas con el conflicto vasco. [. . .] Si los aten-tados del 11-M son una consecuencia directa de la política exterior de España para solucionar el conflicto de Euskal Herria, que considera un problema interno, ha tenido un efecto boomerang. El Gobierno de Aznar, en vez de hacer frente el problema, ha escapado de él convirtiéndolo en un problema mayor. (The PP Government has placed a firm bet in favour of internationalizing the Euskal Herria conflict. Among the benefits that Aznar hoped to obtain in exchange for his loyal subordination and collab-oration with the Bush Administration was the end of the Basque conflict. [. . .] If the March 11 attacks are a direct consequence of Spain's foreign policy to end the conflict of Euskal Herria, an internal problem, it has had a boomerang effect. The Aznar Government, instead of facing the problem, has evaded it, converting it into an even bigger problem). (García-Abadillo 2005, 90)

Despite the Minister of the Interior announcing the new evidence to the media, he still insisted that ETA was responsible and that he was convinced that new clues would prove that ETA perpetrated the attacks. In a new press conference Aznar again sustained the hypothesis that ETA was responsible: "Esa organización terrorista [se refería a ETA] está hecha para matar todo lo que puede, y es lo que hace y, a veces, lo consigue" (That terrorist organ-ization [referring to ETA] is made to kill everything it can, it's what it does, and sometimes, it achieves it) (García-Abadillo 2005, 88). But the govern-ment's narrative was increasingly weakened in the face of PSOE attacks.

According to Olmeda, the PSOE adopted a familiar Janus-faced political communication tactic: "its leader and prime-ministerial candidate, Zapatero, would ask for unity and solidarity, while his party secretary attacked the government for hiding information" (2008, 72). Early on March 12, on the television network Antena 3 TV, the PSOE accused the PP administration of hiding information and demanded that before the March 14 election it tell the Spanish people who was responsible for the attacks. Aznar responded to such allegations by stating that: "No hay ningún aspecto de la investigación que conozca el Gobierno que no se haya puesto en conocimiento de la opinión pública" (There is no aspect of the investigation that the government is aware of that has not been provided to the public) (García-Abadillo 2005, 89).

By March 12 there was evidence that a significant number of Spaniards were angry at the government. In one hospital, a mother who lost her 19-year old son in the attacks, screamed at the Minister for the Economy: "Hijo de puta, la bomba te la tenían que haber puesto a ti" (They should have bombed you, you son of a bitch!) (102). The radio station *Cadena Ser* was beginning to question the government's according of blame when it discovered that the government had ordered its embassies around the world to blame ETA for the attacks after it had received information that implicated Islamic terrorists (103). But it was the mass demonstrations witnessed across Spain in protest to the massacre in Madrid that heated the political atmosphere.

The demonstrations were conceived by the PP who wanted to repeat the mass demonstrations seen after the assassination of Miguel Ángel Blanco in July 1997 (see Chapter Two). In Barcelona, more than a million and a half people were estimated to have participated in the demonstration, which quickly turned aggressive. Many protesters began calling the PP representatives, including high profile PP members Rodrigo Rato and Josep Piqué, "asesinos" (murderers) and yelled "El Gobierno miente" (the Government is lying) and "¿Quién ha sido?" (Who did it?) (105). The PP leaders had to take refuge in a nearby police station. Other slogans included "¡No a la guerra!," (No to war!) and "Madrid y Bagdad, víctimas de la misma guerra" (Madrid and Baghdad, victims of the same war). In Madrid, the situation was the same. Demonstrations that were notably silent in their grief for the victims quickly became animated when Aznar appeared and many in the crowd yelled, "Aznar asesino" (Aznar murderer) and "Aznar culpable" (Aznar guilty).

March 13, 2004—The day of reflection

During the "day of reflection" (the day before a general election) any form of political electioneering is prohibited in Spain. But the media battle on March 13 only heated up. The solidarity evident across Spain on March 11, just two days before, had dissipated. The Spanish people wanted to know who was responsible for the attacks and were becoming increasingly sceptical of the government's evasions. Eduardo Haro Tecglen, the *El País* columnist said on *Cadena Ser* in the early morning:

> Es evidente que el Gobierno desea que haya sido ETA, porque es su lucha, es su objetivo desde el principio que ETA es la culpable de todo lo que pasa en el país. Es culpable de mucho, pero no de todo. Se sabe que es un acto de guerra, una respuesta a Europa y especialmente a España, que era agitadora de la guerra en todos los aspectos en las Azores, en la ONU y en todas partes. [. . .] ETA lo ha negado y las organizaciones islamistas lo han afirmado y lo ha afirmado Al-Yazira. [. . .] Pues no hay más vueltas que darle, es un acto de guerra. [. . .] Yo no sé por qué estamos discutiendo sobre quién es. No digo Al-Qaeda, los islámicos. Lo que hay que discutir es sobre qué pasa con la guerra que nos llega a nosotros a Madrid. Cómo vamos a discutir, si no es ETA. (It is evident that the Government wishes that ETA was responsible, because it's their fight, their objective since the beginning that ETA is responsible for everything that happens in this country. It's responsible for a lot. But not everything. We know that it's an act of war, a response to Europe and especially Spain, which was in every aspect a key proponent of war in the Azores, in the U.N. and everywhere. [. . .] ETA has denied responsibility and the Islamists have claimed it and *Al-Jazeera* has affirmed it. [. . .] There is nothing else to discuss, it is an act of war. [. . .] I don't know why we are discussing who is responsible. I'm not saying Al-Qaeda, the Islamists. What we have to discuss is what's going to happen with the war that is coming to Madrid. How are we going to argue if it isn't ETA?). (Quoted in García-Abadillo 2005, 160)

The sentiments expressed by Tecglen were being discussed in one way or another across bars and homes in Spain. But the PP administration continued to promote the narrative that ETA was responsible. Acebes, the Interior Minister, while informing the media that these had not been suicide attacks, insisted that logic and common sense pointed to an ETA attack. To complicate the PP narrative script, Acebes suggested a possible cooperation among different terrorist organizations, that is, ETA and Islamic terrorists working together (Olmeda 2008, 73).

On the streets, the mood was palpable. In Pamplona, a policeman shot dead a 61 year-old owner of a bakery for refusing to hang a banner outside his shop reading "ETA No." By 15.00 p.m. *Cadena Ser* reported that its sources in the CNI had confirmed that 99 percent of its resources were being used to follow the Islamic lead, and that they had informed the Interior Ministry on Thursday, March 11, the day of the attacks, that the ETA theory was vague (García-Abadillo 2005, 165). There was, therefore, a significant split between what the government was saying and the statements released by the security and intelligence services. At 20.10 p.m. the Interior Minister announced that the police had arrested five suspects, three Moroccans and two Indians, neither of whom had any relation to ETA. The five men were being investigated for the sale and falsification of the mobile phone found in a backpack on one of the trains used in the attacks. Meanwhile, an anonymous tip was received at Telemadrid by someone with a Moroccan accent that a videotape had been deposited in a bin near a mosque, and that the video indicated who the perpetrators of the attacks were. By 20.30, the police had retrieved the videotape and by 22.30 the tape had been transcribed and translated.

But the official day of reflection was dominated by what were referred to as "flash mobs" of protesters outside PP offices across Spain. By early Saturday, Madrid and many other Spanish cities were experiencing a phenomenon never seen before in Spain: thousands of Spaniards were sending SMS messages on their mobile phones calling for demonstrations outside PP headquarters. An example of these messages was as follows: "Hoy 13M. A los 18H. Sede del PP c/ Genova 13. Sin Partidos. Silencio X La Verdad. Pásalo" (Today March 13. At 18.00. PP Headquarters. 13 Genova St. No political parties. Silence for the Truth. Pass it on).

The messages were attributed to Izquierda Unida (IU, United Left) militants and to green and anti-globalization groups. While the PSOE prohibited its members from participating in any such demonstrations, and although the PSOE was not formally involved with this movement, many of its militants were. By 19.30 p.m. some 4000 people were outside the PP headquarters in Madrid and the numbers were steadily increasing. In Barcelona another 5000 demonstrators were chanting anti-government slogans. The fact that many demonstrators were carrying the same placard with the word "Paz" suggested some kind of organization behind the apparently spontaneous demonstrations. According to García-Abadillo, the mobilization would not have succeeded without the collaboration of *Cadena Ser*, which became the foremost media instrument lashing out against the government (2005, 178). One presenter on *Cadena Ser*, Paco González, stated:

Mañana hay elecciones y yo, que soy ateo en política, voy a ir a votar [. . .] porque no todos los políticos son iguales, [. . .] hay unos políticos menos malos que otros y hay políticos que nos mienten. [. . .] Esta vez, después de lo que pasó el jueves, si no votamos, es que no nos importa nada. (Tomorrow there is an election, and I, a political atheist am going to vote [. . .] because not all politicians are the same, [. . .] some politicians are not as bad as others and there are politicians who lie to us. [. . .] This time, after what happened on Thursday, if we do not vote, it means we do not care about anything). (Quoted in García-Abadillo 2005, 179)

Mariano Rajoy, Aznar's chosen successor, called the protests illegal, illegitimate and antidemocratic. In response, placards at the demonstration read "La voz del pueblo no es ilegal" (The voice of the people is not illegal). Socialist Minister Alfredo Pérez Rubalcaba openly accused the government of lying: "Los ciudadanos españoles merecen un Gobierno que no les mienta, que les diga siempre la verdad" (Spanish citizens deserve a government that does not lie to them and that always tells them the truth) (184). The conspiracy theories circulating on the evening of March 13 were numerous and incredible. *Cadena Ser* reported that police had had the videotape in possession from 12 noon. This was impossible given that the tape was recorded at 16.00 p.m. Another rumour was that the government had prepared a decree suspending the elections. Prominent Spaniards such as the film-maker Pedro Almodóvar promoted the theory that the PP was hatching a coup d'état. Many of the government's enemies, who had felt marginalized in Spanish society during the Aznar years, were taking great lengths to discredit it.

The immediate aftermath

In Madrid there was a real fear that the city would experience another round of attacks, and every North African with a bag or backpack was observed with suspicion. On April 2 an attempted attack on the high speed train link between Madrid and Seville was thwarted after a Renfe employee found a bag of explosives on the tracks. The device was made of the same explosives, and constructed in the same way, as those used on March 11. It was set up professionally, in a way that led investigators to believe that the terrorists had undergone specialist training in bomb-making (Nesser 2006, 328). A day later, clues from the failed attack led police to an apartment in the Madrid suburb of Leganés where a drawn out gun battle occurred between the police and the suspects. At 21.00 p.m. the building exploded, killing all seven suspects who the police thought had directly participated in the Madrid bombings (García-Abadillo 2005, 266). In the remains of the building the police found a videotape recorded on March 27, 2004. The video statement that was pieced together from the rubble of the hideout apartment contained threats of new attacks against Spain unless the Spanish troops were pulled out of Iraq immediately (Nesser 2006, 328). In the same message the group claimed that nothing had changed with the election of Zapatero and his new government:

> Tras comprobar que la situación no ha cambiado y después de que vuestro Nuevo gobernante anunciase la apertura de su mandato con más lucha contra los musulmanes y el envío de más tropas cruzadas a Afganistán [. . .] (After confirming that the situation has not changed and after your new leader announced his new mandate with more war against Muslims and more crusade troops to Afghanistan). (García-Abadillo 2005, 268)

Shattering the image of the evil and barbaric terrorist, the attackers were seemingly assimilated second-generation immigrants to Spain, or immigrants who had lived in Spain, or other European countries, for a long time: "They dressed and behaved like other young Spaniards. Some of them were described as handsome and fashionably dressed, some smoked and drank alcohol, and several had Spanish girlfriends or wives" (Nesser 2006, 329).

On April 15, 2004, Osama bin Laden justified the March 11 attacks in Madrid as a punishment for Aznar's support of Bush in Iraq, Afghanistan and Palestine (García-Abadillo 2005, 272). It was not clear, however, whether bin Laden had ordered the attacks in Madrid. His statement seemed to capitalize on the attacks rather than take merit for them. The Spanish secret services concluded that there were no instructions from Al-Qaeda to attack Spain. What was apparent, however, was that the attacks seemed to have changed the outcome of the national election. This startled the world's intelligence services, including the CIA. Could terrorism change the outcome of other elections around the world? Did terrorists have that power?

For the Bush Administration, the Spanish elections were a PR disaster. One of the USA's strongest allies in the war had been defeated. The election of the PSOE now meant the withdrawal of Spanish troops from the war. Although Spanish troops only made up 0.7 percent of the total military contribution, the withdrawal was a significant symbolic, rather than military, move. But it came at a time when the internal situation in Iraq was worsening and it led to a domino effect whereby other allies such as the Netherlands and Poland also withdrew their troops over the next two years.

Competing narratives

We have long known how fragile human life is and how easily disaster can be sowed in the places that seem safest. [. . .] With [the Madrid bombings and the election results] came scrutiny by those who fail to understand Spain, yet seek to judge us. (Molina 2004, 13)

According to Olmeda national crises are often thought to foster solidarity, a phenomenon commonly known as the "rally-'round the flag" effect (2008, 62). This effect was evident in the USA after the September 11, 2001 attacks, and in the United Kingdom after the July 7, 2005 attacks in London. But in Spain there was no such effect in political discourse. Olmeda argues that this is because "'rally-'round the flag' frames only function when opposition leaders do not criticize the government's policies" (64). A crisis frame, according to Olmeda, "promotes particular causes, consequences, culprits and cures" (64). In the Spanish case, the political parties offered radically different interpretations of the attacks. The PP explicitly suggested that the attacks were perpetrated by ETA and thus attempted to mobilize Spanish society behind the government's antiterrorism agenda (63). The Socialist opposition proposed a different narrative script by framing the attacks as punishment for Spanish participation in the occupation of Iraq. Thus, according to Olmeda, "the opposition managed to replace the initial and official narrative with one of its own" (63).

The single most important factor that determines the effectiveness of government crisis communication, according to Olmeda, is the degree of credibility that a government possesses (2008, 64). A track record of lies and deception, he argues, may undermine the credibility of the framing agent:

If a prime minister mismanages relationships with oppositional elites and journalists and fails to offer a compelling explanation for the impending emergency, he or she may lose control of the meaning-making process. [. . .] Crisis, should, in fact, be viewed as a "tipping point" in a longer process of declining legitimacy of government leaders and their narratives. (65)

The March 11 attacks were undoubtedly a tipping point and the Aznar administration clearly lost control of the meaning-making process. In Olmeda's view, the root of the PP's failure lies in the discourse surrounding Spain's participation in the Iraq War. The PP failed to communicate a convincing narrative to frame its peacekeeping mission in Iraq. The opposition Socialists, however, backed by the great majority of Spanish society

(91 percent), successfully framed the Spanish engagement in Iraq as a war mission.

Why did so many Spaniards want to blame the PP for the Madrid attacks? As García-Abadillo paraphrases an Almodóvar film, many in the PP were asking themselves: "¿Qué hemos hecho nosotros para merecer esto?" (What have we done to deserve this?) (2005, 196). Twelve months after the attacks in Madrid, a study conducted by Narciso Michavila for the *Real Instituto Elcano* (2005) concluded that there were four hypothetical explanations for the unexpected electoral turnaround: (1) a latent desire for a change of government; (2) the shock caused by the attacks; (3) a desire to punish the government for its position on the war in Iraq; and (4) a dual manipulation of information—by the government and against the government (2005, 2–3). After studying these hypotheses and the changes in voting patterns as a result of the attacks, the report concluded that the electoral turnaround necessarily involved the confluence of each of the three first hypotheses, while the fourth (the manipulation of information in both political directions) reinforced them. This means that without a latent desire for change, without the intervention in Iraq, and without the attacks, no electoral turnaround would have occurred on March 14, 2004 (3). Of the four hypotheses, however, the two-way manipulation of information generated the most media attention and citation (21). In a similar study, "Terror and Elections: Lessons from Spain" (2007), Valentina Bali also concluded that the attacks altered the turnout and vote decisions of many Spaniards (670). The event mobilized people who were traditionally less likely to vote, such as the young and the less educated, as well as centrist and leftist voters. The attacks also spurred some voters to switch their party vote (670).

The narrative that Spain was being punished for its participation in the Iraq War remains debatable, as is the argument that the withdrawal of troops from Iraq has made Spain less of a target for Islamic terrorists. Petter Nesser's investigation into the motivations for the March 11 attacks argues that it is highly plausible that the Iraq War was the main factor at the group level (2006, 329). For Nesser, the individual motivations for joining the 11 March terrorist cell are far more difficult to grasp, and probably involved a complex mix of social and religio-political grievances related to the perpetrators' lives in the Muslim diaspora in Europe, as well as perceived attacks on Islam and Muslims in places such as Palestine, Chechnya, Kashmir, and Iraq (329). Moreover, in December 2003, a document on an Islamic message board on the internet, entitled *Jihadi Iraq, Hopes and Dangers*, was discovered by the Norwegian Defense Institute (FFI). The posting identified Spain as the country most likely to pull forces out of Iraq if they suffered "painful blows" close to the general elections, and anticipated that an attack would lead to victory for the socialist party, which had the withdrawal of Spanish soldiers on its electoral platform (Nesser 2006, 331).

Fernando Reinares's study, *El nuevo terrorismo islamista. Del 11-S al 11-M* (2004), however, regards this narrative as an oversimplification. Reinares posits that the war in Iraq was, for the March 11 attackers, a mere pretext to justify the massacre. Radical Islamists consider Spain a target for a number of reasons. Before the Iraq War, arrests between 1997 and 2003 of Jihad militants in Spain made revenge a motivating factor (Jordán & Horsburgh 2005, 175). Other factors included the Spanish intervention in Afghanistan, and the place of Al-Andalus in a pan-Islamic imaginary (Osama bin Laden has referred to "the tragedy of al-Andalus" when speaking about Spain, a tragedy that should not be allowed to recur in Saudi Arabia or Palestine).[2] In October 2003, bin Laden promised "crusader Spain" repercussions for its participation in the Afghan and Iraq wars (Celso 2005, 87). Furthermore, the two Spanish conclaves of Melilla and Ceuta on the Moroccan coast are regarded by some radical Muslims in Morocco as an invasion of Muslim territory.

It is understandable that the PP initially blamed ETA for the March 11 attacks. ETA had both the motive and a history of attacks in Madrid (including railways), and was, for the most part, the only significant terrorist group active in Spain. Other groups such as GRAPO, the military wing of one of Spain's Communist parties, were by comparison minor players, and did not provoke the same levels of outrage as attacks by the nationalist ETA did. But according blame to ETA did go against the fact that ETA had never in its history launched an attack on such a scale, favouring instead target assassinations. Moreover, ETA had been severely weakened during the Aznar years between 1996 and 2004 after successful joint operations between Spanish and French police departments. The PP's blame narrative also failed to take into consideration the post-9/11 context, repeated warnings from Islamic extremists against the USA's allies, and Spain's high-profile participation in the invasion of, and subsequent war, in Iraq. Furthermore, given the increasing numbers of disaffected immigrants from North Africa who reside on the margins of Spanish society and are exploited as cheap labour, the idea that Islamic fundamentalists might execute an attack in Spain was not that far-fetched. Spain once had an Islamic history spanning some 800 years, a source of pride for many Islamic and Spanish scholars, and a place in an Islamic imagination as a lost paradise. Spain was therefore at the nexus

---

[2] Bin Laden is referring to the final stage in the Christian conquest of Moorish Spain in 1492 and the defeat of Granada, the last remaining Islamic kingdom on the Iberian Peninsula.

of world events in the post-9/11 era, in terms of both historical imaginary connections and political-military design.

There is no denying that some of Aznar's actions hurt the credibility of the government. For instance, Aznar wanted to manage the crisis alone; he preferred to meet with his electoral adviser in his crisis cabinet meetings and did not include the head of the Spanish intelligence services; and he did not consult other political parties in the mass demonstration of March 12, placing himself at the front of the demonstration. Furthermore, Acebes's appearances on television were confusing, inconsistent and always denied the obvious, suggesting that the PP government was hiding something or, at the very least, not telling everything it knew. Yet, what matters here is not whether the PP manipulated the media or not, but rather why the PP narrative failed to convince the majority of Spanish people of its realness. Put more simply, why did the PP government insist on such an elaborate narrative? This question is particularly important given that most of the Spanish media reported the government line with little questioning.

Three days before the election, the PP government did not want to admit that the Madrid attack was connected with the wider war on terrorism. Spain's participation in the war in Iraq was controversial enough, but the government was loath to concede that somehow Spain was being punished for it. The message that the PP promoted to the Spanish people was that the government was reclaiming Spain's past glory. The accepted media narratives in the aftermath of the March 11 attacks were that the PP government was voted out of government because it manipulated the flow of information by insisting that ETA was responsible. This became the official narrative of the PSOE government, and was adopted by most of the Spanish and international media. Although some international leaders and media outlets (and indeed some of the Spanish media) interpreted the March 2004 election result as an act of cowardice by the Spanish electorate in the face of the global war on terrorism, there was a general feeling in Spain that the election demonstrated the maturity of the Spanish people, who had rejected the manipulation of the event by the government. Paddy Woodworth also argues that the Spanish electorate responded quickly to a fast-changing and complex crisis:

> Spanish voters did not vote out of fear because Spanish democracy has been intimidated for more than thirty years by ETA's bombings and shootings. Moreover, the maturity of Spanish democracy was demonstrated by the Spanish police and intelligence services, which refused to be misled by the government and quickly and professionally tracked down the most likely culprits. (2004a, 22)

But interestingly, certain Spanish conservative critics offer desimplifying insight into the ways the attacks and the election converged with Spain's longstanding and historically contested narratives of nationhood.

The essay, *Terrorismo y democracia tras el 11-M* (2004) by Edurne Uriarte, a conservative columnist for the right-wing Spanish daily *ABC*, exemplifies the Spanish right's perception of the March 11 attacks and the subsequent PP defeat. Uriarte argues that an emotional discourse about solidarity, and the values and unity of the Spanish people united against terrorism, permeates the official narratives of terror in Spain. The strength of these popular narratives is such that few politicians, media representatives and outlets, or intellectuals dare to question them. As a result, the March 12 demonstrations throughout Spanish cities that were meant to condemn the attack, instead became a condemnation of the government widely considered to be responsible for the attacks. Although the protesters claimed that they only denounced the manipulation of information by the government in the hours following the attack, Uriarte was perplexed by the demonstrators' need to know the identity of the killers (17). For the first time in the Spanish history of terrorism, Uriarte claims, the central point was not the crime itself, or its perpetrators, but the role of the government in identifying, or failing to identify, the perpetrators immediately after the attack (29). Thus, according to Uriarte, the context of panic in the people caused a national obsession with the truth—as if knowing the identity of the perpetrators would alleviate momentarily the reality of the massacre (29). The guilty party is no longer the aggressor but found in the ranks of those meant to protect the people —the government (17). After the attacks, the people wanted to return to a life of tranquillity and security. Thus, they believed that the only way to achieve this would be to eliminate the factor that had provoked Al Qaeda: the presence of Spanish troops in Iraq. Uriarte connects this reaction to the phantom of dictatorship that still shadows Spanish politics. Uriarte regards the idea that there is a phantom of dictatorship as Spain's main weakness, one that leads Spaniards to the margins of the fight against terrorism, and that allows the PP's opponents in the 2004 general elections to accuse the PP of being the inheritors of Francoism.

It was therefore not the manipulation of information in itself that caused the downfall of the PP government, but the phantom presence of the Franco dictatorship in Spanish political discourse. The PP government underestimated the extent to which its re-orientation of government policy in many areas did not coincide with the modern post-Franco narratives of the Spanish state. The transition to democracy in the late 1970s and early 1980s was successful because the various pacts of compromise were bolstered by an unofficial policy of forgetting the ghosts of the past. In 2004, then, the

PP failed to adhere to one of the key rules in political campaigning: to convince the electorate. The PP did not recognize how deeply the narratives of compromise operated in Spanish political society. Nor did the PP recognize that violence was no longer a key to Spanish notions of national identity. The PP continued to promote the historical narratives of Francoism in a nation caught between forgetting the past and recuperating the memory of the victims of the past. In an international context of transnational justice that the Spanish judicial system had helped spearhead, the narrative that the PP wove was an embarrassing misstep.

In this instance, the global War on Terror narrative failed to galvanize and unite the Spanish electorate after the Madrid attacks. Such political unity in the face of terror was readily apparent in the USA after the September 11 attacks, in Australia after the Bali bombings of 2002, and to a great extent in the United Kingdom after the London attacks of 2005. Yet, in Spain, the historical divisions between left and right, republican and nationalist, and centre and periphery, re-emerged to split the Spanish electorate. Although initially the head of the Catalan government Pasqual Maragall said, "We are all Madrileños today," the political fallout of the 2004 national election left deep scars. To what extent the former Spanish conservative government was punished because it manipulated the truth is debatable. However, the March 11 attacks indicate that the former Spanish government perceived a threat to its electoral chances if the perpetrators of the March 11 attacks were Islamists, and thus argued, against all evidence to the contrary, that the domestic terrorist group ETA were the likely perpetrators. Moreover, the Spanish electorate saw the danger in participating in a US-led War on Terror that operates in a state of total or perpetual war; voters embraced the Socialist Party that had promised to remove Spanish troops from Iraq and re-align itself firmly with the peaceful EU. Total war is a hard sell to an electorate struggling to negotiate competing historical narratives and internal schisms and ruptures. The global War on Terror (meta)narrative can neither compete with, nor override, domestic politics still coming to terms with the Spanish state's multiple histories and national narratives.

Conclusion

History does not always have reason, purpose and direction. As Wendy Brown argues in *Politics Out of History* (2001), in the post-Cold War world the past becomes "less easily reduced to a single set of meanings and effects, as the present is forced to orient itself amid so *much* history and so *many* histories, history emerges as both weightier and less deterministic than ever before" [original emphasis] (2001, 5). Yet state institutions, as well as individuals, often operate politically as if the historical constitutive narratives of a state are infallible and perpetual. By attempting to construct narratives based on the presumption that there is only one true and valid history, the PP made a political blunder that cost it dearly. The disavowal of the PP and its narratives by the Spanish people was evidence that the former narratives of the Spanish state were (at least for the moment) exhausted in a state already negotiating with multiple histories and national narratives or imaginaries. The Spanish example, then, is telling in a number of ways. It demonstrates that memories of social terror (Francoism) leave a trace in the politics of the present. In times of national crisis these memories regain potency and are politicized within and through state-mediated discourses. In the Spanish case, the pacts of compromise that characterized the Spanish transition to democracy, although still in operation, have been undermined since the mid-1990s. As a result, the PP's rhetoric in the days between the March 11 attacks and the March 14 election did not coincide with the popular narratives of the Spanish state or national meaningfulness that posited that Spain had jettisoned past Francoist rhetoric and now operated as a cosmopolitan and democratic member of the European Union.

The next chapter discusses the fallout of the March 11 attacks and the March 14 general election in Spanish politics. The three fateful days in March haunted Zapatero's first period in office (2004–2008). The Zapatero years were marked by what the Spanish press referred to as *crispación*, a vitriolic form of political polarization that definitively undermined the transition's consensus politics. Those three fateful days set the stage for a full-scale ideological and rhetorical war between the two Spains and their respective terror narratives.

CHAPTER SIX

The Zapatero Years
(2004–2011)

Crispación and the Return of *las dos Españas*

All in all, PSOE's victory is bad news—bad news for Spain, where the successful anti-terrorist, economic, and foreign policies of the Aznar era might well be overturned; bad news for the international struggle against Islamic terror, which has seen its greatest political victory ever on March 14; and bad news for bilateral Spanish/US ties. (Radu 2006, 163)

Relations between the members of the new PSOE government and the new PP opposition began on agreeable terms in 2004 with the latter's formal recognition of the Socialist victory and the promise of a healthy approach in opposition. But the cordial relations between the two parties quickly became strained. The official PP narratives radically shifted in the aftermath of both the Madrid bombing and the March 14 elections by now sowing doubts as to who was the so-called mastermind of the March 11 attacks, and by insisting that without the attack, the PP would still be the government of Spain. The PP narratives also suggested that there was a connection between the electoral defeat and a conspiracy involving ETA; as proponents of these narratives argued, ETA had everything to gain from a Socialist victory. More conspicuously, the PP intimated that the PSOE itself had something to hide about what happened in those days in March.

According to Spanish historian Santos Juliá writing in *El País* (2005, 2), the purpose of these narratives was to erode and undermine the legitimacy of the PSOE victory. Tellingly, the repetition and the insidious nature of these narratives elided neatly with the traditional conservative narratives of Spanish national identity. By repeating the line that Zapatero refused to lift the veil on the whole truth (what this truth could be remained unspoken), the insinuation was that "something [was] being plotted—some shameful concession to terrorism, or some treacherous surrender to the enemy, or some betrayal of the unity of Spain" (Juliá 2005, 2). The PP considered the

PSOE government's dealings with the regional nationalists, its conciliatory approach to regional government, and its refusal to take legal action against the Communist Party of the Basque Country for allegedly being a political front for ETA, as evidence that the Zapatero administration was breaking the spirit of consensus in post-Franco Spain. The PP's repetition of simple messages, instead of putting forward policy ideas, may have been arrogant but to a certain extent was effective. The repetition of these narratives in radio shows and newspapers fixed them as central questions of political debate. This in turn forced the Socialists to respond to these allegations, even if the allegations pointed to the preposterous idea that the Socialists masterminded the Madrid bomb attack in order to win government.

The Zapatero years (2004–2011) were characterized by what the Spanish press referred to as *crispación*. This literally translates as tension or tensing but probably is best translated in English as polarization. Spanish sociologist and political commentator Enrique Gil Calvo, who blames the PP for provoking the *crispación* of Spanish political discourse, argues that the PP strategy was a remake of the same political strategy that the PP had used during González's last legislature (1993–1996). In that period, however, most of the polarization was a result of the many political scandals that were damaging the Socialists, such as the GAL and Filesa controversies. In Zapatero's first legislature, however, the polarization was mostly due to the manipulation of two main issues: the March 11 attacks, and the PSOE administration's counterterrorism policies. Related to the March 11 attacks, the PP consistently argued that the PSOE's election victory was illegitimate and that the elections were stolen. To prove it a whole range of conspiracy theories were put forward by the PP's media allies. Related to the PSOE's counterterrorism policies the PP projected two main narrative threads: first, the narrative of *España se rompe* (that the Zapatero administration was in secret negotiation with radical nationalists and terrorists to break up Spain); and second, the narrative of *traición a las víctimas* (that by negotiating with terrorists the Zapatero administration was betraying the victims of terrorism). The strategy of *crispación* by the PP attempted to give Spaniards the impression that the current political situation was untenable, and that Zapatero was placing Spain on the edge of a dangerous precipice (Calleja 2008, 266–67). The PSOE, on the other hand, argued that life in Spain had never been better, despite the doomsday narratives promoted by the PP and its media supporters on a daily basis. The truth, however, was that both the PP and the PSOE were partly responsible for the polarization of Spanish politics.

This chapter examines the mass-mediated divisions and narrative battles that circulated in Spanish political discourse particularly during Zapatero's first legislature (2004–2008). This chapter explores in detail the process of *crispación* in two main areas: the polarization of political discourse that stemmed from the March 11, 2004, attacks in Madrid; and the polarization that emerged from the narrative projected by the PP that *España se rompe* (that Spain was being broken up or Balkanized). The narrative of *traición a las víctimas* (betraying the victims), which was tied to the Zapatero government's peace talks with ETA, is explained in the next chapter. The next section first provides a succinct overview of the process of *crispación* and discusses how that process was tied to the long-standing historical narrative of *las dos Españas*.

The process of *crispación*

Zapatero's first legislature (2004–2008) began under tense circumstances. Just three days after the March 11, 2004, terrorist attacks in Madrid and the humiliating defeat of the PP, the relatively inexperienced José Luis Rodríguez Zapatero became Spanish Prime Minister. Zapatero's unexpected victory was accompanied by the familiar cry of *"no nos falles"* (don't let us down), recalling the eventual disenchantment that many Spaniards had of the González era. Many PP supporters considered Zapatero to be an accidental prime minister who fostered discord and anxiety in Spanish society. The media attacks against Zapatero from the right-wing press were insidious and scathing, and far more vitriolic than anything ever written against Zapatero's predecessor, Felipe González. One example by the well-known right-wing journalist/academic Gabriel Albiac is telling. The day after Zapatero won the general election he wrote: "España, ayer, decidió morir [. . .] Al dolor, siguió el asco. Asco por el obsceno uso electoralista que PSOE e IU han hecho de la tragedia, en las 48 horas moralmente más turbias de la España reciente. Empieza, a partir de ahora, lo peor" (Yesterday, Spain decided to die [. . .] After pain came disgust. Disgust at the PSOE's and IU's electoral use of the tragedy, in the most morally murky 48 hours in recent Spanish history. Now comes the worst) (2008, 66). Albiac's statements were actually rather moderate. Others referred to Zapatero as "el peor presidente de Gobierno y el menos preparado de la historia de España" (the worst and least prepared president in Spanish history) (quoted in Palomo 2008, 137) or "el presidente más sectario de la Historia de España" (the most sectarian president in Spanish history) (141). The extraordinary circumstances that led to the defeat of the PP mobilized large sections of Spanish society, particularly among PP voters, to rally against the Zapatero administration in a process labelled by the Spanish press as *crispación*.

Although political polarization is to a certain extent a phenomenon that exists in all political societies, and has always existed in Spanish political discourse, there is agreement by Spanish politicians and journalists that the first Zapatero legislature was a period of four years with an unprecedented level of polarization and political differences not seen since Spain's restoration of democracy. Journalist Graciano Palomo suggests that never before was there a legislature "tan vana, crispada, huera y absurda" (so vain, polarized, vacuous and absurd) (2008, 9). The catchphrase *las dos Españas* became a hallmark of the PSOE government's first term of office, and media commentators went back to their history books in an attempt to explain where such animosity came from. It was as if all the hatred that lingered between the two Spains, dating back eighty years to the Spanish Civil War, finally exploded. Spain was, in Palomo's words, "de nuevo en un enfrentamiento abierto sobre dos formas antagónicas de concebir España" (once again in an open confrontation between two antagonistic visions of Spain) (149).

According to Gil Calvo, political polarization in Spain is more intense than in other similar countries because the media in Spain is primarily used as a vehicle to settle political scores. Conflict has ceased to be a means to resolve civil problems and is now a means in itself (2008, 14). *Crispación* is essentially a politically driven process, manipulated by political elites in order to gain electoral advantage. Since the polarization of Spanish politics is a mass-mediated process, the competing partisan narratives eventually led to a stalemate. The Socialists argued that the PP abandoned the centre and had returned to its right-wing roots, and in the process destroyed the spirit of *convivencia* and consensus, which had been the hallmark of Spain's transition to democracy. The PP argued similarly when it posited that it was actually the PSOE who had broken the spirit of consensus, and in the process destroyed the unity of Spain.

The remit of this section is not to determine which side of the "two Spains" is responsible for fuelling the process of *crispación*. There is ample evidence pinpointing to the radicalism of both the left and right's political ideologies. Instead, this section aims to understand why Spanish politics experienced such intense political polarization during the years 2004 to 2008. One explanation could be the structural makeup of the Spanish electoral system. That is, governments that do not obtain an absolute majority must align themselves with regional nationalists, effectively marginalizing the opposition, and thus leaving the opposition with no other recourse but to resort to extremist political rhetoric and doomsday scenarios in order to damage the credibility of the government. But this is true in most political systems and is not a very convincing explanation. Instead, a more credible argument is the continued presence of historical memories of conflict and violence and the role that such memories continue to play in the current politics of the Spanish state.

In Spain, the memory battles of the Spanish Civil War and the Franco regime are now part of the current political climate. Spanish politics in the Zapatero era, according to Gil Calvo, can be neatly divided into the divisions of the Spanish Civil War, between the *rojos* (reds) and *azules* (blues), and the great division between the victors and the defeated. It is no coincidence, he argues, that Zapatero is the grandson of a Republican who was executed during the Civil War, and that notable politicians of the PP are descendants of former Francoists, indicating that the polarization in Spanish politics is inherited from father to son and mother to daughter (2008, 103). The historical role of the Spanish right in the twentieth century in sustaining the Franco regime has also made it difficult for the PP to shed its extremist and authoritarian past. Santiago Carrillo, the former Spanish communist leader has suggested that the PP is the same as the Spanish right of 1936 (Palomo 2006, 179). More scathing still, he argues that "la derecha de nuestro país continúa pareciéndose más a Le Pen que a Sarkozy" (the right in our country continues to resemble more Le Pen than Sarkozy) (354). Even the bastion of British conservative politics, the *Financial Times*, editorialized that the PP had not entirely overcome its Francoist roots and had yet to become a truly modern centre-right political party ("Spain's Choice" 2008, 8).

The traditional division between the left and right is further complicated by the demands of regional nationalists who, although conservative in nature, tend to have more affinity with the PSOE due to a shared history of exclusion and suffering under the Franco regime. The Spanish right, although united, is therefore isolated in the political arena. The division between the left and regional nationalists on the one hand, and the right on the other, continues to be potent for two reasons: first because each of these groups has a selective memory of history and second, that this selective memory allows each of these groups to believe it is historically innocent and a victim of the misdeeds of others. History thus allows these constituent groups to legitimize their own political struggles. The eternal struggle between the two Spains is in continual replay, many decades after the end of the Spanish Civil War.

Gil Calvo argues that the main cause of this perpetual battle is that the Spanish right, unlike other European right-wing totalitarian regimes such as Nazi Germany, Fascist Italy and Vichy France, has neither symbolically rejected the Francoist excesses nor expressed regret for what occurred during the Franco years. Although other cognate European countries did not repent voluntarily, and were instead forced to publicly recognize the wrongs of their regimes, the process in itself went some way in healing the schism in civil society. In Spain, however, there was no equivalent process to de-Nazification as there was in Germany. Instead, historical regret or guilt have been dealt with in secret and silence through the Catholic ritual of confession. In order for there to be true reconciliation in Spain, argues Gil Calvo, the Spanish right must accept responsibility for the crimes of Francoism. Likewise, the Spanish left must accept the responsibility for the crimes and excesses of the Republican side (2008, 115–16).

The polarization of Spanish politics during the Zapatero years also points to the idea that the constant theme of the Spanish transition to democracy—"nunca más," never again would Spain resort to civil war—has lost much of its potency. Zapatero effectively overturned the González strategy of forgetting the past and getting on with business, a strategy that was successful in establishing and consolidating democracy. During the González years, Spain joined the EU and NATO, experienced immense economic growth and a rise in living standards, avoided a military coup, and even resorted to the use of paramilitary death squads to fight ETA. The Socialists under González also kept Francoist symbols and monuments across Spain in place and did not attempt to remove them. González insisted that he governed for all Spaniards and did not wish to provoke the million or so Spaniards who identified with the extreme right (Gil Calvo 2008, 185). Similarly, the Communist Party did not campaign for the removal of Francoist symbols and joined the Socialists in guaranteeing a secure future for democracy. Thus, by the end of the González years, the need for consensus slowly dissipated, because the possible return to the politics of the 1930s and its Civil War became a remote concern for the average Spaniard. With the narrative of political consensus no longer a necessary and founding narrative of the Spanish state, political confrontation, manipulating controversial historical narratives and settling political scores became effective means to win government.

It is important to foreground some of the issues that the process of *crispación* opened in Spanish politics, whereby the Spanish left and right took opposing positions, in order to demonstrate how their narratives differed. The Spanish right believes that Zapatero attempted to reopen doors that González tried to shut, such as the reformation of the Autonomous Communities and the Historical Memory Law (2007). The PP attitude, according to Palomo, reflects how "¡los perdedores de la Guerra Civil quieren reescribir la Historia! ¡Cobardes!" (the losers of the Civil War want to rewrite history! Cowards!) (2008, 68). What particularly irked the Spanish right was the perception that Zapatero sought to return the spectre of the Civil War and the Franco regime back to Spanish politics when many Spaniards thought that had been relegated to the past. The Socialists referred to this process as "la Segunda Transición" (the Second Transition) accompanied by a return to the values of the Second Republic.

Between 2004 and 2008, both the PSOE and the PP contributed to the process of *crispación*: the PP for not acknowledging the legitimacy of its electoral defeat; the PSOE for tending to exclude the PP on major government reforms that required political consensus. The PSOE, which has more or less abandoned its traditional socialist program in the face of globalization and neo-liberalism, sought alternative issues to distinguish itself from the PP, namely the restructuring of the State of Autonomies, the peace process with ETA, legalizing gay marriage and promoting the Historical Memory Law. The Zapatero administration managed to approve these measures with the support of regional nationalists, effectively marginalizing the PP as the main opposition party. These are arguably significant issues that would require cross party support in order to be introduced successfully and avoid political polarization. However, by initiating these reforms the PSOE set itself up for a full-scale ideological war with the PP and the Catholic Church. Many of the PSOE's legislative changes are therefore regarded as illegitimate by almost half of the Spanish electorate, doing away with Spain's historic spirit of consensus on matters of state and security. Considering that the PSOE did not gain an absolute majority in the March 14, 2004, elections, and that these elections discursively represented a vote against Aznar rather than a vote for the Socialists' electoral program, the Zapatero reforms were a political misjudgement for many political commentators on both the right and the left.

The pursuit of strongly ideological issues by the PSOE after gaining office was a strategy to monopolize the political centre, thus highlighting the extremism of the conservatives and the regional nationalists. Cernuda argues that Zapatero cleverly re-branded the PP as an opportunist, anti-nationalist party of the extreme right (2008, 18). Palomo refers to the PP as the PPN during these years: "el Partido Popular del No (PPN)" (the Popular Party of No) (179). The PP's strategy led to the public perception that the party is always indignant and opposed to possible change: the Historical Memory law, new regional policies, the liberalization of laws to do with sexuality, and so on. Almost every sentence in statements from the PP after the 2004 election began with "El PP no va a tolerar . . . ," or "No vamos a consentir . . . ," or "Bajo ningún concepto estamos dispuestos a . . . " (The PP will not tolerate . . . We will not consent to . . . Under no circumstances are we willing to . . .). The litany of negative phrases painted a picture of an impotent and one-note opposition party (166). To be fair to the PSOE, the PP's image was tarnished by the many demonstrations convened in various Spanish cities throughout Zapatero's first term that denounced a whole series of the government's policies and reforms. For instance, when the *Foro Español de la Familia* organized a demonstration against gay marriage in 2004, it invited the PP and thus put the PP leader Mariano Rajoy in a difficult situation. The demonstration sustained the idea promulgated by the Socialists that the PP was influenced by right-wing groups and could not accept the inevitable changes of a modern society.

The PP, in turn, promoted the narrative that it is the only party that is firm against terrorism, nationalists, and immigrants. That rhetoric aimed to delegitimize Zapatero by casting him as Spain's principal enemy, the person breaking with the tradition of consensus established with the Spanish transition to democracy. By inference, the PP represents the embodiment of what Franco once was: Spain's only salvation, capable of bringing stability back to a Spain under threat of disintegration. It is difficult to say which of the two Spains was narratively more successful during this period. The left argued that the right successfully polarized Spanish society in the image of the 1930s. But electorally, the Socialists managed to maintain their lead on the PP. According to Palomo, thanks to the Socialist's narrative strategy, the terms neoliberal and neoconservative had become, in Spain, pejorative labels (2008, 153). He also suggests that intellectuals on the Spanish left have been far cannier in the propaganda and culture wars, whereas intellectuals from the right have been complacent (153). Typically in such a situation of political polarization, each side accuses the other of illegitimately attacking the other in unprecedented dirty media attacks. Both sides denounce the unfair and partisan interests of the other party's media supporters. The PP routinely attacks the PRISA Group (publisher of Spain's largest newspaper *El País* and owner of the radio station *Cadena Ser*), while the PSOE denounces the newspaper *El Mundo*, which it routinely dismisses as "la prensa amarilla," and the Catholic Church owned radio station *Cope*.

The four years of Zapatero's first legislature were marked by a number of events that strengthened the political polarization. For instance, in June 2006, the opposition leader Mariano Rajoy announced that, due to the government's lies, the PP would break off all relations with the Socialists in parliament. In Spanish political discourse that week was one of the most hyperbolic, vituperative and excessive since the Franco era. The President of the Autonomous Community of Madrid, Esperanza Aguirre, called on Zapatero to apologize for the crimes of Joseph Stalin and the Soviet Gulags. More controversial still, the PP's secretary-general Ángel

Acebes affirmed on June 5, 2006 that "El proyecto de Zapatero es el proyecto de ETA" (Zapatero's project is ETA's project) (quoted in Palomo 2008, 150). On June 10, 2006, in the Plaza de Colón in Madrid, an anti-government protest led by the Association of Victims of Terrorism (AVT) was the largest of its nature ever seen in Spain. The demonstrators protested against the "padre de todas las incertidumbres" (father of all uncertainties) and "el gran traidor" (the great traitor) (151). In a demonstration in Barcelona campaigning for a "no" vote in the referendum for a new Catalan Statute of Autonomy, Rajoy was almost physically attacked by Catalan independendistas, and then again a few weeks later in Ponferrada and Zamora by both militant socialists and Galician nationalists (152). Rajoy was reliving more than thirty years later the ire that the Spanish right inspired in the late 1970s when even walking in public was a dangerous activity (152).

In such a polarized political environment the PP had no other recourse but to attempt to reclaim the Spanish centre. On March 10, 2007, Mariano Rajoy convened a mass demonstration for "gente normal" (normal people, that is, the silent majority), which was orchestrated to allow Spaniards to view him as presidential material in solidarity with the victims of terrorism. Rajoy's so-called normal people reportedly called for Zapatero's death, demanded to know who was really responsible for the March 11 attacks, and claimed that the Catholic radio station *Cope* is the voice of "Verdad y Libertad" (Truth and Freedom). The demonstrators referred to Rajoy as *Presidente*, indicating that three years after the March 11 attacks, the narrative that the elections were stolen by some kind of Socialist masterminded conspiracy was still potent. According to Calleja, there were more shouts against the elected democratic government than against the actual terrorists themselves, and public signs were appearing that denied Islamist involvement in the March 11 attacks (116). About the demonstration Rajoy said: "Me da igual que me critiquen o no. Yo creo en esto, en España, en el Rey, en nuestra bandera. Y es lo que vamos a hacer (I don't care if they criticize me. I believe in this, in Spain, in the King, in our flag) (Palomo 2008, 362). A week later, on March 17, 2007, another protest was held by the PP in Navarre where speakers insisted that Navarre had been promised to ETA by the Zapatero administration. As Calleja maintains, the constant repetition of such falsehoods aimed to paint the Zapatero administration as a government of traitors to Spain (117).

The four years of *crispación* demonstrated more than anything that the narratives of terror stemming from the Basque Country and the Basque conflict had become a pan-Spanish phenomenon. According to Calleja:

Al menos en Madrid, ya podemos hablar de síntomas de esa fractura social: grupos de amigos que dejan de hablar de política para evitar las broncas, familias que se lían a gritos en comidas destinadas al encuentro y que terminan en gresca a cuenta de la política, miradas de odio e insultos por la calle, persecución a los lectores de El País. (At least in Madrid, we can already speak about social rupture: groups of friends that stop speaking about politics to avoid arguments, family reunions that end in rows and shouting matches because of politics, hateful looks and insults on the street, persecution of *El País* readers). (2008, 114)

It was clear that the process of *crispación* not only sold newspapers but also provided an efficient way to communicate mixed messages to the Spanish electorate. This was especially true in regards to the aftermath of the Madrid attacks. After the attacks, parts of the Spanish media sensed that there was more to the story than had emerged, and thus continued to dig around for new revelations. Much of the rumour and innuendo came from the PP and, as the next section suggests, the PP's strategy between 2004 and 2008 was to try and win an election that had had already taken place in 2004 and that it thus could never win. This strategy led to disaster. The schism in Spanish political discourse that was opened with the March 11 attacks remains, many years later, unhealed.

The March 11 attacks and blame games

La historia de la España contemporánea mutó en aquella mañana del 11 de marzo de 2004. Nos alcanzó la Guerra. Nos hirió. Nos rendimos. Decidimos que no había sucedido. Y optamos por amar a nuestros asesinos. (The history of contemporary Spain mutated that morning on March 11, 2004. The war reached us. It wounded us. We gave in. We decided that it did not happen. And we opted to love our murderers). (Albiac 2008, 57)

Catharsis after the March 11 attacks proved elusive. The process of looking forward after a crisis, according to Boin, McConnell and Hart, "is hindered because the process of looking back turns out to be inconclusive and contested" (2008, 10). In the aftermath of the March 11, 2004, attacks in Madrid, José María Calleja suggests that nobody could have imagined on that fateful day that the massacre would be used to polarize political discourse, help sell newspapers, excuse an electoral defeat, and insult the victims of terrorism (2008, 39). The Spanish reaction to the

March 11 attacks in Madrid illustrates the severity of political polarization in Spanish political discourse. Unlike the USA and the UK, which came together in impressive displays of solidarity after the September 11 attacks in the USA and the July 7, 2005, attacks in London, the Madrid attacks caused deep hostility between the PP administration and virtually all other sections of Spanish politics. Condemnations were directed at political foes rather than at the perpetrators of the attacks, and both sides believed they were right to feel indignation. The PP was convinced that the March 11 attacks were part of a Socialist strategy, perfectly organized to win votes for the PSOE. According to some sections of the PP, the Socialist government had meticulous, secret plans to prevent the right from again governing Spain. The Socialists were accused of attempting to liquidate "la vieja España" (true Spain). The words most frequently used in their political discourse were "conspiración," "sabotaje" and "tramas" (conspiracy, sabotage and plots) (Palomo 2008, 153). The atmosphere of *crispación* created a political environment of resentment and bitterness with accusations flying from all sides of politics, aided by the victims of terrorism who had become one of the prime stakeholders in Spanish political discourse since 2004 (see Chapter Eight).

Between 2004 and 2008 the PP promoted the narrative that it was not responsible for the March 11 attacks, that the party neither lied about the attacks nor manipulated information related to them, that the attacks were not a consequence of Spain's participation and support of the Iraq war, and, finally, that the PP's defeat had nothing to do with the party's arrogance during its second term in office. Zapatero, this narrative states, was not elected by the will of the people. Rather he was catapulted into office with the help of a constellation of conspirators, which included ETA, Islamist terrorists, sections of the Spanish police, and the Moroccan secret services. Some PP politicians and media even suggest that the attacks were organized by the PSOE (Calleja 2008, 42). This narrative reads as follows. The PSOE had a pact with ETA to allow the destruction of Spain (i.e. Basque independence). To achieve this aim, the PSOE ordered ETA to perpetrate an attack on a massive scale and thus change the electoral result, given that the PSOE knew it had no chance of winning the 2004 general election. The attacks were perpetrated with the assistance of Islamic terrorists, who wanted to pay Aznar back for sending Spanish troops to Iraq, and of the Moroccan secret services because relations between the two countries were strained and Morocco wanted revenge for the Perejil incident[1] (note opposite). The combined result of these events was the defeat of the PP and the victory of the soft-on-terrorism Zapatero. In short, the PP's defeat was nothing less than a coup d'état.

The PP and its media supporters thus project two distinct narratives to explain what happened to Spain after the March 11 attacks. According to Bustelo, the first explanation states that Spanish citizens voted on March 14, 2004, under the influence of fear and that the election results were an expression of cowardice in the face of terrorism (2005, 3). Terrorism managed to achieve its political goal, toppling the PP government and replacing it with one softer in the fight against terrorism, and also willing to remove Spanish troops from Iraq. The second explanation aims to raise doubts over the intellectual authors of the terrorist attacks. This narrative focuses on the suspicion that some link to ETA exists, as well as to persons close to the PSOE, the Moroccan secret services, and even sections of the Spanish security forces. This narrative further suggests that those arrested for their involvement in the attacks were mere instruments who served the darker interests conspiring to defeat the government (3).

Although these narrative charges were not backed by facts or data drawn from the criminal and legal investigations, or from the Investigation Committee of the Congress of Deputies, their power lies in their capacity to question the legitimacy of the 2004 election. The flow of informal rumour and gossip amplified and contradicted the PSOE government's official communications. In 2008, some in the PP still believed that direct connections between the March 11 attack and ETA would be unearthed. The conspiracy theories were numerous and often preposterous. One conspiracy theory argued that *etarras* had trained in Osama bin Laden's camps in Afghanistan and that ETA may have acquired missiles, thus strengthening the narrative connection between Basque and Islamist terrorists. Another theory stated that the Islamist terrorists caught in the Madrid suburb of Leganés did not commit suicide. Rather, they were killed earlier and their bodies were placed in a freezer. When they were needed after March 11, the Spanish police manufactured the shoot up and group suicide. Readily accessible frozen corpses were necessary in order to sustain the thesis

---

[1]   The Perejil incident was a diplomatic crisis between the Spanish and Moroccan governments in July 2002 over the sovereignty of Perejil Island. Perejil Island (Parsley Island) lies just 250 metres off the coast of Morocco and 8km from the Spanish city of Ceuta. On July 11, 2002, a group of Moroccan soldiers set up base on the island. The Moroccan government claimed that the soldiers set foot on the islet in order to monitor illegal immigration. After protests from the Spanish government, the soldiers were replaced by Moroccan navy cadets who then installed a fixed base on the island. On the morning of July 18, 2002, Spain launched Operation Romeo-Sierra, a military attempt to take over the island. The operation was successful and the Moroccan navy cadets were dislodged from the island in a matter of hours without offering any resistance to the Spanish commando attack force (Hooper 2006, 197).

that the bombs were the work of Islamic terrorists and not ETA. Despite their ridiculousness, these conspiracy theories were repeated hundreds of time on radio and in certain newspapers after March 2004 (Calleja 2008, 51). In the second half of Zapatero's first term, Rajoy forbid the PP to promulgate conspiracy theories of the March 11 election. However, various journalists and right-wing groups continued to circulate them.

A notable feature of the PP's post-March 11 narratives was the organization's apparent willingness to disregard the institutions that the party traditionally defended. The PP's campaign against the Socialists included attacks on once-safe targets: the police; the judiciary; and any citizen who sustained the narrative that Islamic terrorists were responsible for the March 11 attacks in Madrid and that the perpetrators were actually those who were either arrested or who committed suicide in the Madrid suburb of Leganés. The Spanish police were accused of destroying evidence that pointed to ETA. The investigating judge, Juan del Olmo, and the prosecutor, Olga Sánchez, were criticized for their "stupidity" and "myopia" (Calleja 2008, 54). The link between the Madrid attacks and the PP's electoral defeat remained a haunting spectre, and it is not an exaggeration to suggest that everything the PP did during Zapatero's first term in office was a result of its electoral defeat in the March 14, 2004, elections, even if that meant discrediting the institutions that the party traditionally defended (41).

But as Martí, Domingo and Ibarra point out, the Zapatero administration made no significant change in counterterrorism laws: hard-line sentencing continued, as did the general application of criminal justice procedures (2007, 134). By contrast, the discourse of antiterrorism did change: "The Zapatero government [. . .] sought to depoliticize the issue (in a partisan sense) and leave the matter in the hands of the police and the judiciary" (134). But this was no easy task. When the PSOE left matters in the hands of the judiciary it was often accused of being soft on terrorism, engendering further PP indignation. This is what happened with the Iñaki de Juana Chaos case. De Juana, a Basque terrorist, was imprisoned in 1987 for killing 25 people. He was technically sentenced to 3,129 years in prison, but due to Spanish constitutional law was eligible for release in 2004. Fresh charges were brought against him once his sentence was due to expire for publishing two articles in the Basque radical press threatening politicians and judges. De Juana protested by undertaking a 63-day hunger strike. He was sentenced to another twelve years and seven months in prison, a sentence later reduced to three years. De Juana again went on hunger strike and the government moved him to a hospital in San Sebastian in March 2007, citing health reasons. This move was severely criticized by the PP, and more than 200,000 people demonstrated against the government on the streets of Madrid. He was eventually released in August 2008.

The De Juana case became a major political scandal that dominated the Spanish press for months. Zapatero's argument that the government must respect the law and human rights was weak against the public disgust that de Juana provoked and the PP's accusations of giving in to terrorists. The PP discourse was able to objectify and to collectivize the historical narrative of unrelenting ETA attacks on Spanish society. Zapatero was accused of cultural relativism and moral ambiguity, and the playing of superfluous rhetorical games continued. It was clear that the potent mix of terrorism and the Basque question were an irresistible combination for the PP and its media supporters.

The narrative of *España se rompe*

The process of *crispación* was not limited to competing narratives about the March 11 attacks in Madrid. Another key narrative promoted by the PP during the Zapatero years was that of *España se rompe*. This narrative rested on two changes in the status of Spain's two significant stateless nations: the new Catalan Statute of Autonomy; and the former Basque President Juan Ibarretxe's Plan for more autonomy and free association with the Spanish state. More than 25 years after the Statutes of Autonomies placed Spain's historic nations on the train toward sovereignty, as Juan Ibarrexte (former President of the Basque Autonomous government) called it, since 2004 that train has appeared to be unstoppable. However, the Spanish journalist Roberto Blanco Valdés calls the increase in autonomous power in Catalonia and that proposed in the Basque Country as signs of "la espiral de locura identitaria" (the crazy spiral of identity politics). That is, he argues, paradoxically Spain as a state consisting of seventeen Autonomous Communities is now more homogeneous than ever before in its history. Travel, the mass-media, technology and Francoism and its legacies have made Spain's regions more similar than they were a hundred or even fifty years ago. Blanco Valdés cynically suggests that what the Guardia Civil could not achieve in thirty-six years (a communal national identity), the magazines *Hola* and *Diez Minutos*, the national football league, the clothing store *Zara*, and the department store *El Corte Inglés* have managed in a mere twenty years (2008, 125).

Given that the PP government adopted an antagonistic attitude towards the regions after it gained an absolute majority in March 2000, the PSOE was able to occupy the nationalist-friendly political space vacated by Aznar.

Since 2004, under Zapatero each region was entitled to request a reform of its autonomy statute, and, provided that any proposed reform commands the broad support of regional parties and remain within the framework of the Spanish Constitution, the PSOE regarded the reforms as beneficial to both the region in question and Spain as a whole (Kennedy 2007, 201). By 2005, the Socialists were promoting a second decentralization process that aimed to integrate the regional nationalisms more firmly into the state structure. This was also the aim of the first decentralization process initiated by the 1978 Constitution. But the respective statutes of autonomies in the first decentralization process did little to stop the increasing demands for more autonomy. Here emerges a Spanish paradox. Whereas non-nationalists view the Autonomous Communities as the cement uniting the country, many nationalists view the Autonomous Communities as the stepping stones towards secession. In the PP's view, the full implementation of the Autonomous Communities signals the end of the devolution process. It wants to keep the constitution unchanged, because constitutional change may lead to the end of consensus democracy. The PP fears that any change in the constitution would lead to calls for further asymmetrical federalism and even the independence of some regions.

A common refrain from the left during Zapetero's first term was, "Aznar tiene la culpa" (Aznar is to blame), for the apparent march towards sovereignty, the implication being that the radicalization of nationalist politics and subsequent territorial tensions were responses to Aznar's hard-line approach to the regions when the PP was in power. A logical conclusion to this narrative was that the defeat of Aznar would alleviate these tensions. With the PSOE government, however, the territorial conflict worsened, at least discursively. At first it seemed that the PP was willing to accept more devolution of powers to the regions after the reform of Valencia's statute of autonomy, which was approved by both the PP and the PSOE in 2006. But the negotiations for a new Catalan statute became a sore point between the PP and the PSOE in what Blanco Valdés calls "el mayor fiasco de nuestra reciente historia democrática" (the biggest fiasco of our recent democratic history) (2008, 96).

One of the most contentious issues in the negotiations for a new Catalan statute that took place in 2005 and 2006 was the use of the word nation to define Catalonia. The Catalan nationalists and the PSOE played down the word, suggesting that it merely had a historical and symbolic role. But the PP argued that in every constitution across the world, the "nation" was identified with the "state," and that the only reason why the Catalans insisted on the word was because their ultimate objective was full independence. Sooner, rather than later, the PP declared, the Catalan nationalists would argue that their nation was rather different to Spain and begin to demand even more national rights. The Spanish right was further infuriated by Zapatero's approach to the Catalan statute negotiations as a bilateral process between two equal national entities. The Spanish parliament finally approved the Catalan Statute on March 30, 2006, in the Congress of Deputies and on May 10, 2006, in the Senate. The PP responded by arguing that the Catalan statute was unconstitutional and campaigned for a no vote in the referendum which took place on June 18, 2006. This was complemented by a nationwide boycott of Catalan products in late 2005 and early 2006. The Catalan Statute of Autonomy was approved and became effective on August 9, 2006. The referendum, however, was noted for its unprecedented high abstention with a voter turnout below fifty percent (Magone 2008, 243). The President of the Generalitat, Pasqual Maragall, was reprimanded by the central government in August 2006 for suggesting that, thanks to the introduction of the reformed statute, the Spanish state now had no more than a "residual nature" in Catalonia (Kennedy 2007, 200). Maragall's statement served to justify the PP's criticisms of the statute, and it seemed that many Spanish people agreed with the PP because support for the PSOE in the polls declined considerably in the subsequent weeks.

For players and commentators on the Spanish right, Zapatero's strategy of not setting limits on the statute debates and his confidence that dialogue would achieve a reasonable agreement was foolish and counterproductive; it actually served to strengthen the self-determination demands from both the Basque Country and Catalonia, and consequently from other regions such as Andalusia and Galicia (Blanco Valdés 2008, 85). This phenomenon was first coined by the Spanish media as *"café para todos"* (coffee for everybody) to describe the devolution process under Felipe González two decades earlier. This phrase refers to the situation in which every region wants the same rights and privileges that other regions have. The granting of self-governance to the historic regions unleashed multiple projects from regions that have not had historical or traditional claims to being different from Spain, such as Andalusia, Murcia, Valencia, and even the capital region of Madrid. Such projects have involved not only seeking autonomy from the central state but also turning dialects into languages (as was the case of Valenciano) and creating newly minted nationalist symbols, most notably a regional flag. Unsurprisingly, according to Encarnación, "the historic communities vigorously opposed extension of home rule to what they disdainfully referred to as the new regions" (2004, 71). From their point of view, new regional demands for autonomy "diluted the claims of the historic regions to constitute national units within, but separate from, Spain" (71). Each Autonomous Community must negotiate its own Statute with the central government. The Basque Country and Navarre enjoy the most rights due to their historical foral rights, and collect their own taxes. On the next level are the historic regions of Catalonia, Galicia, and increasingly Andalusia, which enjoy significantly more autonomy than other Spanish Autonomous Communities. The remaining Spanish regions thus campaign for *café para todos*, the same rights that the historic regions enjoy. As other regions gain more autonomous rights, the historic regions, particularly Catalonia, which has criticized harshly the process of *café para todos*, initiate a new round of demands and autonomy claims, in a process that the Spanish right perceives as interminable and disastrous for Spanish unity. This process has been referred to in Spain as *el cuento de nunca acabar* (the never-ending story). After the approval of the new Catalan statute in 2006, for example, a debate ignited in Galicia for a similar statute so that that Autonomous Community would not be "left behind" (Blanco Valdés 2008, 86). In Andalusia, a new statute was also implemented, a virtual copy in many respects of the Catalan statute, and which referred to Andalusia as a "realidad nacional" (national reality) (Agudo Zamora 2007, 52–53).

But although the train towards yet more sovereignty was moving swiftly during Zapatero's first term, with multiple statutes being approved, the Basque conflict dominated the headlines. On September 28, 2007, the Basque *lehendakari* Juan Ibarretxe made the surprise announcement that he would convene a referendum for self-determination in the Basque Country in October 2008. To be specific, the Ibarretxe Plan called for historic rights, for self-determination, and pacts for free association with the Spanish state by means of a referendum. The Ibarretxe Plan, named after the premier of the Basque Country, was first presented to the Basque public in 2001 and narrowly approved by the Basque Parliament in December 2004. However, the plan was rejected by the Spanish parliament in April 2005. Seeking to establish a status of free association between the Basque Country and Spain, the proposal was viewed as breaching the framework of the Constitution. The plan also clearly broke Spanish law which exclusively grants the central government the power to call referendums.[2] Ibarretxe's 2007 announcement to press ahead with the referendum with a slightly revised plan therefore sparked new political tension in the Basque Country, within the

---

[2] Aznar's PP government passed a law placing severe penalties (including a jail sentence) for an illegal referendum. The PSOE revoked the law in October 2004.

PNV, and also throughout Spain. In September 2008 the Constitutional Court ruled that the planned referendum was illegal effectively halting the Ibarretxe Plan.

The fact that Zapatero took some steps to modernise Spain's State of Autonomies in the face of the PP's vicious attacks and drops in the polls points to the tenacity of his leadership. Originally dubbed "Bambi" by the Spanish right, he was soon referred to as "un maestro de engaño" (a master of deception) (Palomo 2008, 173). Zapatero was able to deliver a new Catalan statute even though it was a watered down version of the original document approved by the Catalan parliament. He successfully stared down Ibarretxe's threats of a referendum by leaving the matter up to the judiciary. His only misstep occurred after the March 27, 2007 regional elections in Navarre. The ruling right-wing party UPN (affiliated with the PP) failed to win an absolute majority. The field was thus open for the Socialists to form a coalition government with the Navarrese-Basque radical nationalist party, *Nafarroa Bai*, which advocates Basque separatism. But it was impossible for Zapatero to stand firm against ETA and also form government with Basque radicals. Zapatero finally chose not to form a coalition government in the Autonomous Community of Navarre as a peace offering to help end the *crispación* in the region.

As is clear from the discussion on *crispación* in this chapter, the twin issues of terror and separatism continued to divide Spanish politics. During the Zapatero years, both issues proved to be electorally irresistible and provided a platform for the PP to attack the PSOE government and put it on the defensive. The PP's attack narratives had an emotive capacity able to counter the legitimacy of the government's narrative. After the approval of the Catalan Statute of Autonomy in early 2006 the PP was steadily closing the Socialist's lead in the polls. The Spanish economy was slowing down. The Catholic Church was stepping up its attack on the government. By 2007, the ETA peace process ended in failure (see Chapter Seven). And as other EU member states one by one elected conservative governments (Greece 2004, Germany 2005, Portugal 2006, France 2007, Italy 2008), Zapatero was increasingly isolated in the continent. On March 9, 2008, the PP had its chance to redeem the Aznar era in the general elections.

Conclusion: From Bambi to Rambo

Throughout Zapatero's first term in office, the PP believed that Zapatero was only Prime Minister by default or accident and thus illegitimate. This idea permeated the PP's opposition strategy and ultimately undid the party's electoral fortunes. The main failure of the PP during the Zapatero years can be summed up in the following statement by Graciano Palomo: "demasiado 11-M, demasiada ETA, demasiado grito, excesiva imagen ultra" (too much March 11, too much ETA, too much shouting, excessive far-right image) (2008, 180). Zapatero was able to exploit the general disaffection in much of Spanish society generated by Aznar's arrogance, authoritarian style of politics, and apparent hypocrisy on such pressing matters as the drives toward more regional autonomy. The PP's mobilization against the Zapatero administration was conspicuous, given that the PP itself granted concessions to Catalonia, such as 30 percent of IRPF taxes, when in government, directly negotiated with ETA in Switzerland in 1998, transferred some ETA prisoners to locations closer to the Basque Country, and pardoned some convicted terrorists, all without damaging the contours or unity of the Spanish state (Palomo 2008, 155). Furthermore, in the relatively short history of Spanish democracy, no other opposition party had taken to the streets as often and with such support as the PP did between 2004 and 2008. Those demonstrations, particularly when directed against the government's antiterrorism policies could not obscure the fact that Socialist government policy was more or less the same as the PP's when in power. In direct contrast, Spaniards were also polarized by a Prime Minister who brought once taboo issues into Spanish public discourse. The processes of *crispación* were complex, mutable, and at times, farcical.

At 13.30 p.m. on March 7, 2008, two days before the general election, a Socialist council member Isaías Carrasco of the town of Mondragón (Guipúzcoa) in the Basque Country, was shot dead by ETA. Yet again, a terrorist event had overtaken the news media days before the general election. The assassination of the council member was not on the same scale as the March 11 attacks in Madrid, but it haunted the rest of the political campaign. Rajoy was the first political leader to respond to the murder on television. His performance was, according to Palomo, serious, serene and brilliant. Rajoy expressed solidarity with the victim of terrorism while at the same time reaffirming the PP's counterterrorism policies (2008, 32). But Rajoy was trumped minutes later by the Socialist Minister Alfredo Pérez Rubalcaba whose face was, according to Palomo, "un auténtico poema" (an authentic poem) in a media performance that was both sentimental and relatable. Many in the PP consider Rubalcaba's appearance the knock-out punch that blew their chances of victory (32). Immediately after his performance, the cry "¡Hemos perdido las elecciones!" (We've lost the elections!) was heard throughout the PP headquarters (Palomo 2008, 32). The PP insisted publicly that after the murder of Carrasco, parliament should withdraw its support for state negotiation with ETA. The result, according to Palomo, was clear: the Spanish right once again was using the corpse of a victim of terrorism to attack Zapatero. Carrasco's relatives ordered the PP to stay away from his funeral. The silence in Mondragón was only broken by shouts of "asesinos" (murderers) to members of the PP, echoing the demonstrations after the March 11 attacks four years earlier (2008, 33). The March 11 narrative was set to repeat itself, yet again.

The strategy of *crispación* adopted by Rajoy and the PP ultimately failed to win the party government. Although the PP increased its overall vote in the March 2008 general elections, so did the PSOE, and Zapatero won another four-year term of office. The result appeared to indicate that the PP suffered from an image deficit. It was unable to sufficiently convince moderate voters that the PP was a modern political party and not under the grip of the Spanish far right. The PP was unable to reimagine and re-narrativize itself by choosing new leaders. Instead, it maintained its monotonous narrative script and thus was unable to counter the narrative description of "ultra" that was pegged to it by the PSOE. The failure of the PP's narrative script was also in part attributable to its refusal to move on from the March 11 attacks and the lost election result four years earlier. In seeking to exonerate the Aznar era, the PP failed to convince the electorate that it had a reasonable electoral program for the Spanish state. The PP did not realize that *aznarismo* was politically dead. The PP also failed to truly represent itself as a moderate political party and its image was damaged in the media by ultra-Catholics and conservatives who frightened the so-called *gente normal*.

Crispación, as it is dubbed by the Spanish mass-media, is an updated version of the narrative of *las dos Españas* that has plagued Spanish political and public discourse since the early nineteenth century. This key constituent narrative drives narratives of terrorism in mass-mediated discourse and is a vehicle for the two major political parties in Spain to project their ideological positions. The repetition of certain narratives of terror by both the PP and the PSOE during Zapatero's first legislature had the effect of creating a reality-making power for their support base. But political parties are subject to the constraints of their historical narratives and in post-Franco Spain the branding of the PP as ultra clearly was more discursively potent than the PP's attempt to brand the PSOE as treacherous and anti-Spain. Nonetheless, *crispación* is a powerful mass-mediated process that forces the PSOE government to always be on the defensive. The next chapter looks at the process of *crispación* during the Spanish government's peace negotiations with ETA in 2006 and 2007. The chapter explores how the polemical nature of the narrative of *las dos Españas* complicated, and ultimately undid, the peace process.

CHAPTER SEVEN

The Beginning and End of the ETA Peace Process (2006–2007)

Between Dialogue and *Engaño*

We deserve a better Spain.
José Luis Rodríguez Zapatero (April 17, 2004)

It's not that we're going fast; it's just that the others are slow.
José Luis Rodríguez Zapatero at a Madrid PSOE rally (April 23, 2006)

Since 1959, the conflict between the Spanish government and the Basque separatist group ETA has, by and large, dominated the political mass-mediated narratives of the Spanish state. Although the significance of ETA diminished due to successful police operations coordinated by Spanish and French authorities in the 1990s and new millennium, it was the September 11, 2001 terrorist attacks in the USA and the March 11, 2004 attacks in Madrid that ultimately made ETA's strategy of targeted assassinations and attacks untenable. On March 22, 2006, ETA unilaterally announced a permanent ceasefire, thus paving the way for negotiations with the Spanish government. This so-called peace process was rapidly politicized by various constituencies in Spain, all of whom were politically invested in the outcome of the peace process.

The Socialist government, together with many regional nationalists, viewed the ETA peace process as a stepping-stone to righting historical wrongs and reforming Spain's State of Autonomies. Zapatero's Socialists absorbed the lesson that the Basque conflict, like most terrorist wars, is political, not just military, and requires a political solution. There was much riding on the success of the peace process. If Zapatero were successful, ETA's demise could guarantee the Socialists a second term in office as well as Zapatero's place in history. Such a prospect understandably terrified the Spanish right. There would have been a satisfying symmetry, however, if a prime minister who was elected after a huge terrorist outrage wrongly blamed on ETA, secured re-election based on the successful dismantling of ETA. For their part, the conservative Popular Party and many victims of ETA increasingly repeated the mantra that Spain must not pay a political price to the terrorists, even for a peace agreement. In 2006, the PP opposition leader Rajoy accused Zapatero of betraying the dead; Rajoy also had an implacable hostility to any proposed Basque peace process. The split between the PP and the PSOE shattered the bipartisanship that had previously characterized Spain's national counterterrorism policy.

Immediately after the ceasefire announcement, the Basque novelist Bernado Atxaga suggested in *The New York Times*:

> Now, after the cease-fire, no satellite can send us a map of the future, but everyone wants to be a weatherman or a prophet. Some lovers of metaphor speak of Pandora's Box and foresee great hatreds let loose. Others believe that pessimism is a sign of intelligence, and they recommend taking ETA's communiqué with many grains of salt. At the opposite extreme are those who call for a reconciliation, right this minute, between the country's two sensibilities. (2006, 23)

The political polarization that continued to plague Spanish politics after the March 11, 2004, attacks in Madrid was set to worsen. Multiple schisms opened up in Spanish society about what such a peace process should look like, and to what extent the government should give in to terrorist demands. One side argued that negotiating with terrorists is akin to surrendering and the Spanish public would never forgive the actors involved. The other side argued that the public would not forgive a government irresponsible enough to avoid taking advantage of the negotiation process. Although there were multiple divisions over these vexing questions, it quickly became evident that once again, terror and the Basque conflict were pitting two Spains against each other in a battle not for peace, but for a re-imagining of the (Spanish) nation. This chapter investigates the mass-mediated narratives generated by the peace negotiations between the Spanish government and ETA in Spanish political discourse (2006–2007), particularly the narrative of *traición a las víctimas* that was projected by the opposition Popular Party in an attempt to derail the government and the peace process. The chapter also posits that since political and media elites perceived the peace process in the historically contested terms of the narrative of *las dos Españas*, those perceptions provide evidence that the ETA peace process was not just about the dissolution of a terrorist group. Rather, the process was concerned with the dissolution of a spectral enemy that the state had utilized for decades to construct, and imagine, a unified Spanish nation.

The perils of negotiation

No creemos que con ETA haya nada que negociar. A ETA hay que combat-
irla con todos los instrumentos del Estado de derecho y derrotarla. (We do
not believe there is anything to negotiate with ETA. ETA has to be
destroyed with all the instruments of the rule of law). (María San Gil,
former leader of the Basque Popular Party, quoted in Calvo Soler 2006,
126)

After 1992, ETA seemed to lose much of its ideological and political direction, and the group entered a new spiral of increased violence that alienated
most of the Basque nationalist spectrum. This situation gave rise to massive
public demonstrations against ETA, particularly after the assassination of
PP Councillor Miguel Ángel Blanco's in 1997 (see Chapter Two).
Successful police operations against ETA during the Aznar years dealt
devastating blows to the organization, and ETA felt obligated to attack or
claim a victim on a regular basis in order to make its presence felt. Calleja
describes ETA's attitude in these terms: "Si no matamos, no existimos; si
no matamos, los medios de comunicación no nos prestan la atención que es
clave para nuestra supervivencia" (If we do not kill, we not exist; if we do
not kill, the mass-media does not give us the attention we need to survive)
(2008, 148). ETA's attacks, however, were becoming less frequent, and as
Zapatero liked to remind Spaniards, ETA had not killed a single victim in
the three years leading up to the 2006 ceasefire. Growing disenchantment
with the organization, coupled with successful police operations, transformed ETA's priorities. The group was now willing to negotiate the
cessation of its terrorist activities.

Negotiation with terrorists is not new in Spain. As, Bew, Frampton and
Gurruchaga put it in their book *Talking to Terrorists*, "Governments talk to
terrorists. This is a statement of fact rather than a critique; it is an acknowledgement of reality rather than a value judgement" (2009, 1). According
to the Spanish sociologist Ignacio Sánchez, however, "negotiation is an
unfinished tale of frustration for successive Spanish governments, and is a
tactic used by the terrorists to achieve their goals" (quoted in Brotóns and
Espósito 2002, 172). Typically, Spanish governments insist that they will
not negotiate politically with groups that are not legitimate representatives
of the people. But as Brótons and Espósito highlight, Spanish governments
have usually maintained a double discourse: "To the public the message is
that the one and only policy in relation to ETA is police action, but they
have also kept the back door open for negotiation with ETA" (2002, 172).
Two former Spanish prime ministers had tried to reach a truce with ETA:

the first, in Algiers, in 1988, was led by Felipe González; and the second, in Switzerland, in 1998–99, by José María Aznar. Both attempts failed.

The ceasefire declared by ETA in September 1998 was known as the Lizarra Ceasefire and lasted fourteen months. ETA's ceasefire announcement began with the Lizarra Pact, an agreement between the different Basque nationalist parties to drive forward the national construction of the Basque Country. The PNV leadership had committed the party to disengaging from Spain and collaborating in building sovereign Basque institutions. In exchange, ETA would abandon armed struggle. Key elements of this pact were the recognition of the right to self-determination, and the inclusion of Navarre and the French Basque provinces in Euskadi, or the Basque Country. ETA broke this indefinite ceasefire in November 1999, partly due to the actions of the Aznar administration, which included the arrest of a key ETA negotiator, Belén González, but also because they felt that the Basque Nationalist Party (PNV) had broken its pledge to work for national construction (Aizpeolea 2006, 4). Although the ceasefire was brief and negotiations failed, the Lizarra Pact ultimately caused consternation in Madrid because the moderate nationalists of the PNV were now also openly calling for self-determination. The peaceful pursuit of Basque sovereignty was perceived during the Aznar years (1996–2004) as a greater threat to Spain than a terrorist campaign and consequently resulted in a torrent of invective from the Madrid media and political establishment.

Analysing ETA's breaking of its 1999 ceasefire, Begoña Aretxaga suggests that ETA's actions were "eliminating a space of mediation necessary for a potential political negotiation" (2005, 242). ETA's continued recourse to violence had the paradoxical effect of reinforcing the appeal of the anti-nationalist Spanish right-wing in the Basque Country, as well as debilitating the social fabric that constitutes Basque nationalism at the local level:

> In other words, rather than *strengthening*, the violence of ETA and of the young activists has the effect of *weakening* nationalist aspirations and the possible political avenues to achieve them [original emphasis]. The harder the radical nationalists try to will into being an independent Basque nation (which they portray as imminent) through discourse and violent action, the lower is the desire for national existence among the Basque population. So bewildering is the new strategy of Basque radicalism, and so much in the profit of the right-wing party in the Spanish government, that it would seem that ETA had been cleverly infiltrated by the Spanish state to provoke the destruction of Basque nationalism once and for all. [. . .] At a loss for

other explanations, the most common reaction of commentators is that radical nationalists have gone totally out of their minds. (2005, 242–43)

To sober observers of the Basque conflict ETA's actions were entering into a realm of madness, projecting narratives that seemed to have no basis in reality. It was difficult to see sense in ETA's actions when the organization had squandered the opportunity for peace with the Lizarra Pact. Moreover, Spanish politicians were understandably running out of patience with what seemed to be ETA's nonsensical actions.

After the end of the Lizarra ceasefire, the PNV energetically condemned ETA's new violence but refused to abandon its own new-found commitment to Basque sovereignty. As a result the PNV was caught in discursively difficult territory. Its dogged pursuit of Basque sovereignty, particularly through the Ibarretxe Plan (see Chapter Six), raised the ire of the major parties and that of much of the Spanish public. On the other hand, the PNV's conciliatory messages and relationships with Spanish institutions and political parties irked ETA and Basque radicals alike. In the meantime, after ETA resumed its attacks, ending their fourteen-month ceasefire, Aznar took a hard line against the organization, and the PP paradoxically increased its vote in the Basque Country. In June 2002, legislation was approved by both the PP and PSOE allowing for the suspension of any political group deemed to serve the interests of a terrorist band. In August of the same year, Batasuna was suspended for three years, but the PP sought a permanent ban, indicating that the government was willing to forego negotiation. Despite widespread support for the ban, many Basques felt uneasy about it, particularly when the infamous Spanish Judge Baltasar Garzón claimed that Batasuna was part of ETA, which made it "guilty of crimes against humanity" ("Bomb Defused" 2002). Joaquin Almunia, a former leader of the Spanish Socialist Party, remarked, "something like this would not have been possible before September 11" (Pontoniere 2003).

The basis for the banning of Batasuna rested on the belief, supported by an overwhelming amount of evidence, that the party constituted a part within the network of organizations led by ETA. According to Alonso and Reinares, the banning of Batasuna was deliberately "presented by the majority of Basque nationalist politicians as a denial of the civil rights of a section of Basque society" (Alonso & Reinares 2005, 269–70). According to Katherine Sawyer, however, "political parties are obliged to operate within the bounds of the Constitution and of established notions of democracy. If a given party, in aligning itself with a terrorist organization, chooses not to do so, it may not, then, invoke those same constitutional principles as a shield nor seek legal refuge in the very provisions that it has chosen to violate" (quoted in Alonso & Reinares 2005, 270). Despite the reservations of some politicians about the banning of a political party (the Irish equivalent Sinn Fein was never banned), Batasuna's illegality did remove the Basque radical left from the political institutions of the Basque Country and subsequently weakened the organization's funding and support base.

In the context of the banning of Batasuna, Aznar's hardline approach to the Basque conflict, and the 2001 attacks in the USA, it seemed that negotiation had once and for all been ruled out in Spain as a solution to the Basque terrorist problem. But two events brought the spectre of negotiation back to the political table. The first was the unexpected victory of the PSOE in the March 14, 2004, general elections. The second was the IRA's renunciation of armed struggle on July 28, 2005. Both events directly and indirectly led to ETA's declaration of a permanent ceasefire on March 22, 2006.

Permanent ceasefire

ETA's declaration of a permanent ceasefire was not unexpected. Zapatero had made the end of terrorist violence one of his new government's top priorities. On February 10, 2006, Zapatero called an unexpected press conference at which he stated that Spain may soon witness the "beginning of the end" of ETA's 38-year campaign of terrorist violence (Eatwell 2006, 1). Zapatero cited the lack of fatal attacks in almost three years as reason to hope for definitive peace. Then, on February 18, 2006, ETA released a communiqué requesting negotiations with the Spanish government, though the communiqué did not mention a ceasefire. In the communiqué ETA called for "dialogue and negotiation" as the "only solution" to the conflict. ETA stated that peace would only come about as a result of a "democratic process," and it cited three conditions to make this possible: giving Basques in Spain and France the right to decide their own future; changing the current political status of the region; and involving all relevant political forces in negotiations. The group argued that the continuation of the Basque Country's current status as an Autonomous Community of Spain would only prolong the conflict.

The Spanish press had been speculating for months about this secret ceasefire announcement. When it seemed that the ceasefire declaration would never arrive, media and political elites began wondering if the supposed ETA truce was a big joke. Zapatero had been giving out so many signals about an end to violence in the Basque Country that his political future was becoming linked to what ETA did, or did not. Finally, on March

22, 2006, the ETA communiqué that the Spanish left had been anticipating finally arrived. ETA had declared a permanent ceasefire. The permanent ceasefire would come into effect on March 24, 2006. According to the communiqué:

> El objetivo de esta decisión es impulsar un proceso democrático en Euskal Herria para construir un nuevo marco en el que sean reconocidos los derechos que como Pueblo nos corresponden y asegurando de cara al futuro la posibilidad de desarrollo de todas las opciones políticas. (The objective of this decision is to propel a democratic process in Euskal Herria to construct a new framework in which our corresponding rights as a nation are recognised and to assure the possibility of developing all political options). (Quoted in Gurruchaga 2006, 164)

The communiqué further stated that at the end of the process, the citizens must decide their own future. Consequently, the French and Spanish states must recognize the outcome of the proposed democratic process without "limitations." Any decision that the Basque "pueblo" makes about its future "must" be respected. ETA wanted a peace based on "justice" in order to create a real "democratic" future for the Basque Country. ETA's use of the expression permanent ceasefire was a direct copy of the IRA ceasefire announcement. The language of the communiqué was much stronger than both the indefinite truce of 1998 and the prolonged partial truce of 1988. Overall the language of the ceasefire was rather moderate compared to the typical ETA communiqué; it did not explicitly mention Navarre and was sufficiently ambiguous to raise hopes that the Basque conflict was finally coming to an end. Yet the breaking of the indefinite Lizarra ceasefire in 1998–99 was still a recent memory. Spaniards were well aware that despite the language that ETA used, it had the power to break any ceasefire whenever it chose if its demands were not being met.

ETA's permanent ceasefire declaration sustained Gabilondo's argument that since 9/11 terrorism has ceased to be a national or domestic issue and has become overdetermined by the spectre of global narratives of terror. As discussed in Chapter One, Gabilondo suggests that the global re-articulation of terrorism since 9/11 means it is difficult for a Western terrorist group to resort to violence as a means to achieve political revolution or utopia (from the workers' revolution to national sovereignty). In this respect and in the foreseeable future, any form of terrorist violence against any political target other than the North American is liable to be interpreted and dealt with as a threat to the USA while at the same time being connected to violent Muslim fundamentalism. This is, according to Gabilondo, "the powerful effect of ideological overdetermination" (2002, 63). To reiterate Gabilondo's argument:

> There is no longer room for any other form of terrorism than the global one inaugurated by bin Laden. Ironically we can no longer talk about 'terrorist movements' around the world; all of them have been overdetermined—terrorised—by bin Laden's actions. Any terrorist action no longer responds to a local, state-based order, so that it can be read from that local context: global terrorism is always the terrorism of the global Other. (2002, 64)

The potency of the global metanarrative of terror meant that ETA had no other recourse but to declare a ceasefire and negotiate the cessation of its terror activities. But once again, in Spain, the constitutive narrative of *las dos Españas* was set to complicate the parameters of the peace process. The two Spains were immediately at odds over a number of questions related to terrorism and the peace process, with each Spain projecting competing narratives over the morality, efficacy and structure of the ensuing peace negotiations.

Immediately after the declaration of the ceasefire, self-declared ETA experts voiced their opinions on what the government's next steps should be. In the following months, many declarations were made through the mass-media by the various parties that felt implicated in the ceasefire, such as political parties, victims of terrorism, public and private institutions, journalists, citizens, and non-governmental organizations (Calvo Soler 2006, 16). Even the terminology of negotiation became a polemical issue. Many Spaniards objected to the phrase "proceso de paz" (peace process) arguing that in order to be a peace process, there must first be a violent conflict between two opposing sides. Instead, many observers, such as the Socialist Txiki Benegas, argued that the correct expression should have been a *proceso hacía un final dialogado de violencia* (process towards a negotiated end of violence) (2007, 19). Others objected to the word negotiation for implying that its interlocutors were all valid and legitimate (21). Rather, they argued, the correct word to use in the process should be dialogue.

The debate in Spain thus raged over what a proper negotiation process should look like and to what extent the government should take steps to bring about the desired peace. The debate was never resolved and every stakeholder invested in the peace process argued different positions. Many valid points were raised. The Spanish right despaired at the fact that ETA was gaining traction in the mass-media (Benegas 2007, 23). Never before had ETA dominated the Spanish mass-media to such an extent, and many on the right were concerned that ETA's message was being broadcast throughout Spain, even though the group had not killed anyone in three years (23). Some critics questioned if the permanent ceasefire was a trap, like the Lizarra Pact, while others wondered if the government should even be negotiating with ETA if the group was really on the brink of defeat. This argument was posited by the historian Stanley Payne and promoted in the newspaper *El Mundo*. Payne's position was linked to the Spanish right's narrative line that there was no underlying Basque conflict in the Spanish state; rather, there was a campaign of violence launched by an illegitimate non-state group. A host of other questions were posed in the news media and on TV chat shows: What are the limits of negotiation with a terrorist group? What is the point of the antiterrorist pact? Can a peace process with a terrorist group be initiated without the support and consent of the main opposition party? How can the government be sure that ETA truly abandoned political violence? (Benegas 2007, 23). Again, the debates around these questions raged in the mass-media, yet no consensus was forthcoming.

Most constituent groups agreed, however, on the points raised in a statement by Basque Socialists days before the ceasefire announcement. The statement suggested among other things that peace is not the imposition of the Basque nationalist project on a plural society. Nor is it the rejection of the Spanish Constitution that forms the basis of Spanish democracy, or the rejection of the Statute of Gernika, which endows the Basque Country with self-government. Peace, the statement argued, is the triumph of democracy (Benegas 2007, 20–21). These were powerful and emotive words. But ETA's demands could only be met by rejecting the Spanish Constitution and the Statute of Gernika, and it was not clear what the triumph of democracy really meant. The Socialist administration's secrecy about the negotiations only served to irk the opposition and promote even more vitriol. After the acrimony experienced in the aftermath of March 11, 2004, outlandish remarks were no longer out of the ordinary in Spanish political discourse, and caused no political damage to the interlocutor. PP politician Jaime Mayor Oreja suggested that Spain was not in the middle of a peace process, but was instead caught in a process of self-determination, the second step after the recognition of the Basque Country and Catalonia as nations (Benegas 207, 31). Opposition leader Mariano Rajoy suggested that ETA and Zapatero "comparten su proyecto" (share their Project). And the President of the Association of Victims of Terrorism (AVT) said: "Es innegable que a Zapatero no le vale con la Transición y converge ideológicamente con ETA en la valoración de que vivimos en una democracia de baja calidad" (It is undeniable that Zapatero is not content with the Transition and converges ideologically with ETA in the assessment that we live in a low-quality democracy) (Benegas 2007, 48). Moreover, the AVT and its supporters changed its slogan from "with the victims or with the murderers" to "with the victims or with the government." The narrative battle of *España se rompe* was again being played out in the Spanish mass-media.

Overall, the peace process was beset by a number of obstacles. First, Batasuna's illegality ruled it out as a valid interlocutor in negotiations with other political parties. Second, the government was at pains to ensure that it did not appear to be entering a negotiation process that was from the outset conditioned by ETA. The unrelenting opposition by the PP to the possibility of a peace process was an added difficulty (Martí, Domingo & Ibarra 2007, 134). With the PP arguing that there could be no progress until it could be confirmed that ETA had once and for all laid down its arms, there was little room for the Socialist government to manoeuvre. The PP suggested that the permanent ceasefire was only a pause in violence and not a renunciation of criminal activity and repeated its epithet that no political price must be paid in any negotiations with ETA. But more importantly, the biggest obstacle had to do with priorities. ETA wanted to begin a political negotiation before it definitively ceased its violent campaign. The government wanted to negotiate the end of violence before a political agreement could be reached. In order to put pressure on the government, *kale borroka* (street fighting, see Chapter Two) returned to the streets of the Basque Country during the peace process. But street violence by radical Basque youths only served to strengthen the PP's argument that terrorists could not be trusted to end violence. Moreover, ETA returned to its typical rhetoric throughout the peace process, referring again to Spain as a repressive force and asserting that peace is not possible without the end of repression.

The word "engaño" (deception) figured heavily in the PP's rhetoric. Rajoy accused Zapatero of surrendering to ETA and "betraying the dead," and insisted that the PP would not join any political talks involving ETA's political wing Batasuna. The PP felt deceived by the government and argued that all Spaniards were being tricked because links with ETA were made without the preconditions that the *Congreso de los Diputados* had set out: that ETA demonstrate it had renounced armed struggle. The Antiterrorist Pact was also a point of permanent discord. The PP felt that the PSOE had broken one of the principle points of the pact—to inform the opposition party about everything related to the fight against ETA. The PP suggested that Zapatero never wanted to have a pact with the PP but that, on the contrary, his strategy was to isolate the PP, to present the PP to the public as a party that cannot reach an agreement, a party that is gloomy and unstable in its attacks on the government. As a result the PP broke off official relations with the government.

It is difficult to determine to what extent the Zapatero administration sidelined the PP during the peace negotiations and to what extent the PP isolated itself. It was true, however, that the Zapatero administration was taking a secretive approach to the negotiations (apparently recommended by Tony Blair after his experience in negotiating with the IRA). But it was also true that the government's approach was sidelining the PNV, the democratically elected representatives of the majority of Basque citizens. The PNV was making a serious effort to rectify its past errors with victims of ETA violence. The *lehendakari*, Ibarretxe, acknowledged in November 2006 that, in the past, the PNV had not transmitted adequately its support for the victims of terrorism and sent "un mensaje profundo de reconocimiento, de memoria, y de paz" (a deep message of acknowledgement, memory and peace) (Benegas 2007, 201). Moreover, the PNV insisted that ETA did not have the right to deny the Basque Country its own right to live in peace and freedom, and that it would not negotiate while ETA violence persisted and called on Batasuna to speak out against *kale borroka* (149). The President of the PNV Josu Jon Imaz summed up the PNV position: "Ningún encapuchado va a negociar el futuro de mis hijos" (No hooded person is going to negotiate the future of my children) (181).

The Zapatero administration, despite its best efforts, became estranged from both extremes in the conflict. The PP accused it of being weak in the face of terrorism, giving up Navarre, Balkanizing Spain and betraying the victims of terrorism. The Basque *abertzale* left lambasted the Zapatero government for its failure to make a gesture, and broke the conditions of the peace process. But despite PP allegations, the Zapatero administration was not flexible on ETA's demands. Zapatero was unequivocally clear that, "Nadie puede poner encima de la mesa algo que no existe" (Nobody can put something on the table that does not exist), which suggests that he does not regard self-determination as a right in the Spanish democracy (Benegas 2007, 105). It is not difficult to understand the PP's opposition to the peace process. It is generally understood in Spain that the prime minister able to bring an end to the violence in the Basque Country would guarantee him or herself an electoral victory. But as Ramoneda points out, "history shows that leaders with the courage needed to resolve such extreme situations often end up paying for it at the ballot box" (2006, 2). It was therefore surprising that the PP took such a hostile attitude to the peace process, given the fact that all previous attempts at negotiating with ETA had failed and that the PP, from the start, had forecast failure.

ETA's declaration of a permanent ceasefire and the ensuing peace process thus highlighted the conflict between the narrative of *las dos Españas* and the global metanarrative of terror. The post-9/11 global context offered the Spanish state an opportunity to negotiate the end of a localized, domestic terror group which no longer fit into a discursive space overdetermined by bin Laden and the September 11 attacks in the USA (Gabilondo 2002, 64). Unlike negotiations between the British government and the IRA, however, the historically constituent narrative of *las dos Españas* further overdetermined the politics of terror in the Spanish state. The conflicting ideological interests between the two Spains haunted the peace process, burdening negotiations with partisan politicking that was linked to the process of *crispación* operating in mass-mediated discourse after the March 11 attacks. The discursive conflict over the peace process could be further traced to the divisions of the two Spains in regards to their idea of what Spain is. As discussed in Chapter Five, the PSOE considers Spain a "nation of nations." Although cultural pluralism and political sharing of power with regional administrations is accepted by the PSOE, Spain is the only entity allowed to have full sovereignty (Núñez 2001, 736). PP discourses, on the other hand, deny that the nationalities have the capacity to be sovereign, and reject the idea of "divided sovereignty" proposed by minority nationalist parties (734). The PSOE's attempted peace process with ETA came dangerously close to making divided sovereignty a permanent political reality, a process that the PP considers will lead to the break-up of Spain. The next section sets out the key narrative that the PP projected during the peace negotiations, the narrative of *traición a las víctimas* (betrayal of the victims) and considers this narrative in the context of these narrative divisions.

The narrative of *traición a las víctimas*

ETA's ceasefire announcement made it evident that the pain and hatred caused by terrorism were still palpable, testament to an unresolved civil confrontation. Many sections of Spanish society were waiting for signs of regret and repentance by ETA members. Zapatero recognized from the very beginning of the peace process that the victims of terrorism would be a "delicate" issue (Benegas 2007, 27). Due to the fact that ETA's attacks were relatively recent, many victims and their families found it difficult to accept the government negotiating with the killers of their relatives. Although there have been victims of terrorism in Spain for more than forty years, including during the 1989 and 1998 ceasefires, those victims were more or less invisible in the mass-media. Since the March 11, 2004, attacks, however, the profile of victims of terrorism in political discourse in Spain has become more visible (Benegas 2007, 199). As a result, the victims of terrorism have been positioned at the forefront of the mass-mediated debates on terror in Spain. The victims of terrorism are the key constituency in Spanish politics that have been caught between the narrative division of *las dos Españas* and the global metanarrative of terror. During the peace process, the victims quickly became the key plot point in both the PP and PSOE's rhetorical narrative scripts about the attempted peace negotiations.

Raúl Calvo Soler argues that in the resolution of conflicts where there have been deaths, two difficulties can block a successful outcome. The first is the confusion between a discussion about the viability of a peace process and the morality of the peace process. The second difficulty is the bias against whatever proposal that includes reference to negotiation with a movement, group or political party that has used and justified violence as a method to attain its objectives (2006, 18). In Spain, much of the mass-mediated debate centred around the morality of negotiation and the political price that must be paid in order to achieve some kind of negotiated outcome. In Spanish political and media discourse, political price referred to any compromise agreed to by the government in order to attain peace and the cessation of violence. It was an epithet constantly repeated by the PP throughout the peace process. The PP position was that the Spanish state should not have to compromise on any ETA demands. Compromise would constitute a political price, and that was unacceptable. This rhetoric put the Zapatero administration on the defensive, forcing it to exhaustively argue that the Spanish government would not cede any ground in its negotiations with ETA.

It quickly became evident that the problem with negotiation was a problem of respecting memory, not only the memory of victims but the memory of all families that had lost loved ones, including the families of *etarras*. A debate on the issue emerged in the mass-media: Do the families of *etarras* have the same moral equivalency as ETA's victims? The Basque regional parliament in Vitoria was singled out for treating ETA's victims in the same way it treated the families of *etarras*, by calling the organization that was established to compensate victims of terrorism, "Ponencia de víctimas" (Blanco Valdés 2008, 190). Hence the word victim refers to victims of ETA and victims of the state; in other words, any victim of the conflict. According to Valdés, the PNV's approach aimed to treat victims objectively in a situation that will only end when the so-called conflict ends (190). As already discussed, the Spanish right considered the argument that the Basque Country and the Spanish state were in a "conflict" as a misnomer and offensive. For example, the Commissioner for the group "Apoyo a las

Víctimas del Terrorismo," Gregorio Peces-Barba, regarded the change in name as a perversion of language that offends victims of terrorism (190).

Apart from the logistics of the peace process itself, what quickly emerged in the mainstream media was a debate about Basque society and its role in conditioning violence in the Spanish state. *El País* correspondent in the Basque Country, José Luis Barbería, for example, suggested that in the aftermath of ETA's permanent ceasefire, Basque society must "revise and analyse what actually took place" and thus undergo "moral regeneration" and a "return to normality" (2006, 4). It is telling that Barbería uses the phrase "return to normality." The placing of responsibility on Basque society as a whole, rather than on some of its constituents, opened up a moral divide in Spanish society. Traditional and democratic Spanish society was narrativized as morally superior to the degeneracy of Basque society, which allowed violence to flourish because ordinary Basques either sympathized with terrorists or were too scared to speak up and defend common decency. In order to sustain this narrative of moral superiority, the victims of terrorism were discursively appropriated for political ends. How could a civilized person not feel empathy for the victim of a terror attack? In the face of the potency that victims narratives were having in Spanish society, Arnaldo Otegi, the leader of ETA's outlawed political wing Batasuna, had no choice but to describe his party's long-standing disregard for the suffering of the Basque terrorist group's victims as an "error." In an inter-view published in the Catalan-language daily *Avui*, Otegi expressed "regret" over ETA's 38-year campaign of violence, saying that "We always gave the impression that the suffering of [the victims] didn't bother us and that the means justified the end. That was evidently an error" ("Otegi Voices Regret" 2006, 1).

The ETA peace process replayed the same debates, and evoked the same national narratives, that occupied Spain during its transition to democracy. That is, to what extent should a society remain silent and forget the tragedy and violence of the recent past? And does Spanish society have a collective responsibility for the effects of the conflict? The victims of ETA's attacks called for memory, dignity and justice. They argued that there is no such thing as collective responsibility, only individual responsibility for those who chose to utilize violence. Many Basques were clearly excited about the opportunity to close that chapter of Spanish history with an agreement to sanction, by identifying and naming, the existence of an original, under-lying political conflict that would exonerate blame (Barbería 2006, 4). These Basques also proposed a collective amnesty and called for more generosity toward the victims. They did not feel it was necessary to draw any further political conclusions about what had occurred (4). Given that it was generally accepted in the Spanish mass-media that Basque society was permeated by fear and silence, and had a deficit of sensitivity to and empathy for the victims of terrorism to the point of moral perversion, the two ideological positions could not be reconciled during the peace process.

Spanish philosopher Fernando Savater was more cynical about the desire of many Basques to forget the past. He suggested that the popular narrative that the "peaceniks" ran with was as follows:

> Let's start from zero, forget the past (especially the killings, which tend to have unpleasant consequences such as long prison sentences). Let's call all sorts of community meetings and assemblies, where those who have been killing and those who have been living in fear will have a right to speak on an equal basis. Let's call a referendum, and ask the public if they want the killers back with guns in their hands, or unarmed and treated with public respect. Put Batasuna leader Arnaldo Otegi and his people in jail? But circumstances have changed!
>
> Now is the time for firmness. There can be only one answer to the question "what do we owe?" Nothing, nothing, nothing. (2006, 2)

As with the end of Francoism, the negotiations with ETA were embroiled in a narratological struggle between memory and forgetting. This time, however, many Basques were arguing for amnesty and forgetting, while the majority of Spanish society argued that the damage caused by ETA violence must not be erased from public consciousness. Barbería argued that it was contradictory to argue that the appeal to bury the past in order to secure future peace excluded the need to address what has occurred in the Basque Country. He stated that "the memories, the sounds, the voices and the images—the echoes of past nightmares—will live on for many long years" (4). Openly addressing and evaluating what occurred in the Basque Country will help avoid the return to violence and from resentment to settle in permanently (4). There was common sense in the idea that terrorists who had killed should pay for their crimes. But the epithet—*What do we owe? Nothing!*—became a problematic mantra for the Spanish right and for many on the Spanish left as well. Owing something meant paying a political price. Paying a political price meant betraying the victims of terrorism. And so on.

The concept of not paying a political price to the terrorists, that is, not compromising on ETA's demands is a deep-seated mantra with victims' groups. Their attitude is that government concessions to terrorists signal that terrorism can achieve its political aims, thus providing fertile ground for other fanatical groups to consider using the method of killing innocent people. Concessions were seen as unacceptable to groups like ETA that acted outside of the rule of law. Interestingly, experts from conflicts in Northern Ireland, South Africa, Colombia, El Salvador, Sri Lanka and Sudan, among others, gave their opinion about the peace process. They suggested that all parties should understand that each side in the equation must compromise in order to reach an agreement (Benegas 2007, 210). PP statements, however, maintained that any concessions to ETA prisoners would be a betrayal of ETA's victims and thus of democracy itself. A common view of many on the Spanish right is that the terrorists should never achieve their objectives simply because they stop killing. This would be a way of winning, to receive a prize for the cessation of violence without anyone taking responsibility for their crimes. The Basque struggle can only continue within existing democratic institutions.

That might be fair, but the arguments of PP opposition leader Mariano Rajoy were becoming circular and nonsensical. He suggested that the government should not do anything until ETA dissolves. And once ETA ceases to exist, there will therefore be nothing that the government need do (Benegas 2007, 90). This tautological argument suggested that terrorism would only cease with a unilateral dissolution of ETA:

> No se puede hablar de política con una organización terrorista. Porque si hablamos de política con ETA, o con su segunda marca, ETA-Batasuna, ya habremos aceptado lo que los terroristas nos están pidiendo, que es la nego-ciación política. (You cannot talk about politics with a terrorist organization. Because if we talk politics with ETA, or with ETA-Batasuna, we would have accepted what terrorists are asking of us, which is political negotiation). (102)

For the Spanish right, then, ETA's presence meant that the greater problem of Basque independence never had to be addressed. According to Aretxaga:

> The ending of ETA's armed activity is the necessary change that opens up the political space to multiple political scenarios. If democratic identity has been forged, in good measure, by its opposition to terrorism, the disap-pearance of the terrorist enemy necessarily forces a redefinition of democracy itself, as regards its own political identity. (2005, 175)

ETA served as a species of internal spectral enemy that had to be contained. This position was a powerful one in a country that worked so effectively to erase violence from its popular narratives. The PP position recognized that the disbandment of ETA ultimately meant that the Spanish state would have to renegotiate the historical pacts of compromise agreed after Franco's death and Spain's transition to democracy, pacts that have served to placate Spanish conservatives and that have, up till now, helped maintain a remarkable level of stability in a country once torn by a traumatic history. In Chapter Nine I evaluate ETA's definitive cessation of its terrorist activities and what that means for the political narratives of the major political parties in Spain.

As a case study, the 2006–2007 peace process between the Spanish state and ETA demonstrates the constraints that the narrative of *las dos Españas* placed on the ritual of Spanish politics. Although the overdetermination of terrorism, to use Gabilondo's term, in the post-9/11 era provided an opportunity for the Spanish state to once and for all defeat ETA terrorism, the play of Spanish politics in terms of the ideological division of the two Spains hindered any attempt at reconciliation and healing. The potency of the narrative of *las dos Españas* in mass-mediated discourse pitted the Basque conflict in a battle between two conceptions of Spain. As long as the narrative division of the two Spains continued to feed mass-mediated discourse, politicize victims of terrorism and circulate nonsensical arguments, then any attempted peace process was bound to be caught in the eternal struggle between memory and forgetting.

Conclusion: Reflections on a broken ceasefire

The permanent ceasefire was short-lived. The peace process was paralyzed by reports of the involvement of suspected ETA members in the theft of weapons in southern France in late 2006, continued disturbances throughout the Basque Country involving ETA sympathisers, and the ongoing extortion of money from businesses in the region (Kennedy 2007, 200–1). Moreover, the government refused to release any of those convicted of having carried out crimes on behalf of the organization, or to transfer them to prisons within the Basque Country, because the organization had failed to show unequivocally that it had abandoned violence. As a result, on December 30, 2006, ETA placed a car bomb in a parking station at Barajas Airport in Madrid, which killed two Ecuadorian immigrants and destroyed 60 percent of the building, effectively ending the ceasefire less than twenty-fours after Zapatero had declared: "Dentro de un año estaremos mejor que hoy" (Within a year we will be better off than today) (Blanco Valdés 2008, 221). It was the first time ETA had executed an attack during a ceasefire without advising of an imminent attack in a communiqué. The two Ecuadorian immigrants were also ETA's first mortal victims in more than three and a half years. The government immediately halted peace negotiations. The PP argued that the attack demonstrated that the PP's position was correct and that ETA had not renounced violence. In her book *Endgame for ETA*, Teresa Whitfield mentions that Deputy Prime Minister Alfredo Rubalcaba would long remember a photograph taken in the hours following the Barajas bomb which showed Otegi and other leaders of Batasuna standing inside a lift, their faces stunned in shock (2014, 180). Rubalcaba read their faces as recognition of the depth of the damage done: "[. . .] I always said to Zapatero, 'Remember that photograph—it's the end'" (180).

Ten days after the attacks on January 10, 2007, ETA released a communiqué in the Basque daily newspaper *Gara*, in which it indicated that while the ceasefire was still in effect, it would nonetheless respond to any aggression against Euskal Herria by the French and Spanish states (Benegas 2007, 250). An *El País* editorial stated that the communiqué was a "masterpiece of inconsistency" ("The Communiqué" 2007, 2). There was clearly an internal conflict between ETA members who wanted to negotiate an end to violence and those who saw violence as the only means to keep their struggle alive. Renouncing its violent struggle would mean that ETA would have to play by democratic rules. ETA formally ended the ceasefire in a communiqué released to the Basque newspaper *Berria* on June 5, 2007.

The PP and its narrative strategy capitalized on the peace process to a certain extent. There was no denying that the PP's tactics during the peace process were to outrage the Spanish public. On January 22, 2007, however, in an interview published in *El Correo*, PP leader Mariano Rajoy admitted that Zapatero neither made concessions against the Constitution nor threatened the future of Navarre (Benegas 2007, 263). This admission was unusual considering that the PP had made such allegations the platform of its opposition strategy. In a survey by the *Centro de Investigaciones Sociológicos* (CIS) in October 2006, only 19 percent of Spaniards believed that terrorism was the principle problem facing the country. More people considered immigration, unemployment and housing to be more pressing issues (Blanco Valdés 2008, 237). Six months later, in March 2007, the number who named terrorism as the most pressing threat to Spain had doubled to 38 percent, indicating that the PP's narrative campaign of making terrorism the single most important issue in Spain had worked. But the PP's standing electorally barely improved in the 2008 general elections, despite the government's failure in the peace process. Zapatero's own words may best explain why the PP failed:

No es creíble emitir opiniones siempre con el mismo tono exagerado, por ejemplo, que nos hemos rendido ante los terroristas. No es creíble para la gente, la primera condición para ser alternativa es ser creíbles. (It is not credible to broadcast opinions with the same exaggerated tone, for example, that we have surrendered to terrorists. It is not credible to the public, the first condition to be a credible alternative is to be believable). (Quoted in Benegas 2007, 112)

Narratives must be convincing for them to work. Once again, the PP's narratives in opposition were not sufficiently convincing for a significant majority of Spanish people.

Part of the reason for this failure was the excess of the PP's criticisms in a political landscape that was rife with absurd commentaries and accusations of madness. Indeed the PP's invective neatly elided with the prevailing madness of the Spanish public and cultural spheres. ETA and Batasuna were accused of madness for their nonsensical actions and demands. The Zapatero administration was accused of insanity for attempting to negotiate with them. The Basque regional premier Juan Jose Ibarretxe accused the Spanish state itself of madness when it took legal action against him for talking with the illegal Batasuna: "only in a country gone mad could a leader be prosecuted for talking to those with different political viewpoints" ("Basque Premier Defiant" 2007, 1). Barcelona comedian Pepe Rubianes, on a TV3 show called El Club, suggested to the Spanish right-wing that they "shove Spain up their ass to see if their balls explode." Subsequently his stage show, *Lorca somos todos*, was pulled from Madrid's Teatro Español. The PP's narrative of *traición a las víctimas* lost much of its political sting in that overloaded political atmosphere, where excessive vitriol was expected.

It was also clear that the placement of the victims of terror at the centre of the terror debate in Spain exposed a moral divide that was difficult for the PP to bridge. Its posture of confrontation with the government often gave the impression that the party was actually pleased with the attacks, an impression that went down badly with public opinion. On this point, Slavoj Žižek asks: "How do you find a bridge between objective social relations and the concrete suffering of the individual? [. . .] It is a conflict between the Particular and the Universal, between the individual's self-experience and the objective social totality" (2005, 14). ETA victim Eduardo Malina effectively demonstrated this moral divide and how it ultimately harmed the PP:

Es verdad que soy una víctima de ETA, pero no solo soy una víctima de ETA: Y he querido dejar todo esto muy claro en mi interior para que no sea ETA [. . .] la que decida mis perspectivas, ponga mis filtros, genere mis críticas y construya mis pensamientos políticos, mis iniciativas, mis reflexiones [. . .]

Estoy convencido de que hay gente dentro del PP que no está de acuerdo con la frase estrella de Mariano Rajoy—'El gobierno de Zapatero está traicionando a la victimas del terrorismo'—Esta es su mayor aportación a la legislatura, su titular, su momento estelar, su hit, su cima más alta, pero ahí se desmontó como político, se convirtió en otra cosa. Se deconstruyó a sí mismo como aspirante a la presidencia de un Gobierno. Él ya no vale para eso después de la frase. (Quoted in Benegas 2007, 207–8)

(It's true that I am an ETA victim, but I am not only an ETA victim: I wanted to make that clear to myself so that it is not ETA [. . .] that decides my perspectives, creates my filters, generates my criticisms and constructs my political beliefs, initiatives and reflections [. . .]

I am convinced that there are people inside the PP who do not agree with Rajoy's star phrase—the Zapatero government is betraying the victims of terrorism—that has been his biggest contribution to the legislature, his headline, his star-turn, his hit, his peak; but that's where he came apart as a politician, he became something else. He deconstructed himself as an aspiring prime minister. He's not cut out for leadership after that phrase)

It was clear that the victims of terrorism and their position in Spanish political discourse would become a troubling and complex phenomenon for the Spanish government. The next chapter takes a deeper look into the role of victims of terror in Spanish society, and discusses their volatile role in shaping government policy and shifting public opinion. The chapter uses the victims of terrorism as a case study to explore how narratives of national identity can be inscribed on the body of the Spanish citizen through the discourses of terrorism, and to explain what this means in the broader Spanish state.

CHAPTER EIGHT

The Semantics and Rhetoric of Victims of Terrorism Groups

> Almost no one appreciated what it meant to be a victim of terrorism.
> (Hirsch 2006, 8)

In February, 2006, Spanish Prime Minister José Luis Rodríguez Zapatero was asked by the mother of an ETA victim what he would do in her place: she did not know what to tell her daughter about her brother's murder (Albiac 2008, 105). Zapatero responded that he understood her position perfectly because his grandfather was also killed during the Spanish Civil War, a conflict that occurred twenty-four years before Zapatero was born. The mere fact that Zapatero dared to equate the historical victims of *las dos Españas* to the current victims of terrorism scandalized many victims' groups. Zapatero was accused of being out of touch with the concerns and realities of victims of terrorism.

The episode was telling in a number of ways. It underscored the precarious position that Spanish leaders faced in the new millennium. Politicians and other public figures were expected to pay tribute to victims of terrorism and consider their feelings when making public policy. The incident also highlighted the ambiguity of victimhood in a country coming to terms with multiple historical conflicts. Were all victims of violence the same, or did some victims deserve more rights and empathy than others, depending on which group had killed or injured them? Finally, the episode illustrated a division between those who saw the victims as a consequence of a localized, isolated and apolitical struggle (the mother), and those who saw the victims as part of a long trajectory of historical injustice and conflict (Zapatero).

Zapatero took the position that it was impossible to separate the victims of ETA's violence from the victims of the Spanish Civil War and Francoism. He, like many descendants of Republicans, regarded the Spanish Civil War as the root cause of the long-suffering conflicts in the Spanish state.

Without the Spanish Civil War there was no Francoism; without Francoism there was no ETA.

In the book *Governing after Crisis* (2008) Boin, McConnell and Hart point out that since the early 1980s, citizens and families affected by crises and disasters have gained a strengthened position in western societies. Victims' associations, they argue, "often turn out to be tenacious and resourceful lobbyists for influence over crisis-induced policy-making processes and decisions. These voices add to the general crisis-induced clamour for political accountability and fuel arguments that leaders should atone for mistakes made, change policies or, in extreme cases, relinquish political office" (2008, 12–13). After September 11, however, there is still very little published material available on the victims' groups formed specifically in response to terrorist attacks in many parts of the world. As Bruce Hoffman and Anna-Britt Kasupski point out in their RAND report, "The Victims of Terrorism" (2007), insufficient attention and analysis have been focused on the victims of terrorist attacks—whether the survivors themselves or their family members, friends, and colleagues directly affected by the violence:

> The deliberate targeting of innocent persons generally plays a central role in the terrorists' ability to "terrorise." Therefore, as the fictional vampire requires blood to survive, the real-life terrorist needs victims. Yet, obvious as this might be, to date, little attention has been focused on the victims of terrorist attacks—whether the survivors themselves or the family members, friends, or colleagues directly affected by this violence. (Hoffman & Kasupski, 2007, 1)

This chapter responds to the dearth of extant analysis by exploring the role of victims' groups in Spanish society and how the mass-mediated debates surrounding the groups are linked to long-standing historical narratives. In Spain victims' groups have widespread influence in the national political arena. More tellingly, they are not only numerous but divided by political allegiances. One of the characteristics of Spain is that absolutely everything somehow ends up becoming politicized: football, education, culture, wine. Victims of terrorism are no exception. In Spain there are several associations, organizations and foundations for victims of terrorism and their families. Each one has a specific, if undeclared, political allegiance. Victims of ETA terrorism tend to gravitate toward the Popular Party because of its hard-line stance against the Basque organization. March 11 victims tend to favour the Socialists, believing that the PP manipulated the 2004 bombings for political gain. Although part of the remit of this chapter is to explore the partisan interests of victims of terrorism groups in Spain, and their influence on Spanish mass-mediated narratives, the chapter also seeks to question the semantics and rhetoric of guilt and innocence surrounding terrorism's victims, and understand how victim narratives also shape and inform contemporary Spanish politics. Such an analysis highlights again how discourses of terror in Spain have a reality-making power because they are caught in a battle between *las dos Españas*.

The complex nature of victimhood

Once an invisible Spanish constituency, the victims of terrorism are now icons in Spanish political discourse and have assumed a role of moral authority in Spanish political life. Spain's leading political actors are now required to adhere to this moral authority or face sanction from extreme elements in Spanish society. For instance, when the former Mayor of Madrid, Alberto Ruiz-Gallardón (PP), urged his party to cease its conspiracy theories about the March 11, 2004, attacks and accept the findings of the March 11 Commission, Federico Jiménez Losantos, a radio shock jock for the conservative *Cope* radio station owned by Catholic bishops, accused him of being a traitor and a liar, and for not caring about the victims of the attacks. Although Losantos was ordered to compensate Ruiz-Gallardón to the tune of 36,000, a sum that he donated to a terrorism victims' association, the implication was clear: ignore the concerns of victims at your peril ("Church-backed shock jock hit with fine" 2008, 1).

In an article expressing the absurdity of this situation, *El País* columnist Soledad Gallego-Díaz opined:

> The politicos in the regional government of Madrid have been speaking for weeks now more of the (non-existent) right of the victims of terrorism to see their political opinions converted into government policy than of the problems of the city's schoolchildren, or the chronic problem of long waiting lists for public healthcare. The strange thing is not how they devote so much attention to one thing and so little to the other. The strange thing is how the public, bombarded by the continual fire of provocation, seems to see nothing strange in it at all. (Gallego-Díaz 2005, 2)

This was a relatively new phenomenon. In the 1970s and early 1980s, victims of terrorism barely rated a mention in the news media, and their funerals were quiet affairs that similarly did not gain much media attention. By the mid-1980s a few small-scale civic groups emerged in the

Basque Country to fight for some recognition of the victims who died for "democracy" and "freedom." The first group to form was the Association for Victims of Terror (AVT), which was founded by Ana María Vidal Abarca in 1981, more than twenty years after ETA's first attacks. It was not until the late 1990s, however, that the victims began to garner wider recognition and support from society and the media, and that change has been attributed to the kidnapping and murder of Miguel Ángel Blanco in 1997. The first book written about the victims of ETA terrorism in Spain was published as late as 1997 by José María Calleja—*Contra la barbarie: un alegato en favor de las víctimas de ETA*. When legal recognition and economic support were forthcoming from the national government in the 2000s, the victims rapidly became one of the most important forces in the Spanish political landscape.

The Zapatero administration recognized that the role of the victims of terrorism had become more important, and Zapatero regularly made remarks to the Spanish media professing, for example, "nos ha unido siempre el espanto ante el terror y la solidaridad con las víctimas" (the horror of terrorism and solidarity with the victims has always united us) (Valdecantos & Rodríguez, 2006, 2). When Zapatero sought authorization from the lower house of parliament to begin talks with ETA in 2006, the government accelerated plans to provide increased compensation to the survivors of terrorist attacks and to the families of victims, and additional assistance to find work and housing.

At the end of 2008, the Zapatero administration proposed a Victims of Terrorism Law to unite all related legislation under one single far-reaching document that would expand the current definition of terrorism victim to include people who are illegally detained, those who suffer "express kidnappings," people affected by terrorist attacks outside Spain, and people who are harassed regularly by terrorists ("Terrorism Victim Status" 2008, 1). This legislation was evidence that the PSOE was attempting in its second term to achieve a careful balance between negotiating peace and assuaging the demands of victims groups, whose sacralized victim narrative and nationally symbolic status cannot be questioned in the Spanish political context of the new millennium. Zapatero's attempts to address the concerns of victims of terrorism were understandable considering the potency of the opposition PP's narrative of *traición a las víctimas* (see Chapter Seven). Yet, as the anecdote in the introduction to this chapter suggests, the Zapatero administration was not able to successfully assuage the fears of some victims of terrorism. As a result its approach was challenged by the Catholic Church, the judiciary, and several different media outlets. More significantly, the Zapatero administration faced the hostility of the Association of Terror Victims (AVT) and of the opposition Popular Party.

In the new millennium, victims of terrorism are courted by politicians and their heart-wrenching stories of loss and despair are given significant coverage on news bulletins. As Zulaika and Douglass argue, "the capacity to instil public fear so that every citizen can imagine him or herself in the victim's stead is an important measure of the efficacy of terrorism and the complex narratives it generates" (Zulaika & Douglass 1996, 139). The efficacy of terrorism is not predicated on the sheer numbers of casualties, since one victim is as sufficient as ten or a hundred (141). Indeed, part of the reason why victims of terrorism are now accorded such a privileged and symbolic position in Spanish society is that, "unlike victims of ordinary crime, the mise-en-scène of modern political terror is essentially sacrificial" (Feldman 2003, 68). According to Feldman, terrorism requires actors who can assume multiple collective meanings and absorb and reflect back to the social polity diverse and often contradictory collective fantasies:

> The victim is recruited from within the targeted social order, the victim may be a social intimate, and the victim is endowed with emissary capacities that are switched on with the application of violence. The victim in sacrificial actions bears messages and alters social reality in the very mutilation of the victim's embodiment. (2003, 68)

This is why Lidia Falcón pointed out in 2002 that although the number of women murdered in acts of domestic violence annually in Spain was more than double the average number of victims of terrorism over the last twenty-one years, they were not accorded the same symbolic and discursive power. As she cynically put it:

> the murder of women will never constitute a threat to the democratic equilibrium of the state. One hundred women are not worth one ETA victim. While social stability and state security are placed in mortal danger every time ETA claims another victim, the women killed by their spouses help maintain the same patriarchal order that our social organization needs to ensure that women remain exploited workers in the system of domestic production. (2002, 21)

Falcón's observation is telling in two ways. First, it reminds us that not all victims are equal. Second, it implies that certain victims gain discursive privilege in relation to the narratives of nationhood, and to the extent to which their death or injuries places the interests of the state above and beyond the individual victim. Two years after Falcón made her statement, the PSOE won government and made the issue of domestic violence one of its top priorities. Interestingly, with the number of victims of terrorism steadily decreasing, the mass-media turned to the stories of these forgotten women on its news bulletins. The media spectacle accorded to the death of each woman at the hands of her husband is exhilarating insofar as it unabashedly shames the patriarchal order. Yet there is a disturbing link in the media's spectacle of exaltation of domestic violence as domestic terrorism. The production and cult of the "victim" thus continues unabated, all-encompassing in its spectacle of trauma, suffering and grief. In such a potent mix of spectacle and mourning, it is unremarkable that victims' narratives are like omnipotent presences that remain sacred and narratively unchallengeable.

Susan Hirsch, herself a victim of a terrorist attack in the US embassy bombing in Dar es Salaam, Tanzania, on August 7, 1998, has described the process by which gaining recognition as victims, especially from state officials, "often becomes a crucial goal for those struggling to bring coherence to a damaged and wildly fluctuating sense of self in the wake of a violent attack" (2006, 44). She adds: "Whether or not one's loss is acknowledged or one's altered self recognized can be key in surviving a tragedy" (44). At the individual level, the memory of having been the victim of a terrorist attack often becomes the sufferer's principal trait of identity; one is a victim forever. This memory, however, is complicated further in societies such as Spain where memorializations of past injustice and violence reaffirm the collective identity of the victims. The more the victims of terrorism are identified as a collective constituency, the more profound becomes the victims' suffering. This is not simply because the victims are newsworthy, but because they have developed their own place, space, role, voice, and capacity to intervene in dominant narratives of the Spanish state and its imagined communities. The victims, by exposing their pain in public, oblige the national political sphere to redefine itself as a system of mourning. The victims, in short, expect nothing less than solidarity from the state.

In such an emotionally charged context, Zulaika and Douglass argue that experiences of victimization and torture are emblematic simply because they move us:

> They reflect embodied terror and are engaged not in moral indignation from the sidelines but in working though the madness of personal experience in the quest for new means of social and political healing. They radically question categorical distinctions between 'us' and 'them,' the saved and the damned. (1996, 192)

Yet the meaning of victimhood is often dependent on the eye of the beholder. It is easy to understand how those injured and killed at the hands of ETA, or by the March 11, 2004 attacks in Madrid, are victims worthy of sympathy. But Slavoj Žižek argues that although the victims are innocent from a moral standpoint, their very innocence is not innocent (2001, 46–47). On this point, Joseba Zulaika attempts to subvert the categories of guilt and innocence by suggesting that a pro-ETA political party like Batasuna in the Basque Country can also narratively define itself as a victim. Borrowing from Michael Herzfeld's notion of "cultural intimacy," (2005) Zulaika points out that Batasuna, bonded by repression and self-victimization, constructs itself as a community of intense intimacy against a world that accuses the group of complicity with terror. The media, he continues, routinely report ETA's more than eight hundred murders during its bloody history, to which the counter-narrative response has been to state the less-known fact that some 40 per cent of Batasuna sympathisers, who regularly made up between ten and fifteen percent of Basque voters between 1980 and 2001, have had problems with the police and fear torture. This tortured body of the Basque nation "becomes a community of loss, fear and mourning" (Zulaika 2005, 280).

But as the anecdote described in the introduction to this chapter suggests, when a mother of an ETA victim is scandalized by Zapatero's suggestion that he understands her position well because his own grandfather was killed during the Spanish Civil War, mass-mediated narratives of terror tend to view the categories of "terror," "guilt" and "innocence" in convenient black and white terms. If we accept the narrative equation that Terrorism = Evil, then the semantics and rhetoric of innocence remain uncomplicated, particularly as they are framed in political and media discourse. But if the narrative equation Terrorism = Evil is subverted, it becomes readily apparent, as Zulaika and Douglass posit, that "the ease with which both terrorist and counterterrorist can manipulate the categories of innocence (for one's own benefit) and guilt (for the other) gives an indication of the extent to which violence introduces its perpetrators into a playlike frame" (1996, 135).

I am stressing here the ambiguous nature and often arbitrary definitions of innocence and victimhood not to downplay the traumatic effects experienced by real victims of terrorist attacks. Rather, my interest is to foreshadow the complexity of questions of guilt and innocence and thus better understand how victims' groups and, by default, political parties and their projected media narratives, become bogged down by messy moral arguments, as witnessed by the Zapatero government's attempted peace negotiations with ETA discussed in Chapter Seven. Questions of guilt and innocence became even more complicated in Spain with the Supreme Court ruling in January 2006 that gave the family of a woman murdered by a right-wing fanatic in 1976 the same right to compensation as relatives of victims of terrorism. The decision set a precedent for the settlement of transition-era crimes, and potentially opened the door for other victims of transition-era crimes to seek the same compensation as terrorism victims. In short, defining who should be considered a victim of terrorism in Spain is a loaded and contested question, due primarily to disagreements between the two Spains about what constitutes terrorism and historical injustice in a post-dictatorship epoch.

On victimhood and recognition

Victims of terrorism seek recognition for the trauma that they have experienced, and no reasonable person should begrudge them that recognition. But as Hirsch points out, exactly what constitutes recognition for those who have been harmed varies tremendously depending on individual and group circumstance, and historical context:

> Is it satisfied by pressing the hand of a dignitary? Receiving an official condolence letter? Hearing an apology? Can money or medical treatment be sufficient? Do victims require press coverage? Information? An explanation? What about a name on a commemorative plaque? A monument? A place of honour at a memorial service? Victims might find any of these constructive and appropriate recognition at one time or another, and might also find that each offering fails to fulfil the deep need to have one's loss and self acknowledged. (2006, 44)

One form of recognition that Hirsch omits from her analysis, but that has been controversial for victims of terror groups in Spain, is political action. Understandably, many victims and their families enter into political debate and campaign for their interests. A victim of an ETA attack might reasonably oppose his or her government for negotiating in their name with their attempted murderers. A victim of the March 11, 2004 attacks in Madrid would be personally invested in the March 11 Commission and thus question whether or not the Popular Party did manipulate the flow of information before the March 14, 2004 election. But when victims' narratives are sacralized by the mass-media their participation in political debate is problematized, as are their motives.

This is not to suggest that victims of terrorism should not participate in the political process. But it is to suggest that terror victims and the narratives they produce are imbricated in broader national narratives. For example, an interview with Maite Pagazaurtundua, President of the Victims of Terrorism Foundation (Ordaz 2005b, 5), explains her views about a possible government peace negotiation with ETA. On February 8, 2003, an ETA terrorist assassinated Pagazaurtundua brother Joseba, sergeant major of the Andoain municipal police and an activist in the grassroots movement ¡Basta Ya!.[1] The interviewer, Pablo Ordaz, questions Pagazaurtundua about why ordinary people feel a certain happiness and hope that ETA might be nearing its end, yet ETA's victims are angered by that prospect. Pagazaurtundua responds:

> More than angry, you could say there is concern and even fear because we don't know what is behind all this. And that generates concern in certain cases and deep unease in others. We don't know what our place in the government's plans is.

It is clear that Pagazaurtundua's victims' group does not simply demand accountability from the government; it also assumes that the victims of terrorism have a place in the peace negotiations. When asked what the victim's place might be, or entail, she continues:

> To demand justice, not impunity. We've reacted democratically, we haven't taken justice into our own hands, we haven't called for the death penalty or revenge; just justice [. . .]
>
>   We're afraid that we might be seen as a nuisance, or that they'll want to hush us up by saying that since we've been affected, we're not in a position to speak. The nationalists always say things like that, and we're afraid that idea could spread.

Pagazaurtundua defends the victims' right to speak and challenges Basque nationalists who criticize victims' groups for stifling peace negotiations.

---

[1] *¡Basta Ya!* is a grassroots organization formed in 1999, headed by the Spanish Philosopher Fernando Savater, that aims to unite citizens with diverse political ideologies. The group's triple objective involves opposing all types of terrorism, supporting victims, and defending the *Estado de Derecho,* the Spanish Constitution and the current Statute of Autonomy in the Basque Country. This activist organization frequently organizes street demonstrations, particularly in the Basque Country. *¡Basta Ya!* opposes Basque nationalism and criticizes the PSOE's counterterrorism approach and policies. In 2007, disillusioned with the Zapatero administration's attempt to negotiate with ETA, it formed its own political party as an alternative to both the PP and PSOE called *Unión Progreso y Democracia* (UPyD).

When asked how she thinks families might react on the day ETA lays down its arms, she responds:

> It depends. It could be a dream or a nightmare. It will be a dream if ETA lays down its arms because we have defeated them socially and through police efforts, especially if we've managed to squash the seed of fanaticism. But if society decides to forget and starts talking about two sides, and how both of them have good intentions, putting the suffering of the victims and the murderers in the same boat [. . .] If that's the case, it will be the worst possible nightmare.

Pagazaurtundua's last observation clearly demonstrates how the victims of ETA terrorism seek recognition. Like the mother remonstrating against Zapatero's comment about his grandfather also being a victim, Pagazaurtundua denies that there are two objective sides to the conflict, hence her phrasing of "the worst possible nightmare." As a sister of a victim, Pagazaurtundua projects, reinforces and re-transmits the *Terrorism = Evil* narrative, and argues that to even compare the suffering of Basque nationalists to ETA victims is not only grossly insulting, but morally taboo. Of particular note is her fear that Spanish society will forget the victims' suffering. Clearly, the recognition that the members of her group seeks is predicated in part on the endurance of their collective suffering as enabled through the persistence of their collective memories. In the semantics of The Victims of Terrorism Foundation, any government action that undermines this narrative morally subverts the purity of their suffering and thus their collective identity.

Morality aside, it is clear that a victim of terrorism must perform his or her victimhood and display his or her vulnerability in what can only be described as a mass-mediated spectacle. There is thus some truth to the adage that describes terrorism, and its aftermaths, as theatre. But a victim's performance is subject to society's silent expectations of how a victim should behave. In his discussion of the war in Kosovo, Žižek argues that the basic paradox of victimization is that:

> the Other to be protected is good in so far as it remains a victim (which is why we were bombarded with pictures of helpless Kosovar mothers, children and old people, telling moving stories of their suffering); the moment it no longer behaves as a victim, but wants to strike back on its own, it all of a sudden magically turns into a terrorist, fundamentalist, drug-trafficking Other. (2006, 148)

What is the proper way for a victim of terrorism to behave? What happens when a victim of terrorism in Spain no longer behaves as a victim, but strikes back on his or her own? To what extent does guilt and innocence matter when politics is a spectacle of mourning? As we shall see in the next section, the politics of victims' groups inevitably involve conflicting moral expectations and subjectivities. How we understand these conflicts turns not so much on ideological identification, but rather on narratives of grief and suffering in relation to broader narratives of state and global terrorism, as the Spanish situation ably confirms.

Victims of terrorism groups: A clash of cosmologies

As a victim of a terrorist attack in which she lost her husband, Susan Hirsch relates that "sharing our stories forged connections among us victims of terror, provided company in grief, kept the dead alive in memory, and moved the events of the past into a present that reshaped their meaning" (2006, 95). Neil Whitehead, moreover, points out that the physicality of violent assault cannot be limited to its destruction of human bodies, "but, necessarily, must also be related to the way violence persists as memory, trauma, and in the intimate understanding of one's self identity" (2006, 232). Victims of terrorism and their families form groups and associations as one method to assist them to cope with their grief and to share their stories. Inevitably many of these groups and associations desire to understand the motivations of terrorists, to seek justice, and to mobilize at a grassroots level for stronger counterterrorism measures. In Spain a number of such groups exist, and the majority have formed specifically to support the victims of ETA terrorism. Some organizations, such as *¡Basta Ya!* and *Foro de Ermua*,[2] while supporting and recognizing the victims of terrorism, have wider objectives that include defending the Spanish Constitution and opposing radical Basque nationalism.

My aim in this chapter is not to discuss every active victim association in Spanish politics. Instead, I want to focus the discussion on two specific

---

[2] The *Foro de Ermua* is a civil association composed mainly of academics and other professionals (politicians, writers and journalists). It was formed on February 13, 1998, in response to the assassination of PP councillor Ermua Miguel Ángel Blanco by ETA. The organization's objectives include helping and promoting the recognition of victims of terrorism, denouncing acts of terrorism, supporting constitutional means to definitively defeat terrorism, preventing any negotiation between the Spanish state and ETA, and defending the Spanish Constitution and current Statute of Autonomy in the Basque Country.

groups: the *Asociación de Víctimas del Terrorismo* (AVT, Association of Victims of Terrorism); and the *Asociación 11-M Afectados del Terrorismo* (11-M, known in English as the March 11 Victims' Association). Despite their affinities, the two groups have been torn apart by partisan and ideological politicking. The Association of Terrorism Victims (AVT) comprises mostly people affected by the acts of ETA. The March 11 Victims' Association consists of family members of victims and surviving victims of the March 11 bombings in Madrid, perpetrated by a group linked to Al-Qaeda. As an article by *El País* succinctly put it, "Both groups have suffered, have been hurt, and have lost loved ones at the hands of terrorists. But their similarities end there" (Granda & Elkin 2005, 3). Some of their disagreements might be considered trifling. For instance, the AVT and 11-M were deeply divided over the impending creation of a memorial to honour the victims of the March 11 attacks. Since there was no memorial to commemorate the lives lost in ETA attacks, the AVT chose to support the creation of a memorial honouring all of Spain's terrorism victims, in contrast to the members of 11-M, who wanted a memorial exclusively for the Madrid bombings (Abend & Pingree 2004). But other disagreements run deeper. These complications indicate that the process of *crispación* and the narrative battle between the two major political parties has been inscribed onto the bodies of the victims and appropriated for political ends.

Most of the differences and disagreements between the AVT and the March 11 Association can be ascribed to the historical context that led to their foundation. The AVT which is the biggest victim association in Spain was founded in 1981, a year during which violent groups, including ETA and GRAPO, killed 42 people. The group's initial agenda was to promote the increase of pensions and other benefits received by victims (Lorant 1991, 35). The AVT is a considerably large organization with delegations in thirteen Autonomous Communities of Spain, including Andalusia, Catalonia, Cantabria, Galicia, Asturias and Castile and León and has over 6,000 members including victims and their families of terrorist attacks by distinct groups such as ETA, GRAPO, the IRA and Al-Qaeda. However, the majority of its membership consists largely of ETA-attack victims and their families. Consequently, the AVT was opposed to Zapatero's attempts to initiate peace talks with ETA in 2006 and is a powerful lobby that was a thorn in the side of the Socialist government's counterterrorism policy throughout the life of the Zapatero administration. The former President of the AVT, Francisco José Alcaraz, railed against Zapatero's efforts to launch a peace process in the Basque Country and accused him of insulting and turning his back on victims when he authorized peace talks with ETA.

The foundation of the March 11 Victims' Association could not be anymore different. The M-11 Victims' Association is the largest victims' association that was inaugurated in response to the March 11, 2004, bombings in Madrid, and has over 1000 victims of the attacks among its members (by comparison the *Asociación de Ayuda a las Víctimas del 11-M* has about 500 members, and the AVT about 300). The Association was founded by Pilar Manjón, the mother of a victim. Having claimed the lives of 191 people, the March 11 attacks were the most fatal terrorist attacks in Europe since the Second World War. Many of the victims of the March 11 bombings were working-class commuters, whose families and advocates tend to support the PSOE. Consequently, this group's politically leftist orientation put it at odds with the AVT since many in the organization generally blame Aznar for his alleged manipulation of the bombings for political gain (Sciolino 2005, 35).

The polarisation of these two victim associations starkly aligns with the narrative division of *las dos Españas* and reflects the process of *crispación* which dominated mass-mediated politics during Zapatero's first term in office. As discussed in Chapter Seven, the years between 2004 and 2008 saw a wellspring of demonstrations in Madrid and other Spanish cities by victims of terrorism groups, mostly organized by the AVT and the PP in what they refer to as a "civic rebellion." According to Calleja, the organization, aesthetics and slogans of these demonstrations were similar and they all shared the same objectives: to overthrow the Zapatero administration, to link ETA to the March 11 attacks, and to demand the truth about the attacks from the Zapatero administration (2008, 149). Many victims of ETA have said that the PP was the first party to show concern for their situation because their leader, José María Aznar, had himself survived a bomb attack by ETA, hence his personal interest in the problem. Consequently, Aznar was made an honorary member of the association. The left-wing Spanish press was particularly harsh in its criticism of the AVT demonstrations, not only because they were heavily backed, encouraged and supported by the PP, but because they attracted the aggressive and highly visible appearance of the traditional extreme right. On this point, one PP member admitted to *El País* columnist, Soledad Gallego-Díaz:

> It is true that these demonstrations are serving as an axis around which the old-time extreme right is organizing; and that some of us, deputies for the PP, who attended the recent demonstration in the Puerta del Sol, found ourselves immersed in groups that were clearly from the extreme right, people, who were monopolizing the whole event. (Gallego-Díaz 2007, 2)

The left-wing press also criticized Aznar's participation in some of the demonstrations that were organized to protest the proposed talks with ETA as ironic, given that when he was leader of Spain, he authorized talks with ETA without consulting Congress. Members of the March 11 Victims' Association and other political parties have tended to stay away from AVT demonstrations.

During the March 11 trial, the 11-M Association sought to legally distinguish itself from the AVT after the judge, Juan del Olmo, issued a writ stating that if the 11-M Association wished to appear as a plaintiff in the trial, it must do so under the legal representation and direction of the AVT. In the writ the judge referred to "a convergence of interests of all the plaintiff associations" ("March 11 Victims' Group" 2005, 3). But the M-11 Victims' Association argued that there was a public and well-known difference between the two associations' approaches to the trial, and an "absolute" and "radical" incompatibility between their interests (3). The 11-M Association sought to distance itself from the AVT after what the group considered outrageous comments and actions by former AVT President Francisco José Alcaraz and his association. Manjón pointed out that the AVT presented a lawsuit on March 12, 2004, for a public admission of responsibility for the March 11 attacks by certain ETA leaders who had been in prison for a number of years, as well as by all those "connected with ETA in its political, youth, labour union and legal-aid organizations" ("March 11 Victims' Group," 2005, 3). The demand echoed the Popular Party's insistence at the time that ETA was responsible for the bombings. The lawsuit was rejected by Judge del Olmo later that month. An extension of the previous claim was filed on March 23, 2004, in which the AVT referred to "countries of Muslim religion and enemies of the Christian world" and to Moroccans as "enemies of our nation in every way." Amongst the measures demanded by the AVT was "the immediate closure of the mosque on the M-30 [Madrid highway], after previous entry and search of those inside" and "entry and search of all premises under the name of mosques or Islamic cultural centres" (3).

The 11-M Association noted that their association was established because the ethical and legal approach of existing associations was unacceptable. According to the former President of the M-11 Commission:

> We have different philosophies and different ways of understanding the terrorist phenomenon. What's clear is that we would never have Mr. Aznar as an honorary member, that is clear. All victims are just that, victims. Mr. Alcaraz says there are different classes of victims and, sadly, until recently in Spain, there were second-class and third-class victims, and I don't want

to continue that. And then it appeared that some people grew envious of
the solidarity that the Spanish population gave [to us] after March 11.
(Granda & Elkin 2005, 3)

The March 11 Association thus insisted that the radically different positions of the two associations, and the open confrontation between them in
the proceedings of the parliamentary March 11 commission of inquiry,
made it impossible for them to appear in court under the legal aegis of the
AVT.

These philosophical differences led to outright hostile confrontation. At
an AVT demonstration against terrorism in January 2005, the March 11
group was invited to attend, but not to participate. During the demonstration, the crowd attacked the Socialist Party representatives in
attendance and insulted the March 11 Association's spokeswoman, Pilar
Manjón. After Manjón testified before the parliamentary commission investigating the attacks, AVT supporters and March 11 victims verbally sparred
for hours outside the Spanish parliament. Manjón later claimed that she
received death threats from AVT members (Ordaz 2005a, 3). At the second
anniversary of the March 11 attacks in Madrid, the estrangement between
the two constituent victims' groups became entrenched. The official tribute
event to the victims of the attack was held in the *Bosque del Recuerdo* inside
Madrid's Retiro Park. However, after a short while, the PP leaders left the
tribute to attend a parallel event in the same park organized by the AVT.

In a powerful and emotive speech, Manjón attempted to bridge the
divide by saying that all victims are united by their pain:

> There are no left-wing members or right-wing victims. There are simply
> victims of terrorism—innocent people who gave their lives for democracy
> in this country [. . .] There is a political manipulation of certain victims,
> and I don't know why that is. If there is something that defined this attack,
> it was its scope, and the youth and diversity of its victims. ("Two Years
> On" 2006, 3)

Manjón seemed to bring back the human element to the tragedy of the
victims' stories, and for a moment shared grief seemed to trump partisan
politicking. But during the Zapatero years the estrangement of the two
victims' associations continued to grow, mirroring the *crispación* between
the two major political parties. The words of Elisabeth Kirtsoglou,
although written about Greek society, are also translatable to Spain:

> [Spaniards] have to deal with not only with the ambiguities of terrorism

and violence but also with the inconsistencies of a harsh and not always straightforward political reality. They do so under the weight of their own historical narrative and in anticipation of a future that at times is envisaged as being no different from the past. Local perceptions of terrorism reveal a culturally and historically rich set of political cosmologies filled with anxiety and mistrust. (2006, 81)

Kirtsoglou's use of "anxiety" and "mistrust" best describes the narrative battle between the AVT and the March 11 Association. Earlier chapters have shown that violent acts often embody complex interpretations of symbols that relate to both order and disorder in a given social context, and these symbolic complexities "give violence its many potential meanings in the evolving formation of the cultural imaginary" (Whitehead 2006, 232). The conflict between the two associations appears to be an imaginary construct deeply embedded in contemporary Spanish culture. It reflects an entire cosmology rooted in deeply held social attitudes, themselves stemming from historical narratives of contestation and division.

There is no escaping from the effects of terror violence, whether or not one is victim, perpetrator or mere spectator. If terror needs to work the imagination and the more general realm of the imaginary, as Strathern and Stewart suggest, then "victims of terror also fit into this imaginary world where ideas shape people's responses to events in terms of cosmologically established or recreated narratives" (2006, 6). For Zulaika and Douglass, "'terrorism' is an enormously efficacious stimulant of the collective imagination, since it clearly garners and hold media attention all out of proportion to the course of actual events" (1996, 183). The narrative battle between the AVT and the March 11 Association is a contest between a set of anticipations and feelings about the effects of violent acts and their meanings.

The Spanish political commentator José Luis Barbería suggests that the figure of the victim emerges from the narrative fog as an uncomfortable witness who questions society:

817 black holes representing those murdered, the traumatic after effects of the 2,000 wounded, the void left open by the 10,000 exiles and the anguish of the 40,000 threatened individuals in high-risk groups. To these figures, we also must also add the terrorist losses: the 32 murdered in the GAL affair, those killed by bombs that went off accidentally or in confrontations with the police; the suicides, the terrible death by torture of Joxean Arregui on February 13, 1981, and the 650 prisoners trapped in the spiral of violence and repression that they themselves helped to generate. (2006, 4)

The stories told by many Spanish victims of political violence and terror, whose ranks are swelled by multiple conflicts and who represent the multiple sides of the political spectrum, often lack narrative coherence, despite the shared suffering of these victims. However, victims' groups and the mass-media often do not have the luxury to live with moral and narrative ambiguity. Instead, many victims of terror and the mass-media seek narrative coherence and moral certainty in order to make sense of such tragedies.

As I have attempted to show, narratives of terror aim to be explanatory. They are employed by victims and the media as a means of composing expedient and coherent explanations not only of historical conflicts, but also of local and international politics and their convergences (Kirtsoglou 2006, 61). With such disparate terrorist attacks, such as the targeted assassinations orchestrated by ETA, and the train bombings in Madrid on March 11, 2004, the narratives projected by the two major victims' associations and their media supporters are understandably in direct conflict. Both associations do not only have a clash of cosmologies; they also battle in a narratological sense for the hearts and minds of ordinary people in their respective campaigns for justice.

Conclusion

Much scholarship on terrorism ignores the local complexities of politics and victims' groups, and thus contributes to our simplistic images of barbarian terrorists. According to Hirsch, "if these images explain little, they impugn whole populations. They also miss the fierce ideological dynamics of local struggles and thus offer little insight into the power of those ideologies, and how to combat or reduce them" (2006, 239). This chapter has not attempted to champion either the AVT or the March 11 Association. Instead, it has attempted to highlight the political character of victims and their associations and their influence on the narratives that dominate Spanish politics. Throughout this book, each chapter has inextricably demonstrated that narratives of terror in Spain are given immense discursive power, not only in politics but also the mass-media. The spectacle of violence feeds into a mass-mediated spectacle of grief and suffering in which the victims inevitable share the centre stage.

The Spanish experience leads to important questions about the nature of victimhood, recognition and commemoration. In a state whose population grapples with multiple historical conflicts, who can be defined as a victim of terrorism? What are the moral responsibilities of the state to give victims recognition for their suffering? To what extent should victims' concerns be taken into account when making public policy? The Spanish experience also challenges us to think about the aftermath of terrorist attacks. Understanding the complex nature of victimhood, and its ambivalent relationship with history and historical truth, goes some way to illuminating the direction of political narratives of terrorism that, at first glance, seem directionless.

Chapter Nine

From Terror to Crisis

Todo lo que era sólido se desvanece en el aire (All that was solid melts in the air). (Muñoz Molina 2013, 17)[1]

The terror narratives examined so far point to the capacity and resilience of both sides of Spanish politics to constantly rearticulate and re-imagine their respective narratives and thus adapt to changing circumstances and times. But at certain periods in Spain's recent history one of the two Spains has projected a more convincing story to the Spanish electorate. In the late 1990s the Aznar government was successful in weaving a narrative script that changed Spaniards' perception of the right and promoted a forward-thinking, confident and rejuvenated Spain. After the March 11 attacks, however, the Socialists were successful in subverting that narrative by branding the Aznar government as opportunistic, regressive and manipulative, rhetoric that fit into the theory of the two Spains.

This chapter sets out the narrative of *las dos Españas* from the beginning of Zapatero's second term in government (2008–2011) until the end of Mariano Rajoy's first term (2011–2015). Those eight years in Spanish politics were tumultuous and eventful. That period oversaw drastic changes in Spanish society particularly due to the ruinous effects of the global economic crisis on the Spanish economy and on the lives of ordinary Spaniards. Most importantly for the remit of this book, in this period terror narratives, which for years had dominated Spanish political and mass-mediated narratives, were somewhat relegated to the background. With more than 25 per cent of Spaniards unemployed, the country's energy was focused on overcoming the destruction of its social and economic fabric. The word "crisis" was not just a political buzzword. It was a devastating social phenomenon with real effects on the living standards of many Spaniards.

---

[1]   Antonio Muñoz Molina's use of Karl Marx and Freidrich Engels' phrase from the *Communist Manifesto* (1848) "all that is solid melts into air" forms the basis of his critique of the Spanish political class and its handling of the economic crisis.

More importantly, the crisis completely changed the political landscape in Spain, destroying the two-party system which had been operating, more or less successfully, since Spain's transition to democracy. The Spain of 2016 has little in common (at least politically) with the Spain of 2007.

In this chapter I argue that the economic crisis, far from tempering the radicalization of Spanish politics, served to exacerbate a host of political tensions. The narrative of *las dos Españas* was thus just as present in Spanish political discourse as ever, except that the post-2008 period saw an unprecedented level of political fragmentation. With young, unemployed Spaniards taking to the streets in cities across the country, it was clear that many young Spanish people were ready to challenge the so-called "pacts" of the transition to democracy. Almost everybody could agree that something along the way had gone wrong: that something was rotten in many Spanish institutions; that the level of corruption had become unsustainable; and that "Spain is different" was an argument no longer worth defending. The problem during those years was not diagnosing the obvious: Spain's social, political and economic problems were evident and plain for all to see. The problem was in deciding how to reform Spanish institutions, to choose: what next for Spain? It was in the process of negotiating those choices that the narrative of *las dos Españas* circulated in mass-mediated discourse, confronting Spaniards once again with the ghosts of the past and the fear of the unknown.

In this chapter, then, I explain how crisis narratives not only operate and circulate in Spanish mass-mediated discourse but in fact *mirror* terror narratives. That is, similar to terror narratives, crisis narratives are inextricably linked with the narrative of *las dos Españas*. Nowhere was this more evident than Zapatero's second term in government. Despite the unprecedented vitriolic attacks against Zapatero and the Socialists by the PP during his first term on a whole array of issues, from "not paying a political price to ETA," to campaigning against the Catalan Statute of Autonomy and to the obstructionist tactics against the "historical memory law," none of those lines of attack were sufficient or narratively convincing to defeat Zapatero. In fact, as I argued in Chapter Seven, the Socialists actually increased their vote in the March 2008 general elections (Botti 2013, 48). What brought an end to Zapatero and the PSOE was the economic crisis, or more precisely, the Socialists' handling of the economic crisis. It is not the remit of this chapter to determine who or what is responsible for Spain's worst economic crisis in eighty years. It is clear, however, that Spain's economic woes are due to structural problems. Spain's economic model based largely on construction, tourism and consumption has been in place for decades and thus both the PSOE and the PP must take some responsibility for it. Rather, my aim in this chapter is to highlight the key narrative battles that emerged in Spanish politics that stemmed from the economic crisis and to understand those narrative battles in the context of the narrative of *las dos Españas*. This chapter provides a brief overview of some of the competing narratives of crisis that circulated in Spanish political discourse between 2008 and 2015 and three key events that occurred in Spain during those years. First, ETA's declaration of a definitive cessation of its armed activity in October 2011; second, the emergence of the 15-M movement and the end of the two-party electoral system; and finally, Catalonia's renewed drive towards independence. By examining these three events alongside narratives of crisis, I argue that the narrative of *las dos Españas* not only remains present in Spanish political discourse, but it continues to adapt, evolve and challenge our idea of what Spain is.

Crisis and history

Perceiving economic crises is not easy because they can grow unnoticed until everything collapses. Then something happens to change society's sense of how the world works, especially after the realisation that all that remains is void and emptiness. In twenty-first century Spain, emptiness manifests itself physically, politically and emotionally. The country is filled with empty buildings, stillborn projects, immobile machines, empty pockets, and idle hands [. . .] No one understands exactly why everything believed to be durable has crumbled. (Vilches 2015, 122)

The effects of the global economic crisis, which first hit the headlines in late 2007 in the USA, were somewhat slow to be felt in Spain. In his book *Todo lo que era sólido* (2013), Spanish novelist and essayist Antonio Muñoz Molina provides a scathing analysis of his country's recent past: "Qué lejos se nos queda ya el pasado de hace sólo unos años" (how far does the past of just a few years ago seem) (9). By 2008, according to Molina, the average Spaniard was wealthier than ever, the Madrid stock market had reached its highest value and the Spanish economy had become the eighth largest in the world. Only a select few voices in the media dared to question the substance of Spain's economic miracle. By examining press articles published between 2006 and 2012, Muñoz Molina discovered that the signs of the impending crisis were apparent but impossible to recognize:

[. . .] necesitábamos imaginar que las cosas eran sólidas y podían ser tocadas y abarcadas sin desaparecer entre las manos, y que pisábamos la tierra firme y no una superficie más delgada que una lámina de hielo, que el suelo no iba a desparecer debajo de nuestros pies. (We needed to imagine that things were solid and could be touched and taken in without disappearing in our hands; that we were walking on solid ground and not on a surface thinner than a wafer; that the ground would not disappear beneath our feet). (2013, 10)

The Spanish economy, however, was anything but solid. Those boom years were built upon reckless spending by local and regional governments on projects aimed to promote *la marca España* and inspire national pride (Vilches 2015, 118). César Molinas, in an article published in *El País*, blamed the Spanish political class for causing the economic crisis by creating and sustaining a system of rent-seeking (2012). Whatever the cause of the crisis, its real and narrative effect on Spanish society would prove to be unprecedented and politically destabilising. As Bonnie N. Field and Alfonso Botti argue in their introduction to the collection *Politics and Society in Contemporary Spain*: "Accustomed to seeing itself (and to being seen) as the architect of a model transition to democracy and economic successes [. . .] Spain is now at the centre of international attention for its economic frailty, extremely high unemployment, and protest movements, such as the *indignados* (indignant)" (2013, 3). This sudden reorientation of internal and external perceptions of and about Spain was the catalyst for a re-examination of Spain's transition to democracy, inciting new political parties and actors to declare a "crisis de régimen" (regime crisis) and to call for a "second transition" (see below).

The enormity of the economic crisis on Spanish society has spurred a renewed interest in economic history. As Elvira Vilches argues in "Witnessing Crisis in Contemporary and Golden Age Spain" (2015), economic historians have sought to examine the extent to which common tropes of financial turmoil can be traced back to the rise and decline of imperial Spain. For her part, Vilches argues that Habsburg Spain "presents twenty-first century society with a compelling and disturbing mirror of another not-so-distant society that grappled with similar financial woes and problematic perceptions of wealth" (109). In a society where the past had come back to haunt Spanish political discourse (see Chapter One) it is perhaps not surprising that the Spanish media turned to an even more distant past to make sense of the current economic crisis. She cites Muñoz Molina who suggests that Spain's adoption of the euro turned the country into El Dorado of Europe; Nick Paumgarten who argues that the flooding of cheap capital with Spain's adoption of the euro created a "modern geo-financial version of the galleons loaded with gold and silver that arrived regularly on Spanish shores 500 years ago"; and Juan Luis Cebrián who suggests that "the weakening financial position of the Spanish government is a reminder of the chaotic royal finances of the 1600s" (quoted in Vilches 2015, 114–115). By attempting to delineate these cyclical historical patterns, economic historians and media commentators have sought to understand the nature of the current Spanish economic crisis and to fit it within a long historical trajectory of boom and bust economics. Indeed, as Vilches points out, "in contemporary Spain the value of past experience to inform the present is held in high esteem" (2015, 126). But as I have demonstrated, although the "past" is valuable in Spanish political commentary, it continues to be contested by the political actors on both sides of *las dos Españas*. These sites of contestation interest my explorations in this chapter.

Crisis and the fall of Zapatero

The electoral victory of Zapatero in the mid-2000s and his successful implementation of manifold social policy reforms were swiftly overshadowed by an economic crisis that seemed to take almost everybody in Spain by surprise. Once a darling of European social democracy, Zapatero quickly became linked to the politics of austerity: cuts in social benefits, reduction of labour rights, unemployment and the reduction of economic prospects and living standards for many (Field and Botti 2013, 1–4). The politics of austerity, of course, betrayed his party's principles, impacting most heavily on Spain's young and poor. As Teresa Whitfield observed: "This was a generation that, for the first time since the Civil War, faced economic prospects worse than their parents" (2014, 215), as a number of cultural texts depicted. The films *Hermosa juventud* (Rosales 2014) and *Techo y comida* (del Castillo 2015) viscerally paint a bleak picture of the crisis's effect on many Spanish youth.

The electoral toll on the Socialists was swift and dramatic. In 2009, the PSOE suffered heavy losses in both the European elections and the regional elections in the Basque Country and Galicia. Anna Bosco suggests that the main charge levelled against Zapatero and his government "was not his incapacity to solve the economic problems, but the way in which he faced up to them. The government's attitude toward the crisis—first denied, then played down, and finally suffered—was a big blow to the prime minister's credibility" (2013, 28). "Progressive voters," insists Bosco, "reproached the PSOE for a lack of coherence between the ideology it professed and the policies it implemented" (28). In one poll, Zapatero received the lowest rating ever achieved by a Spanish prime minister, below González at the height of the GAL scandal or Aznar during the war in Iraq (Whitfield 2014, 238). Botti insightfully suggests that "Aznar's and Zapatero's handling of their respective crises demonstrate that Spanish society does not tolerate being kept in the dark, mocked, or deceived by its politicians" (see Chapters Four and Five) (2013, 42). Faced with the prospect of a massive loss in the May regional elections, on 2 April, 2011, Zapatero announced his decision to stand down at the end of his second term. His announcement, however, did not have the desired effect. The Socialists suffered huge losses in those regional elections, losing key cities such as Barcelona and Seville, and the regions of Extremadura and Castile-La-Mancha, where the Socialists had been in power since 1982.

Zapatero was succeeded by his deputy prime minister, Alfredo Rubalcaba, who at first seemed to enjoy popularity in the polls. But as Bosco explains, the campaign leading up to the general elections on November 20 "was all uphill for the PSOE," who had to deal with increasing state borrowing costs, rising unemployment figures, and with an economy more and more obviously in recession (2013, 33). Neither his campaigning on a more left-wing program than that of the government, nor ETA's historic announcement of an end to terrorism (see below) in which both Zapatero and Rubalcaba had played a key role, could stem the tide against the Socialist government. In the November 20, 2011 general elections, the PP "trounced" the PSOE, losing more than four million voters and attaining its lowest vote share since the transition to democracy (Field and Botti 2013, 9). The PP not only gained a parliamentary majority but enjoyed unprecedented power at the local and regional levels. Field and Botti point out that although the PP only increased its vote by approximately 588,000, that moderate increase in support "produced tremendous gains in terms of real political power" (11). In the 2013 collection of essays *Politics and Society in Contemporary Spain*, most of the contributors agree that the Socialist defeat in the November 2011 general elections was due precisely to the delay in confronting the crisis and introducing the austerity policies to control it (Botti & Field 2013, 217). In other words, Rajoy was not elected in; rather the Socialists were voted *out*.

Despite the PP's unprecedented electoral power in all levels of government, the country they inherited from the Socialists faced what Teresa Whitfield calls "multiple institutional crises"—from a surging pro-independence movement in Catalonia, rampant corruption and high levels of disillusionment with Spain's institutions (2014, 15). Once in power, Rajoy continued the cuts that Zapatero had implemented after pressure from European Union institutions in May 2010. These were the same cuts, Botti reminds us, that Rajoy and the PP had fought against when they were in the opposition (2013, 54). Botti's accounting of Rajoy's spending cuts early in his term include: a reduction of funding of political parties, unions, and employers' organizations by 20 per cent; the freezing of the salaries of public servants; an increase in the hours in a work week; increased income tax; reform of the labour market; a proposed tax amnesty; the negotiation of a 100-billion-euro package from the EU which he called a "loan" rather than a bailout to clean up the banking sector; increased indirect taxes and value added taxes; the elimination of the tax reduction for first home buyers; and the reduction of unemployment benefits (Botti 2013, 55–56). By Botti's estimates, these policies added up to a 65 billion euro hit over two and a half years. The evaluation of the sum of these austerity policies was not positive:

> the government offered higher taxes and nothing, or very little for recovery, growth, and development, notwithstanding the frequent mentions of the opposite during the election campaign and in the investiture speech [. . .] In the space of just a few months, the PP's rise to power has disproven the forecasts of those who maintained that Spain would begin to see the light at the end of the tunnel once it voted out the Socialists. (2013, 57)

This was an exacting economic situation for any government let alone a government (whether socialist or conservative) that had to face multiple institutional crises on many fronts and operate in a climate of mass-mediated *crispación*. César Colino reminded his readers that although public debate seemed to have turned almost exclusively to the problems of the Spanish economy, three main territorial issues remained on the political and media agendas for most of Zapatero's second term (2008–2011): the reform of the regional government funding arrangements and the central and regional responses to the economic crisis; the Constitutional Court's ruling on the Catalan statue of autonomy issues in 2010; and the end of violence in the Basque Country (2013, 81), to which I turn now.

Institutional crisis I: The "definitive" end of ETA

The last vestiges of the Civil War are still being contested here in the Basque Country. (Jesús Eguiguren, ex-president of the PSE, quoted in Whitfield 2014, 31)

In her *Endgame for ETA* (2014), Teresa Whitfield asks: Why is ETA still with us (2)? In Chapter Two I argued, via Joseba Gabilondo, that the ideological overdetermination of the global War on Terror subsumed ETA's theoretical discourse, making it difficult for any Western terrorist group to resort to violence (2002). By the beginning of Zapatero's second term ETA's existence made even less sense. By early 2010 an internal intelligence report described ETA as being "at the edge of the abyss" (Whitfield 2014, 195). The Basque nationalist left, moreover, was also at a low ebb due to the continued illegalization of Batasuna and the fact that most of its leadership was imprisoned. Zapatero was still reeling from his unsuccessful attempt to permanently disarm ETA (see Chapter Seven) and consequently, he began his second term by making it clear that there would be no more negotiation with ETA. As Whitfield put it, "the only news anyone wanted to hear from ETA was that of its own demise" (2014, 3).

The process in which terror narratives have driven mass-mediated political narratives in Spain has been the dominant theme throughout the chapters. Whitfield observes that during Zapatero's two terms as prime minister, ETA killed twelve people, equivalent "to the death toll of a small bus crash" (2014, 15). Yet the Basque "conflict" continued to remain at the centre of political attention and controversy at the onset of the economic crisis; the PP was still insisting that no "political price" should be paid to ETA and that Zapatero was "betraying the victims." Given this narrative impasse it certainly was surprising (on the surface) that the Basque Socialist Party and the PP formed a coalition to oust the Basque Nationalist Party from government in the Basque region.

Juan José Ibarretxe's ten-year rule as Basque regional premier, or *lehendakari*, ended in May 2009 when Socialist Patxi López became the first non-nationalist to lead the Basque Country. Although the PNV won the most votes and seats in the March 1, 2009, election, López was able to become *lehendakari* after the PSOE formed a coalition with its rival, the PP. The coalition government formed by the PSOE and PP in order to oust the nationalists from government in the Basque region might have been surprising considering the general antipathy between those two parties in the climate of *crispación* that had characterized Spanish politics since the election of Zapatero in March 2004. But such a coalition pointed to the potency of narratives of terror in contemporary Spain and the general anti-nationalist mood in the Spanish electorate. In a discursive environment where all Basque nationalists had been narrativized as being complicit in the culture of terror in the Basque Country, the PP-PSOE coalition government was celebrated throughout Spain as the beginning of change and reform in a region that was driven mad by the potent mix of nationalism and violence. The coalition government was also an unexpected outcome, considering the dominant left/right division in contemporary Spanish politics and its manifestation through the two major political parties' narratives of terror. This division, as we have seen, was dubbed by the Spanish media as *crispación*, a reawakening of the dormant narrative of *las dos Españas* that threatened to throw Spain into a vicious cycle of confrontation and violence. But as demonstrated, the narrative of *las dos Españas* is a long-standing historical narrative that can be defined in a Žižekian sense as a hidden counter-narrative, one that has circulated in Spain since the early nineteenth century. The narrative of *las dos Españas* has always been about two different conceptions of what Spain is. In that sense, then, the coalition government in the Basque Country can be explained by the fact that both the PP and the PSOE coincide in their view of a unified Spain in which regional nationalists are allowed to exist, but only within certain limits. The Basque region, since the beginning of the transition to democracy, has tested the tolerance threshold of mainstream Spain. The emotiveness of the narrative of a unified Spain thus trumped the partisan politicking between the PP and the PSOE, hence a coalition to save Spain was not only in order but actively promoted and celebrated. That said, the narrative division between the left and right did not altogether disappear in the Basque Country. The coalition government in the Basque Country was merely a practical measure to sideline regional nationalists and reorient the Basque Country into a more pro-Spanish friendly space.

Although the Socialists and the PP were able to set aside their differences in order to oust the Basque nationalists from regional government, their relationship continued to be fractured in mainstream politics. In fact, the only two other occasions that the PP and the PSOE seemed to align their positions during that period was on the Spanish state's approach to Kosovo and the reform of article 135 of the Spanish Constitution. On the issue of Kosovo, both parties, according to Alfonso Botti, "feared the precedent that Kosovo's independence would represent for the demands made by Basque [and Catalan] nationalists" (2013, 48). On the constitutional reform of article 135, on the other hand, both parties bowed to the will of the "troika" (the International Monetary Fund, the European Commission and the Central European Bank), by introducing the obligation to maintain a balanced budget. The reform was voted on September 2, 2011, just before the November 20 general elections, in the dead of night and as a last act before the dissolution of the Spanish parliament (Botti 2013, 51). These events would later be used, narratively, by new political players to paint the Socialists and the PP with the same brush, as being one and the same (see below). Despite these rare occasions, however, where the PSOE and the PP were able to work together in matters of state, the *crispación* in Spanish politics continued well into Zapatero's second term. Not even the definitive end of ETA's terrorist activities could avoid the intensity of the political polarization in Spanish politics.

By early 2011 behind the scenes talk indicated that ETA was indeed prepared to declare a "permanent ceasefire." And on September 5, 2011, ETA announced to the BBC that it had called a halt to its "offensive armed actions" earlier in the year. On 20 October, 2011 ETA declared a definitive end to its armed activity. As Whitfield affirms, it was an announcement that "even sceptics recognized to be of signal importance in Spain's contemporary history" (2014, 3). The path to ETA's announcement was by no means easy. As with the previous ceasefire, the victims of terrorism were centre stage in the mass-media. Maite Pagazaurtundua, the director of the Foundation for Victims of Terrorism suggested in May 2011 that "the one thing that the victims of terrorism don't want it to end up being the victims of peace" (quoted in Whitfield 2014, 234). The victims rejected the early release of ETA prisoners and also demanded that ETA condemn its entire history, which Whitfield argues was "something quite unthinkable for an armed organisation that, however weakened, retained a deeply ingrained sense of its 'heroic' trajectory and unwavering dedication to its goals" (234).

A new Basque nationalist left party called Sortu (to be born) was created which clearly rejected violence and ETA's violence explicitly. However, the Supreme Court rejected Sortu's statutes by a narrow margin, arguing that Sortu was an unacceptable threat to democracy (it was later legalized in June 2012). As Whitfield contends, "in Madrid the opposition to any party that shared ETA's goals being able to pursue them while ETA was still alive was intense" (215). In May 2011, another new political party was created, Bildu (reunite) which was again opposed by the Constitutional Court. Disallowing the radical left to participate in the Basque regional elections was problematic for the PNV and also for many in the PSOE. After some political manoeuvring the Constitutional Court allowed Bildu to participate in the election, only banning some candidates (215). According to Whitfield, the PP continued its mantra that "everything is ETA," a casuistic reasoning that "because ETA had in December 2008 endorsed the idea of a pro-independence block, all those who worked towards it (regardless of whether their actions constituted a crime or not) were doing so under order" (2014, 216). To complicate matters for Zapatero, there were multiple cases against Spain's star judge Baltasar Garzón. The most indicative of the narrative of *las dos Españas* was a case brought against Garzón by the Falange and other extreme entities. Garzón was accused of "abusing his judicial powers in an investigation he had launched into the thousands of deaths and disappearances during the Franco period as possible crimes against humanity" (222). The case received widespread condemnation internationally and from many in Spain as well.

Although a decades-long struggle to defeat terrorism was finally won by the Spanish state, the PP found it difficult to overcome the impasse of its own narratives that had become deeply ingrained in its very being. Whitfield observes:

> the introduction of Sortu's charter vividly illustrated the extent to which Madrid and the Basque Country were two different worlds where Basque politics were concerned. In Madrid, popular opinion remained largely uninformed about the evolution of relations between the nationalist left and ETA, not least because it had been for years told that they were one and the same [. . .] In the Basque Country, meanwhile, most political actors recognized the change within the nationalist left to be genuine and its legalization as a step that would favour the end of ETA. (236)

In the May 2011 elections in the Basque Country, Bildu won 25.5 per cent of the vote. The seeming defeat of ETA was thus accompanied by a resurgence of the traditional radical left. This was a frightening scenario for both major parties in Madrid, prompting Rubalcaba to suggest "what we cannot allow is that they win the peace" (quoted in Whitfield 2014, 241). The implication of ETA's definitive cessation of its activities for the narrative of *las dos Españas* was that in mainstream Spanish politics it is not enough to end political violence but rather to put an end to the whole Basque radical left movement. The definitive end of ETA violence has thus not brought to a close the narrative impasse between the two Spains. Basque regional nationalism continues to be a threat to a democratic and unified Spanish state. In the aftermath of the so-called peace, recriminations and controversies remain in mass-mediated narratives, particularly on the issue of Basque prisoners who continue to be scattered in prisons across Spain and the process in which the memory and forgetting of the Basque conflict is undertaken. On these issues, mainstream Basque society remains at odds with much of the rest of the Spanish state.

The Spanish government's immobility on the issue of Basque prisoners may seem counterproductive in view of the fact that ETA is finally defeated. But for the Spanish right, it was the very "immobility" of the Spanish government which had been responsible for defeating ETA. Florencio Domínguez, writing in *El Correo*, argues that despite criticism, the government's antiterrorist policies, including the banning of Herri Batasuna, was effective (2013). The government's immobility, suggests Domínguez, challenged ETA and the Basque radical left to take unilateral steps to move forward with its dissolution. The Spanish state's intransigence and steadfastness on the Basque issue is thus perceived as a complete success. By the end of Rajoy's term in 2015, therefore, the end of ETA violence meant that the Basque "conflict" ceased to be situated at the centre of political massmediated discourse. That said, the memory of the conflict continued to be palpable in Spanish society as witnessed by the controversy over Jordi Évole's interview of ex-*etarra* Iñaki Rekarte on his TV program *Salvados* in May 2015. Rekarte was responsible for placing a car bomb in Santander in 1992 which killed three people. Despite his repentance in the interview— "la violencia de ETA no ha servido para nada, sólo para llenar de mierda a tres generaciones" (ETA violence was for nothing; it only served to fill three generations with shit)—his appearance on Spanish prime-time television, was, for many Spaniards, scandalous, especially because, when prompted by Évole, he could not name his three victims. Yet the absence of terrorist attacks and the onset of the economic crisis meant that the Spanish media's focus shifted away from terror to ideological posturing about the economic crisis; attempting to explain what caused the economic mess and to determine how to clean it up. Moreover, corruption scandals continued to be broken in the media on an almost weekly basis, scandals which included high-ranking PP politicians, Socialists in Andalusia, and even King Juan Carlos's son-in-law, Iñaki Urdangarin. In the meantime, the first signs of political fragmentation began to appear with the emergence of the 15-M movement and new political parties and the institutional crisis that the 15-M movement spearheaded.

Institutional crisis II: 15-M—From *Indignados* to Podemos

On Sunday May 15, 2011, at 6 P.M., a popular demonstration took place in 60 Spanish town squares by a newly formed group of associations called Democracia real ya (Real Democracy Now). Those taking part were asked not to carry any symbols of a political or trade union nature. This demonstration was hugely successful: tens of thousands of people marched through Madrid. When the demonstration in Puerta del Sol, the central square in Madrid, came to an end, a spontaneous sit-in was staged in Plaza de Callao; when the police intervened and made a few arrests, a group of protestors decided to stay and occupy the square. (Adagio 2013, 144)

Young people taking to the streets and occupying plazas throughout Spain calling for real democratic change in a state suffering endemic corruption and the worst economic crisis in eighty years, appears now, five years later, as inevitable. At the time, however, the movement that came to be known as 15-M, seemed spontaneous, inspired by the Arab Spring and the Occupy Wall street movement; it also romantically recalled images of May '68 Paris. Even Pablo Iglesias, whose face came to symbolize the movement and who would later lead the new political party Podemos (We Can) associated with 15-M, affirmed that just weeks before the eruption of the movement, he and his colleagues had become frustrated with the failure of Spanish society to mobilize in any meaningful way (Gil and Barcía 2015, 50). The non-violent demonstrators came to be known as *los indignados* (the indignant) and they voiced the malaise and frustration of an increasing number of Spaniards. That period saw the emergence of what the media dubbed the *ni-ni* (neither-nor) generation: young people who neither work nor study, are unable to live independently and despite excellent educational backgrounds their best hopes are poor work contracts, low salaries and precarious working conditions (Adagio 2013, 147). As Iglesias never tired of pointing out in his interviews, more than 80 per cent of Spaniards agreed with 15-M's critique of the economic power-holders and the political class (Iglesias 2015, 13).

The "occupations" spread from Madrid to other cities and towns across Spain. By May 18, 2011, they had already spread to 52 localities, aided by social network activity (Adagio 2013, 144). The movement was leaderless with a horizontal structure and encompassed a large number of educated, middle-class participants (148). As Carmelo Adagio observes: "Zapatero's entire second mandate was [. . .] marked by continuous protest movements, which [. . .] challenged the social and economic policies of the PSOE and also of the European Union, whose commanding influence on Spanish national policies was seen to be growing" (150). Whether the *indignados* movement arose as a consequence of the political fracturing of the Spanish state that occurred in that period, or whether it was a catalyst for that very political fracturing, is difficult at this point to determine. What we can ascertain is that the 15-M movement, and later the creation of Podemos, would serve to reorient political debate on the crisis in the media and to also put both the PP and the PSOE on the back foot. Both parties scrambled in their attempts to be perceived by the electorate as caring for the plight of Spain's increasing underclasses, often appropriating the language of the *indignados* into their political discourse. The emergence of the 15-M movement indicated that the division of the two Spains as defined by the *crispación* of the period between the PP and the PSOE, was a division that no longer spoke to a large section of Spanish society. Instead, the discourse of 15-M, and later Podemos, attempted to subvert the narrative of two Spains beyond the politicking of the two major parties, into a conversation about the material future of Spain's youth.

In their article "Electoral Epidemic" Anna Bosco and Susannah Verney argue that "to govern has become electorally very costly in Southern Europe" (2012, 129). As they demonstrate, the year 2011 saw the ousting of the incumbents of all four countries in "core" Southern Europe: Portugal, Greece, Italy and Spain. Via Peter Mair (2011), they note that political parties in contemporary democracies increasingly find it difficult to exercise the basic functions of modern democracies: to govern and to represent (2012, 132). Mair argues that "in contemporary democracies these two functions have begun to grow apart, with many of today's parties downplaying, or being forced to downplay, their representative role, and enhancing, or being forced to enhance their governing role" (2011, 8). It is important to reiterate Bosco and Verney's argument, via Mair, here, because it goes some way to explaining the emergence of the 15-M movement in Spain and the creation of Podemos. Their main point is that: "[political] parties seem to have become less and less able to reconcile the demands for responsiveness (and therefore representation) with the demands of responsibility which are at the basis of party government" (Bosco and Verney 2012, 132). Political responsiveness has become difficult to attain, suggests Mair, because political parties have moved away from civil society, homogenous electorates have fragmented and voters have become more volatile, thus making it challenging to mobilize and persuade voters (2011, 10). He adds that responsiveness has also come into conflict with responsibility "whereby leaders and governments are expected to act prudently and consistently and follow accepted procedural norms and practices" (11). Functioning as a modern democracy, therefore, involves "an acceptance that in certain areas and in certain procedures, the leaders' hands will be tied" (11). In southern Europe, central banks, courts, international agencies and organisations, and European Union institutions are among the actors that have contributed to tying the leaders' hands. As a consequence, Bosco and Verney posit, "parties are not only less capable than in the past of listening to and representing their voters, but also when in office they are unable to craft and implement the policies their voters asked for, since governments' freedom is severely constrained" (2012, 132). This is a dilemma that southern European states such as Spain find difficult to escape from:

> The economic storm that has broken out in Southern Europe has shown that when incumbents are 'responsible'—abiding by the agreements with

the external actors—they end up neglecting their voters' demands. [. . .] On the other hand, when incumbents avoid being 'responsible' and/or try to be primarily responsive to their voters, they lose international credibility, with dangerous consequences for the management of national sovereign debt and hence for the economic health of the country. (133)

Both the PP and the PSOE were caught in this dilemma during those years, forced to placate the "markets" and abide by European Union protocols. Hence, both parties were successful, in a sense, in fulfilling their "responsibility" role, even if that meant massive austerity which hit Spain's poor harshest. Consequently, neither major party was able to be perceived by the electorate as being "responsive" to citizens' concerns. Podemos, via the 15-M movement, was thus able to capitalize on that failure, damaging (at least for the meantime) the two-party system in the process (see below).

The 15-M movement's optimistic mantra *sí se puede* (yes we can) was a hopeful message that Spanish politics could be transformed through consultation and participatory democracy. The movement was accused, however, of being ideologically weak, and for merely providing convincing critiques instead of any real policy proposals. Both the PP and the PSOE challenged the 15-M movement to create their own political party if they indeed wished to challenge mainstream politics. Nobody imagined that a small group of academics would take up that challenge and create the political party Podemos. Podemos's leader, Pablo Iglesias, is a politics lecturer at Madrid's Complutense University. The son of Socialist parents, he is named after the founding father of the PSOE, the party which has most to lose if Podemos continues to grow electorally. Similarly to the 15-M movement, Podemos took full advantage of social media in order to get its message across and "challenge the all-pervasive media presence of the major parties" (Kennedy 2014).

Unlike cognate countries in Europe, which have seen the emergence of Eurosceptic far-right parties, in Spain Podemos has received not only the most media attention, but also the best electoral results out of all the new political parties formed to challenge mainstream Spanish politics. Formed just two months before the May 2014 European elections, Podemos secured eight per cent of the vote and five seats. Although Podemos and the 15-M are not necessarily one and the same (and Podemos's leadership stresses this point) it is undeniable that the party is the political embodiment of the 15-M movement. Podemos thus attests to Bosco and Verney's argument above that the existing political establishment failed in its fundamental duty to genuinely represent the electorate. Podemos's objective is, according to Kennedy, "to challenge a political and economic status quo based on the acceptance of EU-imposed austerity policies" (2014). Ian Parker posits that because the project of Podemos "was precisely that of academics in political science" it is a form of "anti-politics" (2015, 156). Parker suggests that *"Podemos* has so far succeeded in implanting its discourse in the wider political field, succeeded in making its 'anti-polit- ical' discourse resonate with an 'anti-political' suspicion of the anti-austerity movement" (157).

The success of a political party formed in the corridors of universities has given Podemos a firm theoretical basis. Its leadership is not only well versed on the theories of Karl Marx and Antonio Gramsci, but particularly fond of Ernesto Laclau's theories on discourse analysis and communica- tion. In an attempt to appeal to as many Spaniards as possible, the Podemos leadership painstakingly avoids describing their political pro- gram as on the "left." As Geoffrey Fox surmises: "Instead of presenting a class analysis, they continually denounce 'the caste'—*la casta* -, a vague category for anybody thought to have privilege, as against 'the people'— *la gente*—which means everybody else" (2015). This media strategy has been immensely successful and the Podemos leadership has been able to paint both the PP and the PSOE as belonging to *la casta*, responsible for the endemic corruption in Spanish politics and society. Of course, the sim- plicity of Podemos' communication strategy means that it is accused of populism. As Kennedy observes, "'Weirdos'; 'populists'; 'catastrophic, offering Hugo Chávez-style utopias which would lead to unmitigated dis- aster' are just some of the [. . .] examples directed at Iglesias and Podemos" (Kennedy 2014). Nonetheless, Podemos represents both hope for a significant minority of Spaniards (around 20 per cent of the electorate in 2016) and a threat to both the PP and PSOE and the traditional way of doing politics. Yet it is the Socialists who have the most to fear from the rise of Podemos. By branding them as part of *la casta* and for selling out "normal people" to big business, the Socialists are delegitimized as a viable alternative to the PP. But as we will see below, fragmented bipo- larism in Spanish politics has made it difficult for any political party to gain the significant momentum needed to achieve a workable majority in government. As much as the Socialist are distrusted by many for belong- ing to *la casta*, Podemos's pony-tailed leader Iglesias and his party represent an ideological extremism that many Spaniards have come to fear. As much as they are disappointed in bipartisanship, the two-party system represented some kind of political stability. In lieu of any workable majorities, Spanish political parties have thus been forced to pact and form coalitions and as will see below, historical narrative battles continue to be played out in the mass media in the attempt to form those pacts. But first it is important to turn to another institutional crisis that has also had a significant role in the political narratives of that period: Catalonia's renewed drive for independence.

Institutional crisis III: Catalan independence

If many Spaniards supposed that the definitive end of ETA terrorism would mean the deflation of regional nationalisms and self-determination initiatives, they were mistaken. Aided by the devastating effects of the economic crisis on Spain and an intransigent Rajoy government that steadfastly refused to cater to regional nationalists and instead initiated a re-centralizing agenda, the Catalan independence movement had never been so electorally potent. Apart from the 2008 economic crisis itself, perhaps no other issue dominated Spanish political and mass-mediated discourse as the "Catalan issue" did. An examination of those years would be remiss without a consideration of how the renewed drive for independence in Catalonia intersected with narratives of crisis. As the "Catalan issue" is still currently being played out in Spanish politics, my aim here is to consider how the drive for Catalan independence, as an institutional crisis, helped define the positions of the major Spanish political parties as well as the narratives propagated by new political players Podemos and Ciudadanos (Citizens).

The event that catapulted the Catalan independence movement into a viable political proposition was *Convergencia i Unio*'s (Convergence and Union, CiU) adoption of an overt "pro-sovereignty lexicon" in September 2012 (Gillespie 2015, 5). As the main nationalist Catalan political party CiU had hitherto sought Catalan accommodation within the Spanish state. *Esquerra Republicana de Catalunya* (Republican Left of Catalonia, ERC) had traditionally flown the flag for independence. There are various reasons why CiU radically shifted its position under the leadership of Artur Mas. First, Catalan elites had to respond to stronger mobilization demands from below (4). As Kathryn Crameri argues, the apparent radicalization of CiU since 2012 "is substantially attributed to civil pressure" (2015, 99). She adds: "Catalan nationalism has undergone a significant shift since the middle of the last decade, away from the mass political apathy that characterized that particular period (as demonstrated by the low turnout in the 2006 referendum on Catalonia's new Statute of Autonomy), and towards mass participation in civil action for independence" (111). For instance, on 11 September 2012 (Catalonia's National Day), some 1.5 million Catalans marched in favour of independence. Second, that mobilization can be directly attributed to the Spanish Constitutional Court's striking down of key provisions of that Catalan Statute in June 2010. There was widespread outrage in Catalonia over a Statute that was popularly approved by Catalans (even if the final document was a watered down version of the original document approved by the Catalan parliament) and over the fact that many of the provisions of the statute which were struck down were also included in other autonomous statute's such as Andalusia's, thus ensuring that Catalans perceived themselves as second-class citizens within the Spanish state. Mas (and many other Catalans) pinpointed that decision as the moment in which he shifted his support from Catalan autonomy within Spain to supporting Catalan secession from Spain (Elias 2015, 88). Third, Rajoy and the PP's refusal to negotiate with Catalonia a new fiscal pact led to Mas overtly calling for Catalan independence through what César Colino calls "effective populist rhetoric," which focused on the "plundering" or "pillaging" of Catalonia by Spain (2013, 98). Fourth, Madrid's mishandling of the economic crisis contributed to Catalan grievances. Diego Muro argues that Spain, under Rajoy's leadership, effectively initiated re-centralizing processes (2013). The strategy of fiscal consolidation, which Rajoy argued was "rationalization" and "harmonization," effectively capped regional government's spending, leading to a decline in health and education services. Moreover, a new education law, popularly called *Ley Wert* after the Education Minister José Ignacio Wert, gave greater powers to the Ministry of Education to standardize the curriculum and dispute the model of "language immersion" (35). Wert's infamous comment that "nuestro interés es españolizar a los niños catalanes" (our interest is to Spanishize Catalan children) reeked of the worst excesses of the Franco regime (Sanz 2012). Finally, apart from the deterioration of Spanish-Catalan relations, political expediency also probably contributed to Mas and CiU's policy U-turn. With public sentiment moving towards independence (support for independence was 15.9% in November 2006 and 44.3% in October 2012), Mas and CiU had a lot to gain by overtly pushing for a referendum (Elias 2015, 89). The independence issue also took attention away from Catalonia's own problems and austerity policies.

The developments above have not been a one-way, top-down, process. The increase in support for a referendum on independence has provoked political polarization in Catalonia. While the support for independence has increased, so too has the support for the pro-Spanish political parties, the PP and *Ciutadans*. *Ciutadans* (known as Ciudadanos in Castilian Spanish) has managed to transform its anti-Catalan independence movement into mainstream electoral success, both in Catalonia and in the rest of Spain, under the leadership of Albert Rivera (see below). The political polarization intensified after CiU made self-determination an election pledge in 2010 and also after CiU unilaterally called a non-binding referendum on 9 November, 2014. The central government appealed the legitimacy of the referendum with the Constitutional Court which suspended the process while it considered the appeal (Field 2015, 117). Nonetheless, the Catalan government insisted on the referendum, calling it a "citizen participation process run by volunteers." The turnout was around 37 per cent and 81 per cent voted in favour of independence.

What this new drive for independence in Catalonia has achieved is to spur a debate in the Spanish media about reforming the Spanish Constitution in order to reinforce a federalism that can better accommodate some of the Catalan demands (Colino 2013, 99). The Socialists, Podemos and Ciudadanos have all called for some kind of constitutional reform, though the PP still remains hesitant to reform the post-1978 order. While Basques and Catalans demand more devolved powers on a sub-state level, many in Madrid and in other regions, according to Gillespie, complain that "decentralization of the state may have gone 'too far' and become an obstacle to economic recovery" (2015, 4). Moreover, Gillespie points out that although "the most vehement reactions" over the question of sovereignty come from the Spanish right, the Socialists "have reacted with equal intran-sigence" and that "neither the PP nor the belated or rediscovered federalism of the PSOE connect with the confederal aspirations of many 'moderate' Basque and Catalan nationalists" (13). The Basques are treading more care-fully on the issue of sovereignty given that there still has been no "normalization" in Basque politics post the dissolution of ETA and also because any modification of the Spanish Constitution may risk the special privileges that the Basques already have, especially on fiscal rights (Mees 2015, 54). Catalan nationalists, on the other hand, suggests Mees, "already [feel themselves] at the end of this process of negotiation and without any real option of settling the problem by mutual agreement" (54). The "Catalan issue" is thus an institutional crisis that will continue to destabi-lize Spanish politics into the near future. The discussion below explains how the theoretical "breaking up" of Spain feeds into the narratives propagated by the four main political parties and how those narratives recall the divi-sion of *las dos Españas*.

Crisis and *las dos Españas*

Es muy difícil llevar la contraria en España. (In Spain it is difficult to have an adverse opinion). (Muñoz Molina 2013, 128)

In *Todo lo que era sólido* (2013) Antonio Muñoz Molina opens his essay by reminding his readers of the years just before the onset of the global economic crisis, when Spaniards seemed to be richer than ever, but political differences were irreconcilable in the charged atmosphere of *crispación* where insults such as "red" or "fascist" returned to the public sphere (11). He questions why fragments of the past held such power in Spanish mass-mediated discourse during that time, from the death of García Lorca to Guernica and any number of tragic events in the past century. He suggests that this process of Spaniards attempting to correct the past reeked of gratuitous phantasmagoria and he fails to understand how pre-crisis Spaniards could have attained such high living standards while public political discourse had become so violent and civil life so aggressive (12).

Muñoz Molina reminds his readers of the chilling narrative of *las dos Españas* that circulated during the Spanish Civil War. There was a binary division, he affirms, between a Spain and an anti-Spain with no middle ground (81). Recalling the division between the left and the right in his youth, Muñoz Molina suggests that the right represented purity, origins, the autochthonous, loyalty, land and blood. The left, represented for him and his friends, development, improvement, the universal and internationalism (73). In the aftermath of the economic crisis Muñoz Molina subverts the traditional narrative of *las dos Españas* that are divided along such a conservative/liberal axis. Instead, he suggests that the real division in Spain is between a "real" or "austere" Spain which includes hard-working Spaniards who do the best they can, look after the ill, raise children, educate, pursue delinquents, judge crimes, research in laboratories, cultivate the earth, work in libraries, and create and sell necessary goods and services (53). Above this Spain, there is another, more visible Spain, which is a country full of simulacra and mirages. This is the Spain of global exhibitions; public works that have no real use but serve merely to promote the politicians that inaugurate them and the hicks who feel worthy because of them; regional television stations that squander unlimited funds on sectarian propaganda; and the exaltation of the lowest form of mediated vulgarity transmuted into a species of collective pride (53). The more money available meant that the simulacra would perfect themselves to the point that ordinary citizens could no longer distinguish between reality and representation (106). This narrative division is why, Muñoz Molina suggests, Zapatero and the Socialists were so reticent about admitting that Spain was suffering an economic crisis. The Spanish left accused the right of promoting propaganda in order to damage the government. Or as Muñoz Molina suggested "quien hablara de crisis estaría haciéndole el juego de la derecha" (whoever spoke of crisis was playing into the right's hands) (139).

Muñoz Molina's subversion of the narrative of *las dos Españas* recalls the central message of the 15-M movement that Podemos later rearticulated as "*la casta*" (the caste) and "*gente normal*" (normal people). Podemos's message of "la casta" was even broader than Occupy Wall Street's slogan "We are the 99%" which successfully transmitted the message of income inequality in the USA and in a globalized world. Podemos's formulation of "*la casta*" was broad enough to encompass not only Spain's oligarchy, but the monarchy, politicians in both the PP and the PSOE, and anybody who had taken advantage of their public position. As the endless corruption scandals in Spain attested, the list of people that could be interpreted as belonging to "*la casta*" was sufficiently long enough to be able to subvert dominant mass-mediated narratives. If anything, Podemos's communication strategy was successful in bringing the concerns of the 15-M movement into mainstream political debate where they remained until the run up to the December 20, 2015, general election.

The December 2015 elections were contested in the shadow of the economic crisis and the three institutional crises detailed in this chapter. It is not my aim here to examine the main four political parties' electoral programs; nor is it to determine the correct policies that the Spanish state must adopt in order to confront those crises. My aim, rather, is to consider the main narratives propagated by each political party and to understand those narratives in the context of the traditional narrative of *las dos Españas* and also in the context of the subverted narrative of *las dos Españas* as outlined by Muñoz Molina above. In doing so, I want to understand how those narratives led to the pact of compromise post the election and to question where to next for Spain.

Fragmented bipolarism

> Crises take place with a certain time lag, so it's clear the Spanish system of political parties has entered a transition, but not clear how long that transition will take. (Antonio Barroso quoted in Minder 2016c)

The general elections on December 20, 2015, were the most hotly contested and fraught since 1978. Crisis, corruption and austerity had taken a big toll on the electorate and for the first time political support was more or less evenly split between four parties: the PP, the PSOE, Podemos and Ciudadanos. Although the PP usually led the pre-election polls, its support had plummeted dramatically and it was clear that the PP would not be able to govern on its own. The PSOE struggled to convince Spaniards that it was a viable alternative to the PP, and Podemos and Ciudadanos took advantage of the disenfranchisement of the electorate to capture the imagination of frustrated voters. Both Podemos and Ciudadanos avoided the rhetoric of the "left" and the "right," attempting to convince voters that Spain needed a change and fresh faces in order to steer that change. There was an implicit understanding from both new parties that the left/right divide in Spanish politics was narratively toxic. Despite their best efforts to position themselves in the "centre," however, Podemos was narratively marginalized in the mass-media as belonging to the "radical left" a la Alexis Tsipras and Syriza in Greece or Nicolás Maduro in Venezuela. Ciudadanos was rather more successful in gaining that centre ground, though both Podemos and the PSOE continuously attacked Ciudadanos for belonging to the Spanish right, for being, in essence, the PP in sheep's clothing. Ciudadanos' *raison d'être*, after all, was its vehement opposition to Catalan secessionism and defence of the unity of the Spanish state, a position closely aligned with the PP. As it was clear that no political party would win an outright majority in parliament, the media became obsessed with the logics of "pacts." Pre-election analysis questioned what a shift from a two-party system to a multi-party system would mean for the country. But it was generally assumed that the new Spanish government would either be a coalition between the PSOE and Podemos or PP and Ciudadanos. The political fragmentation of the Spanish electorate, however, was even greater than the media commentariat had dared to suppose. Neither hypothetical formation gained sufficient seats in parliament to form an outright majority. As expected, the PP won the elections with 28.7% of the vote (123 seats); the PSOE came second with 22% of the vote (90 seats); Podemos third with 20.7% of the vote (69 seats); and Ciudadanos fourth with 13.9% of the vote (40 seats). The resilience of the PP and the PSOE was remarkable considering the mass-mediated attacks from both Podemos and Ciudadanos were so electorally potent and the fact that corruption scandals in both of the major parties had received wide media attention. Ciudadanos's result was especially lower than expected indicating that its potential voter base came from disaffected PP voters, who in the end were reticent of supporting a new and inexperienced political party. The Spanish electorate had voted for a Spanish parliament that would have to put many of its ideological differences aside in order to form pacts and a workable government. This was not an easy task for four parties whose campaign narratives were full of so-called "red lines"—ideological positions that each party would refuse to negotiate on, to which I turn now.

Mariano Rajoy and the Popular Party

The essence of the PP's electoral campaign message was that the PP represented experience and stability and that voting for Rajoy would ensure Spain remained in "safe hands." Called an "enigmatic leader" with "professorial countenance" by the *The New York Times*, Rajoy symbolized the "old guard" of Spanish politics who could act as a bulwark against his untested and "dangerous" rivals (Minder 2015b). Rajoy's principle message was that he is the custodian of Spanish unity and continuity in the face of secessionist challenges in Catalonia. Moreover, the PP argued that its economic policies, although tough, were working, as the Spanish economy was set to grow at 3 per cent in 2016. Changing leaders thus risked derailing that economic progress.

Rajoy refused to take part in a live televised political debate with his three rivals, instead agreeing to only one debate with the main Socialist opposition leader Pedro Sánchez. That decision indicated that he wholeheartedly rejected the legitimacy of fragmented bipolarism, suggesting that Ciudadanos and Podemos were ephemeral, one-man organizations that are only "the product of a television show or a marketing campaign" (Minder 2015b). Rajoy's narrative thus reiterated Bosco and Verney's argument detailed earlier, that the incumbent PP government was "responsible" in fulfilling its international commitments (2012, 133). The PP's problem, however, was its deficit in being "responsive" to citizens' concerns. In an attempt to bridge that gap, the worst excesses of *crispación* were toned down during the campaign. One episode was particular telling. On the program *Salvados* (December 6, 2015), the president of the Autonomous Community of Madrid, Cristina Cifuentes, debated Catalan independence with some pro-independence Catalans in their homes. Although she was steadfastly opposed to independence, her bearing was rather agreeable, admitting that the PP had failed to communicate its message adequately to the electorate, especially in Catalonia. She even hinted that the Spanish Constitution could be modified in the future based on consensus, perhaps pointing towards the PP's openness to a federalized Spain. In sum, the PP's campaign narrative promoted the idea of regime stability ("responsibility") while belatedly attempting to be perceived as "responsive" to citizens' concerns.

Pedro Sánchez and the PSOE

The Socialists perhaps had the most challenging electoral campaign out of the four political parties. Its fresh-faced leader Pedro Sánchez had to fend off attacks from the two new political parties, Podemos and Ciudadanos, as well as its traditional nemesis the PP. Moreover, Sánchez had to distance himself from the economic policies of Zapatero and the pall that the economic crisis had placed over his party. Sanchez's narrative strategy was threefold: he attacked the PP's record vivaciously even accusing Rajoy during the election debate of not being a "decent" man and who should have quit over the corruption scandals of his party; branded Ciudadanos as being of the "right" unlike the progressive Socialists; and fear-mongered about the "radical" Podemos who were a risk to Spanish stability. The Socialists walked a fine line between the left–right axes of Spanish politics. Similar to the PP, the Socialists defended the territorial unity of the Spanish state, refusing to grant Catalonia a referendum if elected, while at the same time adopting many of Podemos's critiques of government policy. Unlike the PP, however, the Socialists were open to re-negotiating the post-1978 order and usher in a Spanish federation. It was a brave attempt to capture the so-called "centre" of the Spanish electorate but which ultimately failed. The PSOE was unable to capture disenfranchised PP voters nor was it able to stem the tide towards Podemos on the left. Presenting itself as a traditional social-democratic party in the European tradition was not enough to erase memories of the PSOE's mishandling of the economic crisis. It was, in sum, an effort to balance both "responsibility" and "responsiveness" but the PSOE lacked the credibility to turn that narrative into an electoral win.

Albert Rivera and Ciudadanos

If the Spanish electorate was accustomed to a two-party system character-ized by a *crispación* (polarization) that could be traced back to the narrative of *las dos Españas*, Ciudadanos made every effort to distinguish itself from those long-running narratives of "left" and "right" by claiming for itself the "centre." In a *Guardian* article published in March 2015, Ciudadanos was extolled as a centrist party yet simultaneously referred to as the "Podemos of the right" (Kassam 2015). Launched in Catalonia in 2005 as a staunch defender of Catalan anti-secessionism, its anti-Catalan sover-eignty message was able to spread to the rest of the Spanish state during Mariano Rajoy's term of government when the drive for Catalan inde-pendence movement had intensified. Yet, given that the PP government was also staunchly anti-Catalan sovereignty, as were the Socialists, it is perplexing how Ciudadanos managed to turn their anti-Catalan sover-eignty message into a mainstream political party. Its electoral success is probably due to the support it received from disenfranchised PP voters and also from swinging voters who considered Podemos too much of a risk. Accusations against Ciudadanos also suggested that political and media elites aided the rise of the party in order to challenge Podemos's position as the option for change and regeneration (Iglesias 2015, 198). Ciudadanos is economically liberal but staunchly anti-corruption and it successfully transmitted that message to the Spanish electorate.

José Pablo Ferrándiz from the polling group Metroscopia, attributes Ciudadanos's success to the groundwork laid by Podemos who planted the idea that the anger against bipartisanism could be tackled by politics (Kassam 2015). Although many commentators were able to point out the similarities between Ciudadanos's policies and those of the PP, Ciudadanos was successful in blurring the traditional lines between left and right. Albert Rivera averred during the campaign: "Podemos answered the question, 'What went wrong?' but we're here to answer the question of 'What to do now?'" (Minder 2015a). Rivera's principle message was that of reform, but it was a reform tempered by political realities, promising change, but not radical change. The Catalan sovereignty issue, remained however, Ciudadanos's "red line." Rivera warned that it would not enter into a coalition government with any political party which would allow a referendum in Catalonia. Ciudadanos, moreover, also considered the post-1978 regime as antiquated and supported negotiations on a new federalized state, although Rivera argued that no region should have any special "historical" privileges, as it is "citizens" who have rights, not "territories" (Gil 2015). Ciudadanos's support in the electorate was slightly overestimated indicating that the "centrist" message of Ciudadanos was not as electorally convincing as its left and right counterparts.

Pablo Iglesias and Podemos

Podemos argued that the economic meltdown led to a "regime crisis": the exhaustion of the political social system that emerged from the post-Franco transition (Iglesias 2015, 180). Consequently, Iglesias suggested that the traditional left/right division in Spanish politics no longer accounted for such a regime crisis. Hence, a new ideological framework, such as the one witnessed by the 15-M movement, was needed to articulate that crisis and show the way forward. As much as Podemos aimed to avoid the left/right narrative division in Spanish politics, however, it was difficult for the party to be perceived in mass-mediated narratives as anything other than of the far-left. The mainstream media, the PP, the Socialists and Ciudadanos all successfully situated Podemos on the far left of the political spectrum and argued that it represented a radical change that risked destabilizing and balkanizing the Spanish state. Iglesias himself characterized the constant refrain against his party as follows: "you want to vote Podemos? Look what's happening in Greece" (Iglesias 2015, 206). Podemos's horizontal structure means that Podemos is a kind of coalition of disparate, regional groupings which include Compromís in Valencia En Comú Podem in Catalonia and En Marea in Galicia. As explained above, Podemos's main target was "*la casta*" and thus both the PP and the PSOE came under fire. Rivera and Ciudadanos were attacked for supporting many of the PP's policies. Iglesias revindicated the plurinational nature of the Spanish state on multiple occasions during the election campaign and was the only political party which openly supported a referendum on Catalan sovereignty in Catalonia, arguing that if Podemos was in government Catalans would not wish to leave. Podemos thus represented the political party which advocated a complete break with the post-78 consensus, calling for political, social and economic renewal. Although its electoral result was respectable it was far from the number of votes it needed to form a government. In local elections, however, Podemos affiliated activists took over the town halls of key cities such as Madrid and Barcelona.

Narrative clashes

In more than a century of the narrative of *las dos Españas* circulating in Spanish political and mass-mediated discourse, that narrative witnessed a civil war, a military dictatorship, Spain's entry into the European Union, political *crispación* and an economic implosion. A careful re-reading of key events in the history of the Spanish state can uncover how the narrative of *las dos Españas* has circulated in mass-mediated discourse, often being the catalyst for violent and non-violent conflict. I have been particularly keen to highlight how the narrative of *las dos Españas* intertwines with narratives of terror in all its manifestations. The legacy of ETA terrorism still lingers, as does the memory of the March 11, 2004 attacks in Madrid. The Paris attacks on November 13, 2015 also cut close to home. As in cognate western states, antiterrorism remains a critical area of government policy. Yet in this chapter I observe how "terror," as both event and discourse, can no longer be considered the key issue driving mass-mediated political narratives in the Spanish state, having been superseded by narratives of "crisis."

The global economic crisis and the three events detailed in this chapter (the end of ETA terrorism, the emergence of the 15-M movement and the renewed drive for Catalan sovereignty) demonstrate how the narrative of *las dos Españas* continues to circulate in Spanish mass-mediated discourse, particularly through the narratives propagated by the four main political parties. The difference in 2016 is that bipolar fragmentation has dispersed the narrative of *las dos Españas*, with some political actors like Iglesias and Rivera claiming the left and the right formulation as politically bankrupt. At least in mass-mediated discourse and in the political narratives propagated by Iglesias and Rivera, the narrative of *las dos Españas* as understood in the Civil War context, as between a Republican Left and a Nationalist Right, is no longer the potent division it used to be. Instead, thanks to the economic crisis, the narrative of *las dos Españas*, resembles Antonio Muñoz Molina's subversion of that narrative, that is, a division between a "real" and an "ephemeral" Spain. It is *la casta* which has promoted "ephemeral" Spain and it is thus up to *gente normal* to reclaim "real" Spain. That is not to suggest that the left/right division no longer exists in Spain but rather that the narrative of *las dos Españas* is capable of adapting to current circumstances. In that sense, I would argue that what we see occurring in Spanish political discourse in 2016 is the age-old battle between the "old" and the "new," between different conceptualizations of where Spain is now and where it should be heading into the future. There might be more than "two" conceptualizations of "Spain" and each political party and each Spanish citizen might not be situated neatly on either side of this divide, but we can witness how the long-running narrative of *las dos Españas* informs current Spanish politics and how it brought Spain to the electoral result of the 2015 general elections: a narrative impasse making political compromise both desirable and unattainable, usually due to the narrative dead-ends occupied by the four main political parties.

Despite winning the election, the PP was, in a sense, the big loser. Not only did it not win sufficient votes to form a government, its only potential coalition partner was Ciudadanos. Yet both those parties did not attain sufficient votes in order to form a government majority. The PP's anti-regionalist rhetoric ruled out the support of any regional party such as the PNV or CiU. Moreover, it was not exactly clear what Ciudadanos had to gain in supporting a PP government it had so vehemently opposed. The PP's numerous "red lines" on almost every issue meant that politics had become "the PP against the rest." Its staunch defence of a "true" Spain against "everybody else" had isolated itself in the political arena. On the other hand, in order for the PSOE to govern, Pedro Sánchez would either need to enter a coalition with Podemos and Ciudadanos or to create a coalition of "progressive" parties. The first option was off the table since both Ciudadanos and Podemos refused to enter into any coalition that included the other; Ciudadanos rejected Podemos's support of a Catalan referendum on sovereignty, while Podemos rejected Ciudadanos's economically liberal program. Yet to gain an outright majority the PSOE would need to pact with Podemos, Izquierda Unida (United Left) as well as the regional nationalist parties. It was a risky strategy for the PSOE to negotiate with regional nationalists and Podemos in order to wrest government from the PP.

Faced with defeat and the prospect of a left-leaning government composed of regional nationalists, Rajoy proposed a "grand coalition" between the PP, the PSOE and Ciudadanos in order to transmit within and outside of Spain a message of stability, security and certainty. As we saw with the formation of a coalition between the PP and the PSOE in the Basque Country in 2009, the PP is willing to put aside its differences with the Socialists in order to sideline the regional nationalists. The PP was thus also willing to enter into a "grand coalition" with the Socialists in order to sideline Podemos who represent to the traditional PP voter a return of the chaos of the Second Republic. By the end of March 2016, negotiations among the four political parties had yet to come up with a workable coalition. Pedro Sanchez's attempt to form a government with Albert Rivera's Ciudadanos failed two investiture votes. By the time this book is published either a workable coalition would have been formed or Spaniards would have returned to the polls in new elections.

What is important to consider here, however, is how fragmented bipolarism has impacted on the narrative of *las dos Españas*. The politics of *crispación* that embittered the Zapatero years had now transmuted into a consistent and narratively potent opposition against Podemos and what it represented. The spectre of terrorism (Podemos was accused of terrorist apologia) and the Catalan referendum (Podemos was narrativized as being in favour of the breaking up of Spain) created a new division in Spanish politics. The PP, Socialists and Ciudadanos, despite their differences and charged rhetoric, could be situated on one side of the divide: they agreed that the sovereignty issue was a "red line" that could not be crossed. On the other side, Podemos and the regional nationalist parties were branded as being beyond the pale. With neither major political party gaining sufficient votes to form a government it remains to be seen how this new division in Spanish politics can be reconciled.

Conclusion: A tenuous future or a politics of hope?

A significant section of this chapter has reiterated many of the ideas expressed by Antonio Muñoz Molina in *Todo lo que era sólido* (2013). As a writer proud of many aspects of Spanish culture he is also aghast at many of Spain's intractable problems. Most of his scorn is directed at Spain's political class, whether from the left or the right. He is at pains to understand why the Spanish political class has spent most of the past thirty years exaggerating political differences, or even inventing differences where they had not previously existed (225). With the onset of the global economic crisis and the emergence of the 15-M movement, Muñoz Molina posits that the simulacrum that the political class had manufactured in their interest has broken (235). It is up to ordinary Spaniards to ensure that political elites do not remain in that simulacrum (252). Muñoz Molina suggests, perhaps facetiously, a "reduction" of about twenty or twenty-five per cent of nationalist and ideological "identities." All Spanish citizens, he argues, must accept to be a bit less of what they are. Twenty-five percent less Spanish, less leftist, less Catalan, less Basque and so on. Such a reduction would not be tantamount to renouncing a part of oneself. Rather, it would permit every Spaniard to accept the part of themselves which they have in common with the rest of the country (227). As he puts it: "Es una vulgaridad decirlo, pero a veces da la impresión de que todavía no nos hemos enterado: estamos, literalmente, condenados a entendernos" (It's in poor taste to say it, but sometimes it seems as if we still don't get it: we are, literally, condemned to understand each other) (228).

If the "centre" has been difficult to locate in Spanish politics then so has neutral political commentary in the media. Spanish mass-mediated discourse in 2016 tends towards the extreme, promoting either narratives of hope or narratives of despair. In *Voces del cambio: El fin de la España de la transición* (2015) a recompilation of interviews with the "new" voices from the Spanish left such as Íñigo Errejón, Manuela Carmena and Ada Colau, it is remarkable how optimistic they are about the future of the Spanish state and the grassroots movements that have sprung up across Spain. Catalan political discourse is also characterized by a certain optimism for the future once a sovereignty process is underway. In 2016, therefore, the lexicon of participation, collectives and regime crisis has returned to public and political discourse. Far from being intimidated by the burden of Spanish history, these new leaders see the possibility of reform and change, and even, in certain cases, rupture with the past. On the other hand, a significant section of Spanish society remains disconcerted not only by fragmented bipolarism but also by where political fragmentation might lead them. With Spaniards no longer trusting their political institutions and with the European Union also in crisis due to myriad institutional pressures, it is no wonder that many Spaniards feel demoralized. If the political landscape in 2016 resembles little the political landscape of 2007, what will Spanish politics look like in another eight years? Out of the three institutional crises discussed in this chapter, only the definitive end of ETA can be considered somewhat resolved, even if there remain recriminations in the peace. The Pandora's Box that the 15-M movement opened and the Catalan march for sovereignty continue to be politically destabilizing. And the effects of the economic crisis itself are far from over. Although the Spanish economy in 2016 is growing, unemployment remains high and many Spaniards who can find work are living in precarity.

If the sum total of the developments in Spanish politics discussed in this chapter is the perception that political polarization continues to divide Spain in two then the outlook must surely be bleak. Yet, there have been many positive developments in that period which have served to subvert the narrative of *las dos Españas* into a more manageable and mature framework for many ordinary Spaniards. Whether populist or not, the emergence of both Podemos and Ciudadanos into the political landscape has helped reorient the stark division between the two Spains away from a liberal/conservative divide into a conversation about the future of Spain and Spain's place in the world. Moreover, there is evidence that, at least in popular culture, Spanish society has matured enough to take a light-hearted look at many of the issues brought to attention in this volume. In his film *Negociador* (Negotiator) (2014), Borja Cobeaga utilizes black comedy to find common ground between *etarra* Jokin (Josean Bengoetxea) and an independent government representative Manu (Ramón Barea) in an attempted peace negotiation between ETA and the Spanish government. Although the negotiations ultimately fail, the film illustrates that the two protagonists, through misunderstandings and comic situations, begin to view each other as human; their ideological differences wither away as they share a beer together in a hotel room and watch a football match.

But it is the film *Ocho apellidos vascos* (Spanish Affair) that best points to a certain kind of reconciliation between the two Spains. Also released in 2014 and co-written by *Negociador*'s Borja Cobeaga, the film was a box-office sensation becoming the second most successful film in Spanish history, second only to *Avatar* (2009). Interestingly, Podemos's Pablo Iglesias incessantly referred to this film and its sequel *Ocho apellidos catalanes* (2015) throughout the 2015 election campaign. He challenged his opponents to watch the films and accept the plurinational nature of the Spanish state. The success of *Ocho apellidos vascos* took the Spanish film industry by surprise and indicated that the Spanish public had an appetite for stories that played with stereotypes of regional differences.

Ocho apellidos vascos is a romantic comedy that depicts the story of Rafa from Andalusia and Amaia from the Basque Country. Amaia is at a hen's night in Seville when she encounters Rafa telling anti-Basque jokes.

Offended and unhappy at having been dressed up in the local costume, she gets drunk, and unwittingly spends the night at Rafa's house. The next morning she returns home and Rafa, completely smitten with her, drops everything and searches for her in her native Basque Country. As he tells his horror-stricken friends: "It's not her fault she's Basque." Amaia, already engaged to another Basque man, does her best to fend Rafa off. But through a series of comic events Rafa is forced to pretend to be Amaia's Basque fiancé for the sake of Amaia's father Koldo, a staunch Basque nationalist. The film toys with Basque and Andalusian stereotypes and, conforming to the conventions of a romantic comedy, ends happily; the two protagonists overcome the obstacles that their "regional differences" might have caused.

Ocho apellidos vascos is, in essence, a film that plays with nationalism as performance. The film begins by presenting the quirks of these regions stereotypically, leading the audience to suspect that on the surface it would be impossible for the two protagonists to ever "understand" each other as their preconceptions are so ingrained in their minds and ideology. This is particularly true of Amaia, who as a proud Basque has ingrained attitudes about "Spain" and the south of Spain in particular. Her world view does not allow her to even consider the possibility of falling in love with a *sevillano*. Rafa, on the other hand, while also having ingrained misconceptions of the Basque Country is able to override his fear of the "north" and travel to Basque Country to "conquer" her despite his fears and preconceptions. As the story unfolds it becomes clear that the past is completely informing the present. In toying with regional stereotypes the film is negotiating with the spectres of the past.

Both Rafa and Amaia symbolize, in some sense, two different Spains. My intention here is not to suggest that Rafa and Amaia neatly embody the narrative of *las dos Españas* but there are some verisimilitudes that are important to point out. Although Rafa does not necessarily represent conservative, nationalist Spain, the film does portray him as traditional and masculine (though naïve and foolish) and he is the heterosexual conqueror. He sees a girl he likes and he drops everything to bring her home to Seville. He does not mind that she is Basque even though the Basque Country instils a fear in him. He has absorbed many of the mass-mediated narratives about Basques. Witness the scene where Rafa is arriving in the Basque Country by coach. As he emerges through the other side of a tunnel, the CGI effects show a dark and stormy Basque Country, like a prelude to a Hollywood horror movie. Amaia, on the other hand, again does not necessarily represent Republican Spain. But as a staunch Basque nationalist she is depicted as "othering" Spain as witnessed by her disparaging attitude towards

Andalusians. She is modern and radical but, as the film demonstrates, just as close-minded, if not more so, as Rafa.

The key to reconciling these two ideas of Spain lies in the character of Merche played by Carmen Machi. As a woman from Extremadura who has adopted the Basque Country as her home she provides a neat counterpoint to the situation in which the two protagonists find themselves. Merche is from Extremadura, not quite Andalusian like Rafa, but almost. Her open, charming manner instantly allows her to make a connection with Rafa on the bus as he arrives to Amaia's village in the Basque Country. Although she is represented as a perfect role model for Rafa to emulate—an immigrant from the South who fell in love with a Basque and who has successfully assimilated and acclimatized to Basque life—her success is not due to her adopting the "Basque" way of life. In fact, she has maintained her unique "southernness." It is only at the end of the film, however, that the other characters, and the audience as well, discover that her late husband was anything but an exemplar of Basqueness as defined in the film's context, but rather a civil guard. In the *Ocho apellidos vascos* universe, where the burden of Spanish history is implicitly understood, audiences are aware of the Civil Guard's role in suppressing Basque nationalism during the Franco era. Although this fact is used in the film for comic relief it does demonstrate how Merche's character represents what can be termed "neutral" Spain. Merche sees no contradiction in having married a civil guard in the Basque Country and still keep in her bedroom mementoes not only of the Civil Guard, but also Spanish icons and flags and a portrait of King Juan Carlos, while at the same time begin a flirtatious relationship with Amaia's father Koldo, a staunch Basque nationalist.

It is Merche's role as "mother," however, that is perhaps most telling. As Rafa's family does not appear in the film she becomes his de facto mother, firstly as part of the made up story or plan that Amaia cooks up to convince her father Koldo that Rafa is her fiancé and that she is indeed still marrying him; but she also symbolizes the traditional matriarchal role in her relationship with Rafa, treating him like a son and giving him sound advice, despite having only just met him. But we can take the representation of motherhood in the film a step further and suggest that the Merche character symbolizes "mother Spain"—the mother who has witnessed the intense suffering of the two Spains but sits aside completely non-judgemental of the ideological positions of her children. She is neither the mother of nationalist Spain not the mother of Republican/regional nationalist Spain. She is by her sweet, nurturing nature, simply a mother. In her eyes, the division of the two Spains is not only arbitrary and unnecessary but does not even enter her world view. To symbolize this role Merche could not possibly have been Basque or Andalusian. Her neutrality is paramount and perhaps that is why she is from Extremadura, one of Spain's poorest regions, and arguably, a region that is often discursively forgotten.

The massive success of the film, mostly due to word-of-mouth, attests to the potency of the film's message. This is perhaps why Pablo Iglesias was so keen to mention the film every opportunity he could during the run-up to the general election in December 2015. The film's success also adds credence to Antonio Muñoz Molina's suggestion cited above that what is needed in Spain is for Spaniards to accept to become twenty-five per cent less of what they are. That is the only way in which Spaniards will be able to encounter their shared commonalities instead of focusing on divisions which, he claims, are politically constructed. There was clearly an appetite in the Spanish electorate for such a film indicating that for many ordinary Spaniards perhaps *crispación* had run its course. Yet the mass-mediated narratives driven by political elites continue to look back towards a distant past where a divided Spain fought for an idealized version of a Spain that was never really a real political reality. The period between 2008 and 2015 was a period characterized by political fragmentation. Spurred by the onset of the global economic crisis and radicalized by the definitive end of ETA terrorism, the emergence of 15-M and the renewed push towards independence in Catalonia, the recent political fragmentation is somewhat new for the politics of the Spanish state in the post-'78 order. Many institutional crises will still need to be resolved. But as Merche in *Ocho apellidos vascos* reminded Spaniards, there was much to be gained in ideological fluidity. It was a period characterized by optimism and despair, past and future, crisis and renewal. The events of that period will probably shape the Spanish state for years to come. If the net result of political fragmentation was the dispersion of the narrative of *las dos Españas*, it was clear that as a powerful constituent narrative the idea of two Spains continued to evolve and confront Spaniards not only of the ghosts of their past but also of the shadows of their common future. More than a hundred and fifty years ago Mariano José de Larra wrote: "Here lies half of Spain. It died of the other half." In 2016 the hope is that *all* Spains, despite their differences, can lie side by side, ultimately putting to rest a narrative that has wormed itself through Spanish history, often doing more harm than good. Perhaps the seed to overcome that narrative division was planted during those years.

Conclusion

The multidisciplinary approach adopted has contextualized terrorism and crisis socially and politically, as well as ideologically. Unlike much scholarship on terrorism and crisis related debates that come from political science, I engage with contemporary Spanish history in an attempt to provide deeper context and historicity to the tattered narratives that circulate in Spanish mass-mediated discourse. By ignoring history, extant scholarship into terror/ism and crisis potentially misses the dynamic convergences and disputes of power relations and identity politics, and the national stories they perpetuate. Understanding those convergences, in fact, is necessary in understanding the narrative conflicts in contemporary Spain.

The study uses a narratological model that does not simply assert that history is reduced to texts (Feldman 2003, 61). Borrowing from Feldman, I view the social capacity to narrate the past, to objectify and to collectivize historical experience, "as a cultural process subjected to uneven social and political conditions of constraint and possibility" (2003, 61). The narratological model serves to highlight how modern Spain is caught between a violence that redresses the past and a violence that addresses the future. As such, terror acts and political violence are vehicles for political parties to project their ideological narratives and sell themselves to the Spanish electorate. I thus consider narratives of terror in Spain as a mass-mediated process. That is, I consider terror events as a communicatively constituted process that, when analysed, can provide deeper understanding into how narratives of terror are linked to fundamental and historically constituent narratives (Stohl 2008, 7).

The book has attempted to understand narratives of terror in contemporary Spain even when the narratives in question are dispersed, loaded and complex. I posit that there are two constituent narrative drives that affect how terror in Spain is understood and dealt with in that country. The first is the narrative of *las dos Españas*, the story of two Spains, which battle to refashion the Spanish state in their respective ideological image. As acknowledged in Chapter One, it is overly deterministic to attribute to that narrative the root cause of Spain's long trajectory of political violence. Instead, this study has argued that the narrative of *las dos Españas* has a discursive power in contemporary Spanish politics. That narrative is utilized by the media, politicians and other stakeholders to project their own ideological interests to the Spanish electorate. I have focused on the reaction to violent terror attacks rather than the acts themselves. By highlighting the link between actions and goals, the book has demonstrated that narratives of terror are mediated by interpretations from the media, and also from politicians and many other interested stakeholders. I thus have expanded on Zulaika and Douglass's argument that "far from being a mere mirror of events, discourse may create its own reality" (2008, 29). The narratives, or stories, that political groupings project in the mass-media have a reality-making power, and this ability of discourse to create reality leads to the potency of the division between *las dos Españas* and the conflicts that animate the process of *crispación*.

The second constituent narrative of contemporary Spain in the early millennium is the global metanarrative of terror. As Zulaika and Douglass suggest in their essay, "The Terrorist Subject," the attacks on New York, Madrid and London by Islamists "appear to have made almost obsolete much of the literature on groups such as the IRA or ETA" (2008, 28). My study, accordingly, has posited that since 9/11 Spain is one of the few states that struggled against a localized and classical terrorist group (ETA) while simultaneously coming to terms with a global Islamist attack in Madrid in 2004. In Chapter One I discussed how terror and terrorism are difficult concepts to define. In the book I have avoided what Zulaika and Douglass refer to as "standard procedure" for a terrorism writer to begin by "protesting the glaring flaws in the literature and then to proceed to add his or her own definition, classification, perspective, or theory of the phenomenon" (1996, 98). Instead, I have considered terror as a metanarrative with symbolic and mediated potency. This has allowed me to consider the discursive implications of the new terrorism, as opposed to classical terrorism, on contemporary Spanish politics. The two constituent narratives clashed in the aftermath of the March 11 attacks in Madrid in 2004, and they continue to plague Spanish politics up to the present day through the discursive process of *crispación*.

The book, then, has selectively explored narratives of terror in Spain, providing a historical trajectory from the end of the Franco era until the present day. This approach highlights how the idea of two Spains has always been present in Spanish politics and discourse, albeit taking on different forms depending on the political exigencies of particular historical moments. Chapter Two looked at the long-running conflict between Basque separatists and the Spanish state. That conflict highlighted how narratives of terror in Spain are closely linked to nationalist narratives. I argued that terrorism is likely to be discursively significant when there are problems of continuity in democratic development, as occurred with

Spain's transition to democracy. That transition entailed a series of unofficially negotiated pacts between various political groupings in an attempt to reconcile the extremes of the two Spains and to forge a modern, western democracy. In that sense, the transition to democracy was a success. But the transition coincided with an upsurge in violent terrorist attacks from ETA. Thus the transition failed to confront the ghosts of the past dating back to the Spanish Civil War. So, at the crucial time in history when the Spanish state was seeking to redefine itself after almost four decades of dictatorship, terror, separatism, and later the recuperation of Republican memory, challenged many of those pacts.

The early years of the transition also saw Spain merge into a two-party democracy that reflected, albeit in muted ways, the left and right ideologies of the narrative of *las dos Españas*. The Basque conflict became a prime site of discursive confrontation not only between the two major parties but also between the central state and regional nationalists. The complexity and polemical nature of the Basque conflict made it an ideal vehicle for Spanish politicians and partisan media groups to project their political ideologies about what Spain is, or is not, and to cast a discursive divide between so-called democrats (good) and nationalists (bad). As discussed in Chapter Two, the label terrorist became profane during the transition to democracy, despite the fact that many Basques argued that the real terrorists were the state. The sacred democratic script that erased political violence from Spanish history was further strengthened in the aftermath of the 9/11 attacks in the USA in 2001.

The September 11 attacks were a major shift in terrorism related discourse. Conflicts such as ETA's campaign of terror in Spain were once local struggles, more or less contained within the parameters of state borders. But since 9/11 the metanarrative of terror has made all terror-related events global. Consequently, groups like ETA and the IRA had little recourse but to attempt to negotiate the cessation of their activities. However, the potency of narratives of suffering from both sides of the Civil War and both sides of the Basque conflict, made reconciliation near impossible despite the political realities of the post-9/11 era. Narratives of terror in Spain are thus conditioned by the historicity of personal grief and suffering.

According to Michael Stohl, contemporary research on violence and politics "has traditionally considered government as society's neutral conflict manager and the guarantor of political order" (2008, 6). However, the state may more usefully be considered a party to conflict and not necessarily a neutral one. Without taking the position that "the real terrorist is the state," in Chapter Three I returned to the GAL scandal on Spanish politics in order to re-read its effects on narratives of terror. The GAL scandal was a particularly interesting case study in Spanish politics. It involved state-sponsored paramilitary groups working outside the rule of law to fight terror using the same tactics and *modus operandi* of the group it was attempting to annihilate. In the chapter I argued that the GAL scandal can, and must, be re-analyzed as a sign of what the myth of the peaceful transition had to repress in order to become the dominant narrative of the new democratic Spain. The lingering debates that the official narratives of the transition attempted to erase had come back to haunt the present politics.

The official positions taken by the two major parties over the GAL scandal were particularly telling. The Socialists, the party that allegedly sponsored the paramilitary groups, while denying its involvement in the GAL affair, slyly argued that the paramilitary death squads were justified, and even, heroic. When one considers that the Socialists and the entire Spanish left were branded by conservative Spain during the Franco era as weak, feminine and anti-Spain, it is understandable that the PSOE under Felipe González took that approach in order to silence its critics who argued that the Socialists were soft on terrorism. More astounding was the attitude of the Popular Party under José María Aznar after it won government in 1996 and its decision to *"pasar página"* (turn the page) on the whole affair. This points to how the narrativization of terror events is intrinsically linked to the survival of older, historically constituent narratives, such as that of *las dos Españas*. The survival of the pacts and institutions of the transition (at least at the time) ultimately outweighed the pursuit of the scandal, a process that could have destabilized the founding myths of the new Spanish democracy.

Spain's transition to democracy was built on consensus, a process that relied on an intentional and unofficial agreement to forget the injustices of the past. The Basque conflict and the subsequent GAL affair, therefore, were caught within the confines of the transition's founding myths. But by the late 1990s the pacts of silence and forgetting were beginning to weaken. Chapter Four examined the electoral victory of the Popular Party under the leadership of José María Aznar. For many political commentators, the victory of the conservatives marked the official close of Spain's transition to democracy. After fourteen years of Socialist rule, the Spanish electorate had finally evolved to the point where it could elect a centre-right government. Aznar's first term (1996–2000) produced a rather moderate and conciliatory legislature in which the PP relied on the votes of regional nationalists to pass legislation. But that period coincided with the grassroots movement to recuperate Republican memory and the campaign to unearth Spain's

numerous mass graves dating back to the Spanish Civil War. The fear of a
return to political violence, which characterized Spain's transition to
democracy in the 1980s, was no longer perceived as a danger or threat by
many Spaniards, especially the young. When the PP won an outright
majority in the 2000 general election many of the debates that had
simmered below the surface of public discourse for two decades again resurfaced. This included a new patriotic nationalism that aimed to re-legitimize
national symbols, such as the Spanish flag, as well as a sharp new anti-leftist
rhetoric. With the 9/11 attacks in 2001, and the subsequent war in Iraq in
2003, consensus was no longer a defining characteristic of post-Franco
Spanish politics.

The arguments presented have highlighted how and why terrorism, and
to a lesser extent peripheral nationalism, have been elevated into the single
most important issue (at least discursively) facing and challenging the
Spanish state. It is therefore probably no coincidence that there is a symbiotic relationship between terror narratives and the left/right division in
Spanish politics. Examining narratives of terror are therefore crucial in
understanding how the narrative of *las dos Españas* circulates in Spanish
mass-mediated discourse. On March 11, 2004, when ten bombs exploded
in Madrid, Spain was at the nexus of global terrorism, and subject to a series
of events that not only finally undid the remnants of the founding myths
of Spain's transition to democracy, but also brought the division of *las dos
Españas* back to the centre of Spanish political and public discourse.

Chapter Five explored the competing narratives that the PSOE and PP
projected during the three controversial days between the March 11 attacks
and the March 14 general election in 2004. The PP government propagated
the narrative that the attacks were perpetrated by ETA, despite considerable evidence that it was most likely an attack by Islamists in the context
of the wider global War on Terror. In Chapter Five I highlighted that it is
difficult to determine to what extent the PP "manipulated" the media and
to what extent (if at all) it was hiding information. Instead, I examined both
the PP's narrative line and the PSOE's counter-narrative in an attempt to
determine which narrative line was more convincing and why. I argued that
the PSOE mounted a convincing counter-narrative that rejected the line
that ETA perpetrated the attack and that branded the Aznar government
as manipulative and authoritative. As a case study, those three days demonstrated, again, that in order to understand narratives of terror in Spain, one
must first understand their context and historicity. To outsiders, the electoral defeat of the PP in the March 14 election was perceived as capitulation
to terrorism. But by understanding the evolution of the narrative of *las dos
Españas* in the twentieth century, it is easier to appreciate the narrative

battle that was waged during those three days and to grasp why the PSOE was able to spin their counter-narrative into an electoral win.

Since the March 11 attacks in Madrid, and the subsequent electoral victory by the Socialists under Zapatero, the transition-era pacts have been virtually extinguished. The competing narratives from both sides of Spanish politics left deep wounds and an acrimonious political environment. The fallout of the March 11 attacks still haunts present Spanish politics. Chapter Six explored what the Spanish media has coined the new process of *crispación*, a form of bitter political polarization characterized by vituperative political commentary, which has shaped Spanish politics since 2004. I argue, however, that *crispación*, is far from new. Rather it signifies an updated version of the narrative of *las dos Españas*. By 2004, the PP and PSOE had more or less abandoned any pretence to abiding by the transition's unspoken rule of consensus. Their respective visions of Spain's position in the world, its structural make-up and socio-economic policies, were increasingly at odds. The PP's defeat under such controversial circumstances sparked a rhetorical feud. Chapter Six argued that although both the PP and the PSOE are partly responsible for fuelling the *crispación* in Spanish politics, the PP and its media supporters' repetition of accusations, hearsay and conspiracy theories forced the PSOE to be continually on the defensive. *Crispación* is thus a powerful mass-mediated process, arguably instigated by a terrorist attack (March 11) and constantly fuelled by terror narratives (betrayal, weakness, insensitivity to the victims, surrender). In the post-March 11 era, the hidden counter-narrative of *las dos Españas* ceased to float beneath the surface of public discourse and became, once again, a hotly contested debate in the mass-media, spurring countless articles, books and talk-show programs.

The Zapatero Socialist government sought to reform a number of areas in Spanish politics that the conservatives consider damages the transition's successes and puts the unity of Spain in danger. Foremost among the Zapatero government's reforms were the legalization of gay marriage, the reform of Catalonia's Statute of Autonomy, the withdrawal of Spanish troops from Iraq, and most controversially, an attempted peace process with ETA. In a political environment characterized by excessive, discursive confrontation in the aftermath of the March 11 attacks, the peace process instigated a whole new battleground between the two Spains. The new PSOE government immediately made the end of ETA terrorism a top priority, and after much rumour and waiting, ETA finally declared a cease-fire on March 22, 2006. Chapter Seven explored how that process was hindered by the repetition of certain key narratives propagated by the PP opposition in the mass-media, particularly the narrative of *traición a las víctimas*, which posited that the Socialist government was betraying the victims of terrorism. The peace process that dominated the news headlines in 2006 and 2007 was particularly interesting in understanding narratives of terror in Spain. In that period, terrorism was openly and unabashedly utilized by all sides of Spanish politics in a battle for electoral leverage. The PP sought to convince the Spanish electorate that the Socialists were negotiating the future of Navarre with ETA and, by implication, were secretly undermining the unity of the Spanish state by being in league with terrorists. The Socialists argued that it was within their rights to attempt a negotiated end to the long-running conflict. The resulting conflict between the two major parties demonstrated that terror narratives have become intrinsically linked to the electoral platforms of the major parties. It also demonstrated how the future-oriented narrative scripts of the major parties utilize terror-related events as a vehicle to sell their vision of Spain to the electorate. The peace process ended in failure after a bomb attack at Barajas Airport in Madrid on December 30, 2006. The collapse of the peace process highlighted that a negotiated peace settlement between ETA and the Spanish government was near impossible given the constraints that the process of *crispación* placed on talking to terrorists in mass-mediated discourse.

This book has investigated terror narratives in Spain by paying particular attention to how those narratives are interpreted and rearticulated by the Spanish state and its major political parties. In Chapter Eight, however, I explored the role of victims of terrorism in influencing public policy and public discourse. Victims of terrorism have, over the years, gained a considerable and privileged position in Spanish politics. This is especially the case since the 9/11 attacks in the USA and the March 11, 2004 attacks in Madrid. Victims' groups mirror the division in Spanish politics. ETA victims tend to flock to the PP-affiliated Association of Victims of Terrorism, whereas March 11 victims flock to the March 11 Victims' Association, which tends to support the Socialist Party. The discursive struggle between those two groups is a case in point of how the polarization of Spanish politics has transformed the ritual of Spanish politics into a parody of the narrative of *las dos Españas*. The feuding between the victims' groups demonstrates the reality-making power of discourse to the extent where it is impossible to differentiate between the real and the imagined, truth and fantasy.

Although most of the book deals with selective case studies of terror-related events, Chapter Nine provided a brief overview of the years 2008–2015. I argued that in recent years there has been a significant shift away from terror narratives in Spanish political discourse towards a predom-

inance of crisis narratives. This is partly because there has been no significant terrorist attack in Spain since 2007 and also due to the eventual
cessation of ETA terrorism in 2011. The devastating effects of the economic
crisis on Spanish society thus instigated the emergence of the 15-M movement, which in turn spearheaded the fragmentation of political bipolarism.
The new political parties Podemos and Ciudadanos tapped into the disenchantment the electorate felt towards the post-1978 order which was
characterized by endemic corruption by political elites. The December
2015 general elections thus brought Spanish politics to an impasse. No
political party won an outright majority and at the time this book went to
press, no potential political pact had sufficient votes to form a government.

What was interesting about those years is that although terror narratives
had lost much of their discursive power, crisis narratives were just as intrinsically linked to the narrative of *las dos Españas* as terror narratives were. The
renewed drive for Catalan independence and the acrimonious post-election
pact talks, all suggested that the narrative division of the two Spains was
just as potent as ever, even if more muted and fragmented. As such, I
pointed out that Spanish political discourse tends to project either narratives of optimism or despair. A significant section of Spanish society,
spurred on by the electoral success of Podemos and Ciudadanos is characterized by a remarkable optimism for the future of the Spanish state. On
the other hand, many other Spaniards are justifiably concerned about where
fragmented bipolarism will lead them. Both Podemos and regional nationalists are thus now discursively marginalized in a repeat of the division of
the two Spains. In my discussion of *Ocho apellidos vascos* (2014), however, I
suggest that there are signs that many Spaniards are ready to laugh off the
narrative divisions that once divided them. Where the narrative of *las dos
Españas* will lead Spaniards remains to be seen.

I have consistently argued that most of the division or *crispación* in Spain
is driven by political elites in a mass-mediated process to tell a "story" of
the "nation" to the Spanish electorate. I took an intensive and considered
approach to understanding terror and crisis narratives in Spain. The country
is unique in that it fought a local terror group for over four decades while
also being at the forefront of the global War on Terror since the March 11,
2004, attacks in Madrid. Terrorism and politics are indeed an irresistible
mix. Politicians, the media, so-called terrorism experts, victims, and many
other interested stakeholders, attempt to sway public perception on the
issue. Consequently, numerous mass-mediated narratives of terror circulate
in public discourse. The crisis narratives that emerged with the onset of the
global economic crisis are also utilized by these stakeholders in similar ways.
I have sought to understand the direction and purpose of these narratives

when at first they seem too complex and directionless, to find continuity where others see discontinuity, and to identify purpose and structure where others see incoherence.

In the book I have tried to show that in Spain terror and crisis narratives are not new but have a long historical trajectory. Understanding that trajectory goes some way to demonstrating that there is much at the level of explanation in terror and crisis-related debates that simply does not fit the global rhetoric. In *Paul Ricoeur* Karl Simms writes: "Narrative is the form of discourse which, through its dependence on plot, is richest in human meaning. Discover the meaning of narrative, and you discover the eternal truth of the human soul" (2003, 83). I would like to think that something similar is true in understanding narratives of terror and crisis in Spain. Discovering the meaning of narratives of terror and crisis in Spain may not mean discovering the eternal truth of the Spanish soul. Rather, it may mean that our understanding and reconstruction of the past, in narrative form, may help us understand the present and even illuminate the future. I thus agree with Jacques Le Goff when he suggests that what is necessary "is a constant rereading of the past in relation to the present, which must constantly be questioned anew" (1992, 18).

The rereading of terror and crisis narratives is an ongoing task. Narratives of terror and crisis, unlike this study, do not have an end. At the very least these narratives have been identified, shown how they function and circulate, where they came from, and why they work and persist in mass-mediated discourse. What will become of these narratives remains, for the time being, unknown. What is certain, however, is that these narratives can, and must, be questioned anew.

Bibliography

Abend, L. & Pingree, G. 2004, "Spain's Path to 3/11 Memorial," *The Christian Science Monitor*, Boston: Mass., July 14, p. 7.

Adagio, C. 2013, "Youth Protests and the End of the Zapatero Government" in B. N. Field & A. Botti (eds.), *Politics and Society in Contemporary Spain: From Zapatero to Rajoy*, Palgrave Macmillan, New York, pp. 143–160.

Agudo Zamora, M.J. 2007, *El estatuto de Autonomía de Andalucía de 2007*, Centro de Estudios Andaluces, Seville.

Aguilar, P. 1999, "The Memory of the Civil War in the Transition to Democracy: The Peculiarity of the Basque Case," in P. Heywood (ed.), *Politics and Policy in Democratic Spain—No Longer Different?*, Frank Cass, London, pp. 5–25.

Aizpeolea, L.R. 2006, "The Path to a Historic Breakthrough," *El País (English Edition)*, March 25, pp. 4–5.

Albiac, G. 2008, *Contra los políticos*, Temas de Hoy, Madrid.

Alonso, R. & Reinares, F. 2005, "Terrorism, Human Rights and Law Enforcement in Spain," *Terrorism and Political Violence*, vol. 17, no. 1–2, pp. 265–78.

Álvarez Junco, J. 2002, "The Foundation of Spanish Identity and its Adaptation to the Age of Nations," *History and Memory*, Special Issue, Spanish Memories: Images of a Contested Past, vol. 14, no. 1/2, pp. 13–36.

Álvarez Junco, J. & de la Fuente Monge, G. 2013. "La evolución del relato histórico" in J. Álvarez Junco (coord.), *Las historias de España: Visiones del pasado y construcción de identidad*, Marcial Pons, Barcelona.

Amodia, J. 1976, *Franco's Political Legacies*, Penguin, London.

Anderson, B. 1983, *Imagined Communities*, Verso, London.

Aretxaga, B. 1999, "A Fictional Reality: Paramilitary Death Squads and the Construction of State Terror in Spain," in J.A. Sluka (ed.), *Death Squad: the Anthropology of State Terror*, University of Philadelphia Press, Philadelphia, pp. 46–69.

Aretxaga, B. 2002, "Terror as Thrill: First Thoughts on the 'War on Terrorism'," *Anthropological Quarterly*, vol. 75, no. 1, pp. 139–50.

Aretxaga, B. 2005, *States of Terror: Begoña Aretxaga's Essays*, Centre for Basque Studies, Reno.

"Attacks Called Great Art." 2001, *The New York Times*, 19 September, p. 3.

Atxaga, B. 2006, "The Basque Spring," *The New York Times*, March 29, p. 23.

Aznar, J.M. 2005, *Eight Years as Prime Minister: A Personal Vision of Spain 1996 –2004*, trans. L. Dillman, Planeta, Barcelona.

Balfour, S. 1996, "The Lion and the Pig," in C. Mar-Molinero & A. Smith (eds.),

Nationalism and the Nation in the Iberian Peninsula: Competing and Conflicting Identities, Berg, Oxford, pp. 107–18.

Balfour S. & Quiroga A. 2007, *The Reinvention of Spain: Nation and Identity since Democracy*, Oxford University Press, Oxford.

Bali, V.A. 2007, "Terror and Elections: Lessons from Spain," *Electoral Studies*, vol. 26, pp. 669–87.

Barbería, J.L. 2006, "The Ailing Fatherland," *El País (English Edition)*, 9 May, pp. 4–5.

"Basque Premier Defiant After First Court Appearance." 2007, *El País (English Edition)*, 1 February, p. 1.

Bastida, X. 1998, *La nación española y el nacionalismo constitucional*, Ariel, Barcelona.

Baudrillard, J. 2002, *The Spirit of Terrorism*, Verso, London.

Bay, M. (dir.) 1998, *Armageddon*, Film, M. Bay, J. Bruckheimer & G.A. Herd, USA.

Benegas, T. 2007, *Diario de una tregua*, Espejo de Tinta, Madrid.

Bew, J., Frampton, M. & Gurruchaga, I. 2009, *Talking to Terrorists: Making Peace in Northern Ireland and the Basque Country*, Hurst & Company, London.

Blanco Valdés, R.L. 2008, *La aflicción de los patriotas*, Alianza Editorial, Madrid.

Blakeley, G. 2005, "Digging up Spain's Past: Consequences of Truth and Reconciliation," *Democratization*, vol. 12, no. 1, pp. 44–59.

Boin, A., McConnell, A. & Hart, P.t. 2008, "Introduction: Governing After Crisis," in A. Boin, A. McConnell & P. t' Hart (eds.), *Governing After Crisis*, Cambridge University Press, New York, pp. 3–32.

"Bomb Defused after Basque Party Ban." 2002, *BBC News*, 27 August, viewed 30 August, 2009. <http://news.bbc.co.uk/2/hi/europe/2218252.stm>.

Bosco, A. 2013, "The Long *Adiós*: The PSOE and the End of the Zapatero Era" in B. N. Field & A. Botti (eds.), *Politics and Society in Contemporary Spain: From Zapatero to Rajoy*, Palgrave Macmillan, New York, pp. 21–40.

Bosco, A. & Verney S. 2015, "Electoral Epidemic: The Political Cost of Economic Crisis in Southern Europe, 2010–11," *South European Society and Politics*, vol. 17, no. 2, pp. 129–154.

Botti, A. 2013, "From Opposition to Government: The Popular Party of Mariano Rajoy," in B. N. Field & A. Botti (eds.), *Politics and Society in Contemporary Spain: From Zapatero to Rajoy*, Palgrave Macmillan, New York, pp. 41–59.

Botti, A. & Field, B. N. 2013, "Conclusions" Botti, A. 2013, "From Opposition to Government: The Popular Party of Mariano Rajoy," in B. N. Field & A. Botti (eds.), *Politics and Society in Contemporary Spain: From Zapatero to Rajoy*, Palgrave Macmillan, New York, pp. 217–224.

Brassloff, A. 1996, "Centre-periphery Communication in Spain: The Politics of Language and the Language of Politics," in C. Hoffmann (ed.), *Language, Culture, and Communication in Contemporary Europe*, Multilingual Matters, Clevedon, UK, pp. 111–23.

Breen Smyth, M., Gunning, J., Jackson, R., Kassimeris, G. & Robinson, P. 2008, "Critical Terrorism Studies—An Introduction," *Critical Studies on Terrorism*, vol. 1, no. 1, pp. 1–4.

Brooks, D. 2004, "Al Qaeda's Wish List," *The New York Times*, 16 March, p. 27.

Brotóns, A.R. & Espósito, C. 2002, "Combating Terrorism: Strategies of Ten Countries," in Y. Alexander (ed.), University of Michigan Press, Ann Arbor, pp. 163–86.

Brown, W. 2001, *Politics Out of History*, Princeton University Press, Princeton.

Burke, A. 2008, "The End of Terrorism Studies," *Critical Studies on Terrorism*, vol. 1, no. 1, pp. 37–49.

Burke, P. 1989, "History as Social Memory," in T. Butler (ed.), *Memory: History, Culture and the Mind*, Basil Blackwell, Oxford, pp. 97–113.

Burkitt, I. 2005, "Powerful Emotions: Power, Government and Opposition in the 'War on Terror'," *Sociology*, vol. 39, no. 4, pp. 679–95.

Bustelo, M.G. 2005, *Terrorism and Democracy: Spain and the Terrorist Attacks of March 11*, Centro de Investigación para la Paz, CIP-FUHEM, Madrid.

Calleja, J.M. 1997, *Contra la barbarie: Un alegato en favor de las víctimas*, Temas de Hoy, Madrid.

Calleja, J.M. 2008, *Cuatro años de crispación. Cuando la derecha se echó a la calle*, Espejo de Tinta, Madrid.

Calvo Soler, R. 2006, *La negociación con ETA: Entre la confusión y los prejuicios*, Gedisa Editorial, Barcelona.

Carr, R. 1982, *Spain 1808–1975*, 2nd ed., Clarendon Press, Oxford.

Celso, A. 2005, "The Tragedy of Al-Andalus: The Madrid Terror Attacks and the Islamization of Spanish Politics," *Mediterranean Quarterly*, vol. 16, no. 3, pp. 86–101.

Cernuda, P. 2008, *Contra el talante: Rajoy y la oposición a ZP*, Random House, Barcelona.

Chomsky, N. 2005, "Simple Truths, Hard Problems: Some Thoughts on Terror, Justice and Self-defence," *Philosophy*, vol. 80, pp. 5–28.

"Church-backed Shock Jock Hit with Fine for Slandering Madrid Mayor." 2008, *El País (English Edition)*, 17 June, p. 1.

Clark, R.P. 1990, *Negotiating with ETA: Obstacles to Peace in the Basque Country, 1975–1988*, University of Nevada Press, Reno.

Cobeaga, B. (dir.) 2014, *Negociador*, Film, B. Cobeaga, E. Gozalo, & N. Ipiña, Spain.

Colino, C. 2013, "The State of Autonomies between the Economic Crisis and Enduring Nationalist Tensions," in B. N. Field & A. Botti (eds.), *Politics and Society in Contemporary Spain: From Zapatero to Rajoy*, Palgrave Macmillan, New York, pp. 81–100.

Connolly, W. 1995, *The Ethos of Pluralization*, University of Minnesota Press, Minneapolis.

Conversi, D. 1997, *The Basques, the Catalans and Spain: Alternative Routes to Nationalist Mobilisation*, Hurst, London.

Courtois, M. (dir.) 2004, *El lobo*, Film, J. Fernández & M. Miralles, Spain.

Courtois, M. (dir.) 2006, *GAL*, Film, A. Avila, M. Miralles & V. Ripoll, Spain.

Crameri, K. 2015, "Political Power and Civil Counterpower: The Complex Dynamics of the Catalan Independence Movement," in Gillespie, R. & Gray,

C. (eds.) *Contesting Spain?: The Dynamics of Nationalist Movements in Catalonia and the Basque Country*, Routledge, London, pp. 99–115.

Croft, S. 2006, *Culture, Crisis and America's War on Terror*, Cambridge University Press, Cambridge.

Cromer, G. 2001, *Narratives of Violence*, Darmouth Publishing, Aldershot.

Cué, C.E. 2005, "The Two Spains: The Divided Legacy of Franco's Rule Means Dictator Still Lives On," *El País (English Edition)*, 21 November, p. 2.

Davis, B. 2003, "Activism from Starbuck to Starbucks, or Terror: What's in a Name?," *Radical History Review*, no. 85, pp. 37–57.

Davis, M. 2005, "Is Spain Recovering its Memory? Breaking the Pacto del Olvido," *Human Rights Quarterly*, vol. 27, no. 3, pp. 858–80.

De Azúa, F. 2006, "Whose Side are You on?," *El País (English Edition)*, 11 March, p. 2.

De Larra, M. J. 1836, *El día de difuntos de 1836. Fígaro en el cementerio*, Proyecto Mariano José de Larra en Internet, viewed 19 March, 2016 <http://www.irox.de/larra/articulo/art_diad.html>.

Del Castillo, J. M. (dir.) 2015, *Techo y comida*, Film, G. García & A. Santapau, Spain.

Derrida, J. 2001, *Acts of Religion*, Routledge New York.

Díez-Medrano, J. 1995, *Divided Nations: Class, Politics and Nationalism in the Basque Country and Catalonia*, Cornell University Press, Ithaca.

Domínguez Iribarren, F. 2000, "El Enfrentamiento de ETA con la Democracia," in A. Elorza (ed.), *La Historia de ETA*, Temas de Hoy, Madrid, pp. 277–419.

Domínguez Iribarren, F. 2013, "Inmovilismo Eficaz," *El Correo*, 27 August, viewed 20 March, 2016, <http://paralalibertad.org/inmovilismo-eficaz/>.

Drennan, L.T. & McConnell, A. 2007, *Risk and Crisis Management in the Public Sector*, Routledge, Abingdon, UK.

Durkeim, E. 1961, *The Elementary Forms of the Religious Life*, trans. J. Swain, Collier, New York.

Eatwell, A. 2006, "Zapatero Believes the 'Beginning of the End' of ETA Violence is Near," *El País (English Edition)*, 11 February, p. 1.

Edles, L.D. 1998, *Symbol and Ritual in the New Spain*, Cambridge University Press, Cambridge.

Ekaizer, E. 2004, "José María Aznar, adiós a las armas: del cénit de las Azores y la derrota del PP," *El País*, 18 April, viewed 26 August, 2009, <http://www.elpais.com/articulo/portada/Jose/Maria/Aznar/adios/armas/elpdompor/20040418elpdmgpor_1/Tes >.

Elias, A. 2015, "Catalan Independence and the Challenge of Credibility: The Causes and Consequences of Catalan Nationalist Parties' Strategic Behaviour," in Gillespie, R. & Gray, C. (eds.) *Contesting Spain?: The Dynamics of Nationalist Movements in Catalonia and the Basque Country*, Routledge, London, pp. 79–98.

Emmerich, R. (dir.) 1996, *Independence Day*, Film, D. Devlin, USA.

Encarnación, O.G. 2004, "Democracy and Federalism in Spain," *Mediterranean Quarterly*, vol. 15, no. 1, pp. 58–74.

Encarnación, O.G. 2007, "Democracy and Dirty Wars in Spain," *Human Rights Quarterly*, vol. 29, pp. 950–72.

Encarnación, O.G. 2007/08, "Pinochet's Revenge: Spain Revisits its Civil War," *World Policy Journal*, vol. 24, no. 4, pp. 39–50.

Engene, J.O. 2004, *Terrorism in Western Europe: Explaining the Trends since 1950*, Edward Elgar, Cheltenham.

Falcón, L. 2002, "Violent Democracy," *Journal of Spanish Cultural Studies*, vol. 3, no. 1, pp. 15–28.

Feldman, A. 1991, *Formations of Violence: The Narrative of the Body and Political Terror in Northern Ireland*, Chicago University Press, Chicago.

Feldman, A. 2003, "Political Terror and the Technologies of Memory: Excuse, Sacrifice, Commodification, and Actuarial Moralities," *Radical History Review*, no. 85, pp. 58–73.

Ferrándiz, F. 2006, "The Return of Civil War Ghosts: The Ethnography of Exhumations in Contemporary Spain," *Anthropology Today*, vol. 22, no. 3, pp. 7–12.

Field, B. N. 2015, "The Evolution of Sub-State Nationalist Parties as State-Wide Parliamentary Actors: CiU and the PNV in Spain," in Gillespie, R. & Gray, C. (eds.) *Contesting Spain?: The Dynamics of Nationalist Movements in Catalonia and the Basque Country*, Routledge, London, pp. 116–134.

Field, B. N. & Botti, A. 2013, "Introduction: Political Change in Spain, from Zapatero to Rajoy," in B. N. Field & A. Botti (eds.), *Politics and Society in Contemporary Spain: From Zapatero to Rajoy*, Palgrave Macmillan, New York, pp. 1–20.

Flynn, M.K. 2001, "Constructed Identities and Iberia," *Ethnic and Racial Studies*, vol. 24, no. 5, pp. 703–18.

Foucault, M. 1972, *The Archaeology of Knowledge*, Routledge, London.

Foucault, M. 1979, *Discipline and Punish: The Birth of the Prison*, trans. A. Sheridan, Vintage Books, New York.

Foucault, M. 1982, "The Subject and Power," in H.L. Dreyfus & P. Rabinow (eds.), *Michel Foucault: Beyond Structuralism and Hermeneutics*, Harvester, Brighton, pp. 208–26.

Fox, G. 2015, "Podemos: Threat or Promise?," *Counterpunch*, February 13, viewed 7 August, 2015, <http://www.counterpunch.org/2015/02/13/podemos-threat-or-promise/>.

Frank, S. 2001, "The Art of Politics, the Art of War," *The Yale Herald*, 28 September, viewed March 19, 2016, <http://www.yaleherald.com/archive/xxxii/09.28.01/opinion/p8art.html>.

Funes, M.J. 1998, "Social Responses to Political Violence in the Basque Country," *The Journal of Conflict Resolution*, vol. 42, no. 4, pp. 493–510.

Fusi, J.P. 2000, *España: La evolución de la identidad nacional*, 3rd ed., Temas de Hoy, Madrid.

Gabilondo, J. 2002, "Postnationalism, Fundamentalism, and the Global Real:

Historicizing Terror/ism and the New North American/Global Ideology," *Journal of Spanish Cultural Studies*, vol. 3, no. 1, pp. 57–86.

Galán, L. 2006, "Not Flying the Flag: The Young Grow Restless with Spanishness," *El País (English Edition)*, 16 May, p. 2.

Gallego-Díaz, S. 2005, "Archives or Youth Care?," *El País (English Edition)*, 14 June, p. 2.

Gallego-Díaz, S. 2007, "Back to the Pact, Impossible," *El País (English Edition)*, 9 January, p. 2.

García-Abadillo, C. 2005, *11-M la venganza*, La Esfera de los Libros, Madrid

Gellner, E. 1983, *Nations and Nationalism* Basil Blackwell, Oxford.

Gibbons, J. 1999, *Spanish Politics Today*, Manchester University Press, Manchester.

Gil, A. 2015, "Rivera presenta su 'Pepa' en Cadiz: derechos sociales garantizados, nueva ley electoral y el fin del Senado y el CGPJ," *El Diario*, 7 November, <http://www.eldiario.es/politica/RiveraPepa-Cadiz-derechos-sociales-garanti-zados-fin-Senado-CGPJ_0_449705119.html>.

Gil, A. & Barcia J. V. 2015, *Voces del cambio: El fin de la España de la transición*, Roca Editorial, Barcelona.

Gil Calvo, E. 2005, *11/14-M: El cambio trágico de la masacre al vuelco electoral*, Adhara Editorial, Madrid.

Gil Calvo, E. 2008, *La lucha política a la española: Tragicomedia de la crispación*, Taurus, Madrid.

Gillespie, R. 2015. "Between Accommodation and Contestation: The Political Evolution of Basque and Catalan Nationalism," in Gillespie, R. & Gray, C. (eds.) *Contesting Spain?: The Dynamics of Nationalist Movements in Catalonia and the Basque Country*, Routledge, London, pp. 1–21.

Golob, S.R. 2002a, "'Forced to be Free': Globalized Justice, Pacted Democracy, and the Pinochet Case," *Democratization*, vol. 9, no. 2, pp. 21–42.

Golob, S.R. 2002b, "The Pinochet Case: 'Forced to be Free' Abroad and at Home," *Democratization*, vol. 9, no. 4, pp. 25–57.

González, F. 2001, "Chile, Argentina y las Comisiones de la Verdad," *El País*, 22 April, viewed 26 August, 2009, <http://www.elpais.com/articulo/opinion/Chile/Argentina/Comisiones/Verdad/elpepiopi/20010422elpepiopi_8/Tes?print=1>.

Graff, J. 2004, "The Zen of Zapatero," *Time Europe*, 27 September, 28–33.

Graham, H. 2004, "The Spanish Civil War 1936–2003: The Return of Republican Memory," *Science and Society*, vol. 68, no. 3, pp. 313–28.

Granda, E. & Elkin, M. 2005, "Mob Attack on Minister Shows Up the Rifts between Spain's Associations of Terror Victims," *El País (English Edition)*, 26 January, p. 3.

Gupta, S. 2002, *The Replication of Violence: Thoughts on International Terrorism after September 11th 2001*, Pluto Press, London.

Gurruchaga, C. 2006, *El fin de ETA*, Editorial Planeta, Barcelona.

Gutiérrez, C. (dir.) 2005, *El Calentito*, Film, Á. Augustín & T. Cimadevilla, Spain.

Hardt, M. & Negri, A. 2000, *Empire*, Harvard University Press, Cambridge.

Hardt, M. & Negri, A. 2004, *Multitude*, Hamish Hamilton, London.

Hegel, G.W.F. 1977, *Phenomenology of Spirit*, Oxford University Press, Oxford.

Heiberg, M. 1989, *The Making of the Basque Nation*, Cambridge University Press, Cambridge.

Herzfeld, M. 2005, *Cultural Intimacy: Social Poetics in the Nation-State*, 2nd ed., Routledge, New York and London.

Heywood, P. 1995, *The Government and Politics of Spain*, St. Martin's Press, New York.

Hirsch, S.F. 2006, *In the Moment of Greatest Calamity: Terrorism, Grief, and a Victim's Quest for Justice*, Princeton University Press, Princeton and Oxford.

Hobsbawm, E.J. 1992, *Nations and Nationalism since 1780: Programme, Myth, Reality*, Cambridge University Press, Cambridge.

Hoffman, B. & Kasupski, A.-B. 2007, *The Victims of Terrorism: An Assessment of Their Influence and Growing Role in Policy, Legislation and the Private Sector*, RAND Centre for Terrorism Risk Management Policy, Santa Monica, CA.

Hooper, J. 2006, *The New Spaniards*, 2nd ed., Penguin Books, London.

Humlebæk, C. 2014. *Spain: Inventing the Nation*, Bloomsbury Academic, London.

Iglesias, P. 2015, *Politics in a Time of Crisis: Podemos and the Future of a Democratic Europe*, Verso, London.

Jackson, R. 2007, "An Analysis of EU Counterterrorism Discourse Post-September 11," *Cambridge Review of International Affairs*, vol. 20, no. 2, pp. 233–47.

Jaúregui Bereciártu, G. 1981, *Ideología y estrategia política de ETA: Análisis de su revolución entre 1959 y 1968*, Siglo XXI, Madrid.

Jordán, J. & Horsburgh, N. 2005, "Mapping Jihadist Terrorism in Spain," *Studies in Conflict and Terrorism*, vol. 28, no. 3, pp. 169–91.

Juliá, S. 2004, *Historias de las dos Españas*, Taurus, Madrid.

Juliá, S. 2005, "A Year in Opposition," *El País (English Edition)*, 2 May, p. 2.

Kagan, R. 2003, *Paradise and Power: America and Europe in the New World Order*, Atlantic Books, London.

Kassam, A. 2015, "Ciudadanos: 'the Podemos of the Right' Emerges as Political Force in Spain," *The Guardian*, 13 March, 2013, viewed 10 December, 2015, <http://www.theguardian.com/world/2015/mar/13/ciudadanos-podemos-of-right-political-force-spain-albert-rivera>.

Kennedy, P. 2007, "Phoenix from the Ashes. The PSOE Government under Rodríguez Zapatero 2004–2007: A New Model for Social Democracy?," *International Journal of Iberian Studies*, vol. 20, no. 3, pp. 187–206.

Kennedy, P. 2014, "The Breakthrough of Podemos in Spain Poses a Serious Challenge for the Country's Two-Party System," *LSE Europp Blog*, viewed 10 December 2014, <http://blogs.lse.ac.uk/europpblog/2014/06/09/the-break-through-of-podemos-in-spain-poses-a-serious-challenge-for-the-countrys-two-party-system/>.

Kirtsoglou, E. 2006, "Unspeakable Crimes: Athenian Greek Perceptions and International Terrorism," in A. Strathern, P.J. Stewart & N.L. Whitehead (eds),

Terror and Violence: Imagination and the Unimaginable, Pluto Press, London and Ann Arbor, pp. 61–88.

Kurlansky, M. 2001, *The Basque History of the World*, Penguin, New York.

Laqueur, W. 1979, *Terrorism*, Little Brown New York.

Le Goff, J. 1992, *History and Memory*, trans. S. Renall & E. Claman, Columbia University Press, New York.

Lemon, M.C. 2003, "The Structure of Narrative," in G. Roberts (ed.), *The History and Narrative Reader*, Routledge, London, pp. 107–29.

León Solís, F. 2003a, *Negotiating Spain and Catalonia: Competing Narratives of National Identity*, Intellect Books, Bristol.

León Solís, F. 2003b, "The Transition(s) to Democracy and Discourses of Memory," *International Journal of Iberian Studies*, vol. 16, no. 1, pp. 49–63.

Linz, J.J., "Los nacionalismos en España: Una perspectiva comparativa," in E. d'Auria & J. Cassassas (eds.), *El estado moderno en Italia y España*, Universitat de Barcelona, Barcelona, pp. 79–88.

Lorant, R. 1991, "Spain's Innocent Victims of Terrorism Battle for Government Support," *Los Angeles Times*, April 14, p. 6.

Machado, A. 1983, *Times Alone: Selected Poems of Antonio Machado*, trans. R. Bly, Wesleyan University Press, Middletown, Connecticut.

Magone, J. 2004, *Contemporary Spanish Politics*, Routledge, London and New York.

Magone, J.M. 2008, *Contemporary Spanish Politics*, 2nd edn, Taylor & Francis, London.

Mair, P. 2011, "Bini Smaghi vs. the Parties: Representative Government and Institutional Constraints," *Robert Schuman Centre for Advanced Studies and EU Democracy Observatory*, EUI Working Paper No. 2011/12, European University Institute, Florence.

"March 11 Victims' Group Seeks Legal Separation from Hard-line Rival." 2005, *El País (English Edition)*, 6 August, p. 3.

Mar-Molinero, C. 2000, *The Politics of Language in the Spanish-speaking World: From Colonisation to Globalisation*, Routledge, London and New York.

Martí, S., Domingo, P. & Ibarra, P. 2007, "Democracy, Civil Liberties, and Counterterrorist Measures in Spain," in A. Brysk & G. Shafir (eds.), *National Insecurity and Human Rights: Democracies Debate Counterterrorism*, University of California Press, Berkeley and Los Angeles, pp. 118–36.

Martínez Lázaro, E. (dir.) 2014, *Ocho apellidos vascos*, Film, A. Augustín, G. Barrois, G. Salazar-Simpson, Spain.

Martínez Lázaro, E. (dir.) 2015, *Ocho apellidos catalanes*, Film, A. Augustín, & Salazar-Simpson, Spain.

Marx, K. & Engels, F. 2008 [1848], *The Communist Manifesto*, Oxford University Press, Oxford.

Medem, J. (dir.) 2003, *La pelota vasca. La piel contra la piedra*, Film, Spain.

Mees, L, 2015. "Nationalist Politics at the Crossroads: The Basque Nationalist Party and the Challenge of Sovereignty (1998–2004)" in Gillespie, R. & Gray,

C. (eds.) *Contesting Spain?: The Dynamics of Nationalist Movements in Catalonia and the Basque Country*, Routledge, London, pp. 41–59.

Michavila, N. 2005, *War, Terrorism and Elections: Electoral Impact of the Islamist Terror Attacks on Madrid (WP)*, Real Instituto Elcano de Estudios Internacionales y Estratégicos, Madrid.

Miller, G.D. 2007, "Confronting Terrorisms: Group Motivation and Successful State Policies," *Terrorism and Political Violence*, vol. 19, no. 3, pp. 331–50.

Minder, R. 2015a, "In Spain, New Political Party Makes Gains from Surprising Place—the Centre," *The New York Times*, 28 November, 2015, viewed 10 December, 2015. <http://www.nytimes.com/2015/11/29/world/europe/in-spain-new-political-party-makes-gains-from-surprising-place-the-center.html>.

Minder, R. 2015b, "Spain's Enigmatic Leader Faces New Generation in Election" December 18, viewed March 20, 2016. <http://www.nytimes.com/2015/12/19/world/europe/spains-enigmatic-leader-faces-new-generation-in-election.html>.

Minder, R. 2015c, "Spanish Election Marks another Rejection of Austerity" *The New York Times*, December 21, viewed March 20, 2016. <http://www.nytimes.com/2015/12/22/world/europe/spain-elections-government.html?_r=0>.

Molina, A.M. 2004, "We Don't Want to be Alone," *The New York Times*, 20 March, p. 13.

Molinas, C. 2012, "Una Teoria de la Clase Política Española" *El País*, viewed 24 January 2016, <http://politica.elpais.com/politica/2012/09/08/actualidad/1347129185_745267.html>.

Muñoz Molina, A, 2013, *Todo lo que era Sólido*, Seix Barral, Barcelona.

Muro, D. 2015, "When do Countries Re-Centralize?: Ideology and Party Politics in the Age of Austerity," in Gillespie, R. & Gray, C. (eds.) *Contesting Spain?: The Dynamics of Nationalist Movements in Catalonia and the Basque Country*, Routledge, London, pp. 22–40.

Muro, D. & A. Quiroga. 2005, "Spanish Nationalism: Ethnic or Civic?" *Ethnicities*, vol. 5, no. 1, pp. 9–29.

Narotzky, S. & Smith, G. 2002, "Being Politico in Spain," *History and Memory* Special Issue, Spanish Memories: Images of a Contested Past, vol. 14, no. 1/2, pp. 189–228.

Nesser, P. 2006, "Jihadism in Western Europe after the Invasion of Iraq: Tracing Motivational Influences from the Iraq War on Jihadist Terrorism in Western Europe," *Studies in Conflict and Terrorism*, vol. 29, no. 4, pp. 323–42.

Núñez, X. M. 1993, *Historiographical Approaches to Nationalism in Spain*, Breitenbach, Saarbrücken.

Núñez, X. M. 2001, "What is Spanish Nationalism Today? From Legitimacy Crisis to Unfulfilled Renovation (1975–2000)," *Ethnic and Racial Studies*, vol. 24, no. 5, pp. 719–52.

Olick, J.K. 1999, "Collective Memory: The Two Cultures," *Sociological Theory* vol. 17, no. 3, pp. 333–48.

Olmeda, J.A. 2008, "A Reversal of Fortune: Blame Games and Framing Contests after the 3/11 Terrorist Attacks in Madrid," in A. Boin, A. McConnell & P.T. Hart (eds.), *Governing After Crisis*, Cambridge University Press, New York, pp. 62–84.

Ordaz, P. 2005a, "The Champion of Terror Victims is also the Government's Bane," *El País (English Edition)*, 28 June, p. 3.

Ordaz, P. 2005b, "Maite Pagazaurtundua / President of the Victims of Terrorism Foundation 'The Role of Terrorism Victims is to Demand Justice, Not Impunity,'" *El País (English Edition)*, 22 September, p. 5.

"Otegi Voices Regret for Pain Caused by ETA." 2006, *El País (English Edition)*, 9 May, p. 1.

Palomo, G. 2008, *Rumbo a lo desconocido. Historia secreta de los años más convulsos del PP*, MR Ediciones, Madrid.

Parker, I. 2015, "Podemos as Event or Not: What it Looks Like from Manchester," *Revista Teknokultura*, vol. 12, no. 1, pp. 153–160.

Pontoniere, P. 2002, "Batasuna Outlawed as Freedoms Curtailed around the World," *Euskal Herria Journal*, viewed April 18 2003, <http://www.ehj-navarre.org/news/n_batasuna_b_article3.html >.

Pradera, J. 2005, "Historical Revisionism," *El País (English Edition)*, 25 March, p. 2.

Pradera, J. 2006 "The Stone and the Hand," *El País (English Edition)*, 11 January, p. 2.

Preston, P. 1990, *The Politics of Revenge: Fascism and the Military in 20th Century Spain*, Routledge London and New York.

Puig, V. 2004, "Spain's Atlantic Option," *The National Interest*, vol. 76, pp. 69–74.

Radu, M. 2006, "Spain's Socialist Surrender," in *Dilemmas of Democracy and Dictatorship*, Transaction Publishers, New Brunswick, pp. 160–64.

Ramazani, V. 2002, "September 11: Masculinity, Justice, and the Politics of Empathy," *Comparative Studies of South Asia, Africa and the Middle East*, vol. 21, no. 1–2, pp. 118–24.

Ramoneda, J. 2006, "The Price of Peace," *El País (English Edition)*, May 29, p. 2.

Rees, W. 2007, "European and Asian Responses to the US-led 'War on Terror,'" *Cambridge Review of International Affairs*, vol. 20, no. 2, pp. 215–31.

Rein, R. (ed.) 2002, *Spanish Memories: Images of a Contested Past*, Special Issue of *History and Memory*, vol. 14.

Reinares, F. 2004, *El nuevo terrorismo islamista. Del 11-S al 11-M*, Temas de Hoy, Madrid.

Reiner, R. (dir.) 1992. *A Few Good Men*, Film, D. Brown, R. Reiner & A. Scheinman, USA.

Resina, J.R. (ed.) 2000, *Disremembering the Dictatorship: The Politics of Memory in the Spanish Transition to Democracy*, Rodopi, Amsterdam and New York.

Resina, J.R. 2000, "Short of Memory: The Reclamation of the Past since the

Spanish Transition to Democracy," in J.R. Resina (ed.), *Disremembering the Dictatorship: The Politics of Memory in the Spanish Transition to Democracy*, Rodopi, Amsterdam and New York, pp. 83–126.

Richards, M. 2002, "From War Culture to Civil Society: Francoism, Social Change and Memories of the Spanish Civil War," *History and Memory*, Special Issue, Spanish Memories: Images of a Contested Past, vol. 14, no. 1/2, pp. 93–120.

Rojo, J.A. 2004 "Shedding the Fear of the Franco Years," *El País (English Edition)*, 2 November, p. 2.

Roller, E. 2001, "The March 2000 General Election in Spain," *Government and Opposition*, vol. 36, no. 2, pp. 209–29.

Rosales, J. (dir.) 2014, *Hermosa juventud*, Film, J. Dopffer, B. Díez, J. M. Morales & J. Rosales, Spain.

Rose, J. 1996, *States of Fantasy*, Clarendon Press, Oxford.

Salstad, L. 2001, "A Question of Distance: Three Spanish Civil War Narratives for Children," *Bookbird*, vol. 39, no. 3, pp. 30–36.

Sancton, T. 1996, "War of the Spanish Succession," *TIME International*, vol. 147, no. 10, pp. 12–16.

Sanz, L. A. 2012, "Wert: Nuestro Interés es Españolizar a los niños Catalanes," *El Mundo*, viewed 23 January 2016, <http://www.elmundo.es/elmundo/2012/10/10/espana/1349858437.html>.

Savater, F. 2006, "How Much do We Owe?," *El País (English Edition)*, 24 March 2006, p. 3.

Sciolino, E. 2005, "Spain is Riven by the Sorrows of March," *The New York Times*, March 11, p. A4.

Silva, E. & Macias, S. 2003, *Las fosas de Franco*, Temas de Hoy, Madrid.

Simms, K. 2003, *Paul Ricoeur*, Routledge, London.

Smith, Á. & Mar-Molinero, C. 1996, "The Myths and Realities of Nation-Building in the Iberian Peninsula," in C. Mar-Molinero & Á. Smith (eds.), *Nationalism and the Nation in the Iberian Peninsula: Competing and Conflicting Identities*, Berg, Oxford, pp. 1–32.

Somers, M. 2003, "Narrative, Narrative Identity, and Social Action: Rethinking English Working-Class Formation," in G. Roberts (ed.), *The History and Narrative Reader*, Routledge, London, pp. 354–74.

Somers, M.R. 1994, "The Narrative Constitution of Identity: A Relational and Network Approach," *Theory and Society*, vol. 23, no. 5, pp. 605–49.

Somers, M.R. & Gibson, G.D. 1995, "Reclaiming the Epistemological 'Other': Narrative and the Social Constitution of Identity," in C. Calhoun (ed.), *Social Theory and the Politics of Identity*, Blackwell, Oxford, pp. 37–99.

"Spain's Choice Polarised between a Pre-modern Right and Uninspiring Left." 2008, *Financial Times*, 3 March, p. 8.

Stapell, H.M. 2007, "Reconsidering Spanish Nationalism, Regionalism, and the Centre-Periphery Model in the Post-Francoist Period 1975–1992," *International Journal of Iberian Studies*, vol. 20, no. 3, pp. 171–85.

Stohl, M. 2008, "Old Myths, New Fantasies and the Enduring Realities of Terrorism," *Critical Studies on Terrorism*, vol. 1, no. 1, pp. 5–16.

Strathern, A. & Stewart, P.J. 2006, "Introduction: Terror, the Imagination, and Cosmology," in A. Strathern, P.J. Stewart & N.L. Whitehead (eds.), *Terror and Violence: Imagination and the Unimaginable*, Pluto Press, London and Ann Arbor, pp. 1–39.

Taibo, C. (ed.) 2007, *Nacionalismo español, esencias, memoria e instituciones,* CYAN, Madrid.

"Terrorism Victim Status to be Extended." 2008, *El País (English Edition)*, 6 October, p. 1.

"The Communiqué." 2007, *El País (English Edition)*, 11 January, p. 2.

Todorov, T. 2003, *Hope and Memory: Reflections on the Twentieth Century*, Atlantic Books, London.

Townson, N. (ed.) 2015, *Is Spain Different?: A Comparative Look at the 19th and 20th Centuries*, Sussex Academic Press, Brighton.

Tremlett, G. 2004, "Massacre in Madrid," *The Guardian*, 12 March, p. 1.

Tremlett, G. 2006, *Ghosts of Spain: Travels through a Country's Hidden Past*, Faber and Faber, London.

Tremlett, G. & Arie, S. 2003, "War in the Gulf–Spain/Italy–Aznar Faces 91% Opposition to War," *The Guardian*, 29 March, p. 9.

"Two Years On, 3/11 Ceremony Underscores Widening Political Rift." 2006, *El País (English Edition)*, 13 March, p. 3.

Tusell, J. 1999, *España, una angustia nacional*, Espasa, Madrid.

Uriarte, E. 2004, *Terrorismo y democracia tras el 11-M*, Espasa e Hoy, Madrid.

Valdecantos, C. & Rodríguez, J.A. 2006, "Zapatero pide consenso al PP para una ley de víctimas que proteja a los amenazados," *El País*, 2 March, p. 18.

Vercher, A. 1992, *Terrorism in Europe: An International Comparative Legal Analysis*, Clarendon Press, Oxford.

Vilches, E. 2015, "Witnessing Crisis in Contemporary and Golden Age Spain," in A. M. Kahn (ed.), *Connecting Past and Present: Exploring the Influence of the Spanish Golden Age in the Twentieth and Twenty-First Centuries*, Cambridge Scholars Publishing, Cambridge, pp. 109–132.

Whitehead, N.L. 2006, "Afterword. The Taste of Death," in A. Strathern, P.J. Stewart & N.L. Whitehead (eds.), *Terror and Violence: Imagination and the Unimaginable*, Pluto Press, London and Ann Arbor, pp. 231–38.

Whitfield, T. 2014, *Endgame for ETA: Elusive Peace in the Basque Country*, Hurst & Company, London.

Winter, J. & Sivan, E. (eds.) 2000, *War and Remembrance in the Twentieth Century*, Cambridge University Press, Cambridge.

Woodworth, P. 2001, *Dirty War, Clean Hands: ETA, the GAL and Spanish Democracy*, Cork University Press, Cork.

Woodworth, P. 2004a, "Spain Changes Course: Aznar's Legacy, Zapatero's Prospects," *World Policy Journal*, vol. 21, no. 2, pp. 7–26.

Woodworth, P. 2004b, "The War Against Terrorism: The Spanish Experience from ETA to Al-Qaeda," *International Journal of Iberian Studies*, vol. 17, no. 3, pp. 169–182.

Yee, A. 1996, "The Causal Effects of Ideas on Policies," *International Organization*, vol. 50, no. 1, pp. 69–108.

Žižek, S. 1989, *The Sublime Object of Ideology*, Verso New York.

Žižek, S. 2001, *Welcome to the Desert of the Real*, The Wooster Press, New York.

Žižek, S. 2005, *The Metastases of Enjoyment: On Women and Causality*, Verso London.

Žižek, S. 2006, *The Universal Exception*, Continuum, London.

Zulaika, J. 1998, "Specificities: Tropics of Terror: From Guernica's 'Natives' to Global 'Terrorists'," *Social Identities*, vol. 4, no. 1, pp. 93–108.

Zulaika, J. 2005, "Epilogue: The Intimacy of Violence and a Politics of Friendship," in J. Zulaika (ed.), *States of Terror: Begoña Aretxaga's Essays*, Centre for Basque Studies, Reno, pp. 279–85.

Zulaika, J. & Douglass, W.A. 1996, *Terror and Taboo: the Follies, Fables, and Faces of Terrorism*, Routledge, New York and London.

Zulaika, J. & Douglass, W.A. 2008, "The Terrorist Subject: Terrorism Studies and the Absent Subjectivity," *Critical Studies on Terrorism*, vol. 1, no. 1, pp. 27–36.

Index